For

C000214038

Matt
April 2005

£6.5⁰

St Martin-in-the-Fields

The exterior of St Martin's has not changed in nearly 300 years.

St Martin-in-the-Fields

Malcolm Johnson

Phillimore

2005

Published by
PHILLIMORE & CO. LTD,
Shopwyke Manor Barn, Chichester, West Sussex, England

© Rev. Malcolm Johnson, 2005

ISBN 1 86077 323 0

Printed and bound in Great Britain by
CAMBRIDGE PRINTING

For Robert Wilson

Contents

List of Illustrations

Frontispiece: The exterior of St Martin's.

Acknowledgements

Dick Sheppard thought him a pompous old devil in a skull cap but came to love him and call him 'Jenks', and I also owe John McMaster a great deal because his history of St Martin's, published in 1916, has been a huge help in preparing this book, as have the books by Vera Brittain and Carolyn Scott.

The present vicar, Nick Holtam, whose ministry I have greatly admired since his Stepney days, and his congregation have been very supportive, and I have benefited enormously from the help of Geoffrey Brown who is now in retirement. Thankfully, I was first introduced to St Martin's thirty years ago by Sibyl Allen, who has been a member almost since birth and is now a much-loved dowager in the congregation and a mine of information.

Several enjoyable teas with Daphne Williams, Freda Champion and Patricia Frank (Pat McCormick's daughter) have given me an insight into the heady days of the 20th century, and the advice of David and Alison Hardwick has been invaluable. It was a great pleasure to visit Norman Ingram-Smith, now retired in Wickham Market, to hear more of his ministry at St Martin's. June Wright, who worked with Norman, told me about those exciting days and Neville, her husband, kindly took me to the St Martin's Almshouses where he has been a Trustee for many years. David Say, former Bishop of Rochester, and Trevor Beeson, former Dean of Winchester, gave me memories of their curate days and David Edwards, former Provost of Southwark, sent me a very moving letter which I have quoted in full.

Being a musical numbskull I sent the chapter on the Academy to Sir Neville Marriner for his comments and received a warm, encouraging reply from Lady Marriner saying that it was fine, although she didn't think that Mendelssohn had written *Eliza*. The informative and amusing book on the early days of the Academy by Susie and Meirion Harries helped me greatly. The Archivist at the church, William Young, and Alison Kenney, Rory Lalwan and the staff of the Westminster City Archives have guided my research as have my good friends Margaret and Jimmy Garrod, whose knowledge of the area is extensive. They discovered some superb stories about Mr Kitto. Three wise men – Stephen Green, John Barnes and Robert Thorne – have generously spent time searching for errors and heresies, and Oliver Howard, the Campaign Officer, has been immensely supportive in collecting together and researching the illustrations.

I also owe a debt of gratitude to Simon Thraves and Peter Cook at Phillimore for their guidance and help.

Richard, Bishop of London, wins my award for valour as he has now written two Forewords for me; I am very grateful indeed. Long may he reign!

I have received the gracious permission of Her Majesty Queen Elizabeth II to quote correspondence between Canon McCormick and King Edward VIII, later HRH the Duke of Windsor, concerning his marriage, and also letters from Lord Wigram about visits to Sandringham. I am very grateful.

The author and publisher are most grateful to the following owners and trustees of copyright for their permission to publish these images: Phil Ashley, 39; Belgrave and Portman Photography Ltd, 56; Geremy Butler, 12; Fox Photos Ltd, 28; Guildhall Library and Harry Margary, 3; Kenneth Heath, 57; Oliver Howard, 42; Illustrated London News Picture Library, 14 and 24; Keystone Press Agency, 30; Horace Knowles, 25; Karim Merie, kmphotos.com, 36; Metropolitan Museum, New York, II; National Portrait Gallery, 40; Jaap Oepkes/The Connection at St Martin's, 53 and 54; Eric Parry Architects, 37 and 38; Pictorial Press, 21; Andrew Putler, 41 and 47 (© Andrew Putler); The Radio Times, 29; Lucinda Rogers, IV; The Tate Gallery, cover (© Tate, London 2005); Hazel Thompson, 34; Peter Tucker, 23; Westminster City Archives, III, 7, 8, 9, 10, 11, 12 and 44; and Mrs Daphne Williams, 32.

MALCOLM JOHNSON

Foreword

by the Bishop of London

Situated on a world square, St Martin's is conspicuous as a building and its ministry is also very public. There is no place to hide or shirk. What is done at St Martin's for good or ill reverberates around the globe. This is particularly true in a church which has pioneered the use of modern means of mass communication.

Malcolm Johnson's narrative reveals how greatly the whole church has been blessed by the ministry of successive vicars during the 20th century. The parish embraces those who live in palaces and those who, like Christ himself, have nowhere to lay their heads. It is a remarkable feature of the work at St Martin's how the community has been able to embrace both constituencies without blunting the edge of its social radicalism on the one hand or surrendering to simplistic and economically illiterate rhetoric on the other.

Any story of a church, as well researched as this history, prompts the question, What is to be the contribution of the present generation? Johnson's Dictionary of St Martin's appears at a very opportune time. Under the leadership of Nick Holtam and his team, St Martin's has properly ambitious plans to meet the social needs and the spiritual strivings of the 21st century.

The current chapter of the St Martin's story promises to be one of the most exciting and visionary yet. The Lottery grant of more than £14 million is a fitting recognition of a regeneration plan which cherishes the inheritance of the past while equipping St Martin's to serve more effectively the new multicultural London. Come to St Martin's on a Sunday afternoon, for example, and you will find that the service is in Cantonese. Ask homeless people with any experience of central London and they will almost certainly tell you about The Connection at St Martin's and the hope it holds out to young people at risk.

At the same time there cannot be many churches that have qualified for a Les Routiers award. How St Martin's gained the coveted London Café of the Year Award for 2003 is described in the following pages alongside many other fascinating revelations.

Malcolm Johnson is well qualified to write this history. As Rector of St Botolph's Aldgate, he was himself responsible for a glorious chapter in the life of a parish where social outreach and care for the homeless was also seen to be an essential part of gospel living. For five years before his retirement Malcolm served at St Martin's as the Bishop of London's Adviser on Pastoral Care. I am deeply grateful for the work he did during this period and delighted that those years have led on to the composition of this history. St Martin's has a remarkable story and Malcolm tells it with relish and reasonable discretion. For the past – thanks be to God. For the future illuminated by the compassion of God – yes.

RICHARD LONDIN

Introduction

Sir John Betjeman speaking at Noël Coward's Memorial Service in May 1973 said that he was pleased it was being held at St Martin's – 'Cheerful, wide, welcoming, English Baroque; it is precise, elegant and well ordered, like Noel.' Many would agree because since the 13th century the church has had a special place in people's affections. Not only is it the most famous church in London; it is, because of its broadcasts, known as the parish church of the Commonwealth. Its boundaries have changed considerably over the centuries. If today's vicar took food parcels to Knightsbridge he might get some odd looks, but in 1625 Dr Thomas Mountforde, the then incumbent, hired a cart, filled it with food, and took it to feed the poor living around his chapel of the Holy Trinity which stood where today's Hyde Park underpass emerges into Knightsbridge. This was then the western boundary of a parish which covered a huge area, but it soon grew smaller with the creation of new parishes – St Paul, Covent Garden (1645), St Anne, Soho (1678), St James, Piccadilly (1685), and St George, Hanover Square (1724). Today most of us have a hazy idea where the parish ends, but in the early 19th century Beating the Bounds was a regular ceremony when the St Martin's charity boys would march two abreast to thrash the boundary stones. As the boundary goes through the middle of Buckingham Palace this presented difficulties, although King William IV interrupted a Levée to allow the boys, who were howling and rattling their canes, to be admitted to the courtyard to thrash the boundary stone. The last change in 1990 extended the boundary to Parliament Square, and so now the Prime Minister joins the Queen and Prince Charles as parishioners.

Since the 1820s, when John Nash suggested an open space as part of his plan to provide 'a convenient communication from Marylebone Park to Charing Cross', Trafalgar Square has been at the centre of the centre of London, the scene of meetings, political rallies and national celebrations; no self-respecting politician would refuse to be seen between Landseer's lions haranguing a huge crowd about apartheid, the poll tax, hunting or the wars in Iraq, Vietnam and Suez. The Square is presided over by St Martin's, whose congregation have always struggled to make a connection with these concerns, and 700,000 people visit it each year. Many more will come when the exciting new development is completed.

Having always opened its doors to all sorts and conditions of men and women, it has a tradition of hospitality equalled by none, and it was this which enabled me to find a home there for the last four years of my working ministry when I was Bishop of London's Adviser on Pastoral Care. From my eyrie-office I could open a stained glass window and observe all that was going on in the building, and I was continually amazed at what I saw. The Mission Statement says it all: 'St Martin-in-the-Fields exists to honour God, and to enable questioning, open-minded people to discover for themselves the significance of Jesus Christ.'

Stephen Roberts, one of Geoffrey Brown's curates, described St Martin's as an island in a turbulent sea. The congregation arrive, tie up their dinghies briefly, and then paddle off never to be seen again, all except for the regulars. Mr Kitto expressed the same thought 100 years ago, but now, in contrast to his day, very few worshippers live in the parish. This is a challenge to both clergy and laity. The church attracts people of the very highest calibre, but it also attracts some very needy people not only in the homeless centre – now known as The Connection at St Martin's – but also in the congregation. The quality of pastoral care must be high – and it is. There is a brisk trade in Memorial Services so the great, good and not so good are continually filling the pews. Spike Milligan's Service was held on St John the Baptist's Day, 2002. Nick Holtam told the congregation that John was not as funny as Spike but he had the advantage of only losing his head once.

Links with the United States, where many churches have been modelled on Gibbs' designs, have always been important. Amongst others there is a St Martin-in-the-Fields in Philadelphia, Colombia, South Carolina and Pompano Beach, Florida. The Academy of St Martin in the Fields, founded in 1958, has also made the name known across the Atlantic and beyond, and vergers today have patiently to deal with tourists wanting to meet Neville Marriner.

Over the centuries the vicars have been an interesting assortment: two became Archbishops, Thomas Tenison and Thomas Lamplugh (who like the Vicar of Bray changed his views according to the political climate), and two went to prison, Robert Beste for singing the Litany in English and William Lloyd for daring to send a petition to King James II protesting at his views. He was acquitted after a trial in Westminster Hall 'to a tremendous ovation from the people'. Incumbents over the last 100 years have led a quieter life, but it is amazing how the right man has always appeared at the right time and surrounded himself with a supportive team – lay leaders at St Martin's have always taken their rightful place in parish affairs.

Reading the *Reviews* for the last hundred years has been an informative but also a nauseating experience. There is so much self-congratulation, and previous incumbencies are often surrounded by sentiment; but there is much to be proud of. We value the past but do not live in it. Why is St Martin's important? Other churches have excellent choirs, use their resources to the full, do work with the marginalised, stimulate the brain with sermons and discussion groups and have a care for international affairs, but perhaps not all at the same time, as

St Martin's does. It is the parish church of London; but it does seem odd, as David Monteith pointed out when he left the staff in 2001, that such a grand building which seems so much part of the Anglican establishment should be a place of protest, courageous action, unconventional clergy and sometimes unconventional theology.

The pages which follow describe these tensions and paradoxes and are a gift from someone who has experienced the thrill of being part of it all.

1

Who was Saint Martin?

He is not the patron saint of beggars, as most people think, but of innkeepers and reformed drunkards! He is remembered not as a bishop or theologian but as an Army officer who, seeing an almost naked, half-starved man on a cold winter day, dismounted from his horse, drew his sword, cut his cloak in half and gave it to the surprised beggar – much to everyone's amusement. Although not then a Christian, he dreamt that night that Jesus came to him wearing the half cloak. 'Inasmuch as you do it to the least of my brothers and sisters, you do it to me.' At the time of this incident, which probably happened near Amiens, he had been in the Roman Army for 25 years, having enlisted when he was 15. His father was a soldier, and Martin was born in Pannonia(now Hungary) around 316.

At this time it was not possible for a Christian to be a soldier because pacifism was so strong in the Church, and there would also be a conflict concerning the oaths to be taken, so he left the Army after making a protest that could be considered an early example of conscientious objection to military service. He was baptised and began to lead a reclusive life near Ligugé, Poitiers where he set up a community of believers, the first monastery in France, which existed until the Revolution in 1789. He soon became known as a holy man of prayer and a healer. It was a time of great change as Constantine the Emperor had become a Christian in 312. Christianity became respectable and bishops could now become civic figures who would amass wealth and power. Constantine hoped that their presence would bind the Empire together.

The people of Tours visited Martin in 372 and almost kidnapped him so that he could become their Bishop. Not wanting to be a civic leader he refused to accept a lordly lifestyle, preferring to live frugally with his followers in the caves at Marmoutier outside the city on the other side of the Loire. He showed remarkable gifts of healing and many stories tell of his bringing the dead to life. Christopher Donaldson suggests in his biography of Martin that this may stem from his time in the Army ministering to the wounded.[1] He always opposed the persecution of heretics, and when at Trier in 384 the Emperor Maximus condemned the Gnostic Priscillian and six companions to death he said that civil authorities had no power to punish heresy; excommunication was sufficient. Bishop Ambrose of Milan supported him, but when Martin left the city his fellow bishops persuaded the Emperor to kill the heretics. This was the first time the death penalty was passed and the furious Martin excommunicated the bishops, only receiving them back when the Emperor agreed to stop the persecution.

Death came to Martin on 8 November 397, and that evening the people of Tours and Poitiers argued about where his body should be buried, realising that a shrine would be good for business. While those in Poitiers slept their rivals lifted the body through the church window and took it by boat to Tours, which soon became a major centre of pilgrimage. Martin left no writings, but his life was recorded by his friend, Sulpicius Severus, and the uncritical collection of his miracles by Gregory of Tours added to his fame. He was the first to be made a saint who was a confessor of the faith and not a martyr, and his cult grew rapidly so that today over 4,000 buildings in France are dedicated to him. His fame soon spread to England, the ancient St Martin in Canterbury being the place where King Ethelbert of Kent was baptised by St Augustine in 596. The oldest parish church in Scotland, Ninian's White House, is named after him.

The day of his burial, 11 November, is St Martin's Day. In medieval England meat was salted down for the lean months to come, and fat Martinmass geese went to market – Martin's emblem is a goose. St Martin's summer is a spell of fine weather which sometimes occurs around his feast. In art he is usually depicted dividing his cloak, as in the famous El Greco painting in the National Gallery of Art, Washington DC, which in 1597 was placed above a side altar in the Capilla de San Jose, Toledo. There are numerous representations of him in illuminated books and windows and the most complete cycle of stained glass is in the 15th-century St Martin, York.

In 1997 Nicholas Holtam went on pilgrimage to Tours, 1,600 years after Martin's death, and in the Friends' Newsletter made a connection with the church of which he is incumbent:

> There are quite extraordinary stories of Martin healing the sick and the possessed. His Christian community was distinctive because it attracted the ἐνεργούμενοι, the mentally and physically sick, who were excluded from normal society but who found their place in the church. Every Sunday Martin would bless flasks of oil and members of the church would anoint the sick and housebound. At the Parish Weekend in July we did this for each other and found it a lovely way of praying with and of *being* prayed with. It feels miraculously healing to be anointed in this way.

Collect for Saint Martin's Day, 11 November:

> Lord God of hosts, who clothed your servant Martin the soldier with the spirit of sacrifice, and set him as a bishop in your Church to be a defender of the catholic faith: Give us grace to follow in his holy steps that at the last day we may be found clothed with righteousness in the dwellings of peace; through Jesus Christ our Lord, who lives and reigns with you and the Holy Spirit, one God, now and forever.
> Amen.

2

The First Two Churches

1222-1540

Disputes have always dogged church life but occasionally they can be useful. In 1222 the Bishop of London quarrelled with the Abbot of Westminster about their territorial rights so the Pope appointed a commission consisting of Stephen, Archbishop of Canterbury, the Bishops of Winton and Sarum and the Priors of Merton and Dunstable to determine the boundaries of St Margaret's parish, Westminster. In their decision they exclude 'the Church and burial-place of Saint Martin' and this is the first mention of St Martin's. A small chapel, it probably paid its priest with the alms given by pilgrims on their way to the Abbey. It may have been used by monks working in the nearby convent (covent) garden, or perhaps it was an outpost of the great religious house of St Martin-le-Grand in the City.

This building, known at first as St Martin-nigh-the-Cross, was to the east of the King's Mews, in which the royal hawks were kept, which stood on the site of the present National Gallery, and the cross would have been the one standing in the centre of the nearby village of Charing named after the 'char' or bend in the Thames. Business would have been conducted around this cross and an occasional sermon preached. Built of wood, it was replaced in 1290 by one carved from Caen stone by Richard of Crundale to commemorate the fact that the coffin of Queen Eleanor, wife of Edward I, rested here on its way from Lincolnshire to the Abbey. Similar crosses were erected in other stopping places but this was the grandest. It survived until 1643 when it was demolished. The Accounts record that the workmen were given an extra allowance of ale for this thirsty work.

> Undone, undone, the lawyers are,
> They wander about the town;
> Nor can find the way to Westminster
> Now Charing-cross is down.
> At the end of the Strand they make a stand,
> Swearing they are at a loss;
> And chaffing say, that's not the way,
> They must go by Charing Cross.[1]

The original cross stood on what is now the east side of Trafalgar Square but a replica can be seen in the forecourt of Charing Cross station.

1   *The South Prospect of the church demolished in 1721.*

About 1230 the parish is mentioned in a charter of Richard II as being within the franchise of Westminster, where stood the Royal Palace and the Courts of Law, but the church's first known incumbent is John de Hocelive (1275). Scandal touched the parish at this time when Edward I (1272-1307), hearing that some treasure had been buried in the fields during a plague, sent the Archdeacon of York and Lord Cobham to look for it, but nothing could be found. Soon afterwards Aleyn, the vicar of St Martin's, was imprisoned in Newgate for 'treasure trove and for the death of John-le-Leche'. The National Archives possesses two petitions sent by him from Newgate asking for his release. In 1299 Ralph de Baldock, Dean of St Paul's, cursed all those who had sacrilegiously violated St Martin's for 'an hoard of gold'. Could these events be connected? Many of the problems of the parish at this time were not ecclesiastical: they ranged from the capture of hedgehogs and the care of cows to the imposition of taxes and the upkeep of roads.

St Martin's Lane, a country path which probably came into existence at the beginning of the 13th century, linked the two houses of God 'in the fields', St Giles and St Martin's. There may have been a field path there even earlier. The Agas view (*c.*1560-70) shows no buildings in the Lane apart from those around the church.[2]

2 *The West Prospect of the same building.*

Very little is known about the parish in the 14th and 15th centuries but the vicars are listed beginning from 1352 (John de Kerseye) and 1363 (Thomas Skyn), both of whom were appointed by Westminster Abbey. The next incumbent, John Atwater, and his four successors were appointed by King Richard II. The Abbot of Westminster became patron from 1393 until 1554 when the Bishop of London took over. The patronage still rests in his hands.

Fortunately St Martin's possesses its Churchwardens' Accounts from 1525 to the present time so from the 16th century there is a great deal of information, but the real interest is to be found not in facts and figures but in the people themselves. The first entry refers to £3 6s. 8d. paid 'to John Carvar for the carrying and garnysshyng of the Rode looft and for the makyng of the Image of J'hus and of our lady and the xii p'phetts'. Pews were installed in churches at this time and they obviously caused trouble. In 1530 eight pence was paid for a pair of hinges – garnets – for a pew door and seven years later three pews were purchased from Stretforde Abbey for five shillings and large nails – specknalls – were used to repair them. A puzzling entry refers to garments for Mistress Norice's pew.

The burial registers also begin in 1525 when 37 persons were interred. The first name to be entered was that of Peter Kylks Chylde on 21 September; in 1526 there were 14 burials and in 1527 twenty-two. At nearly all these funerals a charge was made for lights, knells or torches but there was no fixed price – it varied from two pence to two shillings (£4 to £48 today). For burials inside the church the sum of 6s. 8d. was paid for the 'pytt'. Services were held for the monthly or year's mynd and a herse or canopy of wood was set up similar to that used at the funeral. Lights and tapers were placed around it and a hearse cloth covered it. The best cloth cost eight pence but an older 'worst cloth' cost two pence. The registers, which were filled in on a Sunday and kept in a locked chest, also list the address and occupation of the deceased – one woman was a maker of farthingales, an Elizabethan crinoline. During the Commonwealth a paid Registrar was appointed but at the Restoration the clergy took charge of the registers again until 1837, when Parliament established a Department to keep the records.

This first building, which had a steeple, was paved with tiles of various colours and patterns, and probably had three small chapels attached, no doubt built at different times. In 1530 the altar of Our Lady of Pity was given two altar cloths by Mr Humffrey Cooke, and three years later pews were made for St Johan's aisle and an altar cloth was received for St Cuthbert's chapel. The same year King Henry VIII gave some vestments, and between 1530 and 1536 he bought 180 acres of land to the north of Westminster Abbey to build St James's Palace and lay out the Park. At the same time he took over Cardinal Wolsey's large house, York Place, which, because of the white stone used in its reconstruction, was now known as Whitehall. The King had lacked suitable quarters in London since fire had destroyed Westminster Palace in 1512, so this now became his chief London residence. In 1534 the Royal Stables in Bloomsbury were burnt down and King Henry had his horses transferred to the Mews at Charing Cross. This building, where the royal hawks were 'mewed up' at moulting time, occupied the whole area north of the present Trafalgar Square. The parish was becoming busier.

On 17 February 1536 Henry wrote to 'Our wel beloved William Skener, Clarke, Vycar of Saynte Martyns-yn-the-Ffelds and the Gardyans' telling them that he had decided to make St Martin's a civil parish separate from St Margaret's Westminster, and by Letters Patent on 21 March 1542 this was done. King Henry did not care to see coffins being carried past his Palace in Whitehall on their way to St Margaret's, particularly if they contained plague victims, so the obvious thing to do was to create a new parish to the north. Burials could take place there and the risk of infection would decrease.

The new parish consisted mainly of open fields from what is now Oxford Street in the north to the Serpentine and Sloane Square to the west and Drury Lane in the east. To the south the boundary ran from Chelsea to what is now Buckingham Palace and Horse Guards. The King allowed some of his land to be sold or let for housing so the number of St Martin's parishioners began to grow. Thomas Cromwell, Vicar-General of King Henry, ordered that registers of births, marriages and deaths should be kept from 1538, although St Martin's already had a record of burials because in 1525 the Accounts show a payment 'for the paper book for the clerk to write in buryall'.

King Henry, having removed the Church of England from the Pope's jurisdiction, had definite views on liturgy and worship so laid down strict instructions concerning ornaments: no candles, tapers or images of wax were to be set before any image or picture. The wardens of St Martin's accordingly sold their metal candle stands and sticks. When the monasteries were dissolved and their lands and possessions fell into the hands of the King, he gave the vicar, Sir William Skinner, the vestments from the Hospital of St Mary, Rounceval at Charing Cross. This was demolished and its bodies were re-interred in St Martin's, where all three chapels had a tiled floor which was constantly being dug up for burials. Several payments are listed for these in the Accounts and also many more for repairs to the fabric which suggests the building was in a parlous condition.

King Henry allowed pews to be rented, and the first mention of this at St Martin's is an entry in the Accounts for 1537 when £25 1s. od. was received. Presumably the pews were at the side as worshippers stood or sat on chairs in the main body of the church. In 1563 the wardens paid for red silk lace and pale-coloured serges for the Bedford family pew but the auditors made them claim the money from the family. The pews over the next three hundred years had locks and keys and charges for these occur frequently in the Accounts.

1540-1600

A new parish demanded a new church so somewhere around 1544 the old building was demolished. Its replacement was tiny – only 25 feet wide and 45 feet long – which suggests a small congregation. There were few houses in the new parish but some grand houses near the Thames, presumably lived in by members of the Court. Several medieval bishops had their London houses along the Strand, which until the 16th century was the only main road in the parish, linking the City with Westminster, and there were continual squabbles as to who should keep it in good repair. Parishioners did, however, have to pay for their new church and the Accounts record that they gave money, stone, iron, lead and wood. The King did not contribute. Careful records were kept showing payments to Brycklears, Tylers, Carpenters, Plastorers and Laborers.

There is no record of a dedication ceremony or dinner given to celebrate the event, probably because London was in the grip of a plague in 1543-4. The burial book shows how serious the situation was, for in August 1543 eight people from two houses – one the vicarage – died. Robert Beste, the vicar, opened his house to the sick: 'Buried a poor child from the vicarage' is followed shortly afterwards by 'A poor woman from the vicarage'. Two priests assisted him, Sir John Scott and Sir John Michell. The clerical title 'Sir' or 'Dominus' does not denote knighthood but shows that the cleric did not possess a master or bachelor's degree.[3] Soon after the church opened Henry VIII died and was buried at Windsor so the wardens paid for the bells to be tolled including £1 'payd for bread and drinks for the said ryngers'.

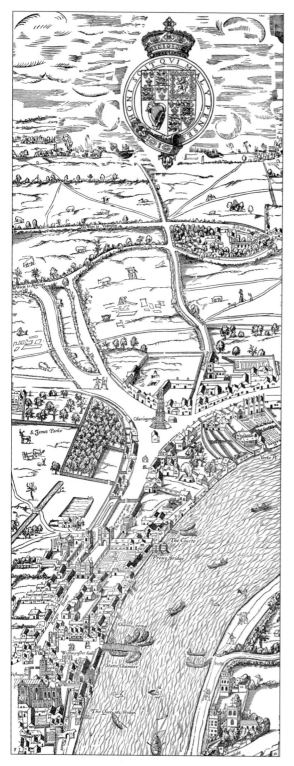

The nine-year-old Edward VI, Henry's only son, was crowned on 20 February 1547 and, being so young, was under the care of the protestant Lord Protector, Edward Seymour, Duke of Somerset. Incumbents were ordered to remove all shrines, images, candlesticks and paintings, and anything that reminded one of Romish practices had to be destroyed. The churchwardens complied with the orders and even removed the stained glass. Some of the Plate was sold 'with the assente and consent of the hole parrysh or the most of the same parryshioners' but some of the silver was used to make a new chalice. The building was whitewashed at a cost of 46 shillings and seven pence and the walls were covered with the Commandments, Lord's Prayer and Bible texts, the painters charging by the yard. A new psalter book cost 20 pence and the 1549 Prayer Book replaced the old Service books which had to be sent to the Bishop to be burnt.

The young King only lived another six years, and everything changed when the Roman Catholic Mary became Queen in July 1553. Dr Weston, the Dean of Westminster was ordered to find out what had been sold and St Martin's former wardens were fined and told to replace the items, so they recorded the purchase of a 'Messe booke, a crosse and a payre of candyll stykes and a holye water stocken with a spryncler'. A statue of St Martin cost 20 shillings and cash was paid 'for wypeng the scriptures owte of the church'. Great excitement surrounded the visit of the Queen early in 1554 to hear Mass and bread, beer and wine were purchased to celebrate. Herbs were

3 *Agas' Map of the parish, c.1560.*

strewn in the nave and brooms were bought to clean the yard. The Queen must have enjoyed her visit because later she donated for the High Altar 'a pair of hangings of needle worke, wrought upon sylke' and also a pair of organs.

Queen Mary died on 17 November 1558 and 'longe torches were given for the buryall'. Her reign had been a bloody one and many of her opponents were executed at Charing Cross as heretics. On 7 February 1554 the Kentish rebels led by Sir Thomas Wyatt arrived in London and advanced on Whitehall from Knightsbridge. The royal troops under the command of Sir John Gage fled into the Palace and bolted the gates. There they remained until the Earl of Pembroke arrived and killed most of the rebels, Wyatt himself surrendering. Many of their bodies were buried in St Martin's graveyard.

The changes of Edward's six years had challenged the inherited religious beliefs of England more than those of his father's reign. Temporarily reversed by his Catholic sister Mary, Edward's reformation was now slightly modified to form the basis of the great Elizabethan Via Media settlement which began in 1559. The new Rood Screen at St Martin's had to be taken down and the walls were once again whitewashed. Jasper the joiner was paid two shillings to frame the Ten Commandments so that they could hang in the church. Priests and people for twenty years had lurched from one royal religious view to another but they had to obey the different directives because their lives were at stake. This was especially so at St Martin's which was under constant surveillance from the nearby royal palace.

The clergy were now ordered to say the Lord's Prayer, Commandments, Creed and Gospel in English and their sermons, often read from a book of other men's homilies, were lengthy. In 1568 an hour glass was purchased and installed near the pulpit which must have been popular and used continually because another was needed twenty years later. The preacher asked the congregation to remain until the glass was empty, but if he continued after that they would leave, not always quietly. In 1576 the Bishop came on his Visitation and rushes and herbs were put down to sweeten the place, as they still are at Guildhall today when a Lord Mayor is elected.

On 25 January 1560/61 Francis Bacon, the future writer, philosopher and statesman, was baptised in St Martin's. His father, Lord Keeper of the Great Seal who lived at York House in the Strand, wanted everything to go well and the wardens paid four pence to 'two poore folks for making cleane of the church lane when the Lorde Keeper's child came to be christened'.

The office of Parish Clerk can be traced back in the Accounts to 1525 when the holder was paid four shillings a year (approximately £96 today). His tasks included playing the organs, watching the sepulchre from Good Friday night till Easter morning and collecting money. The first official appointment was made in 1577 when Robert Forest was chosen in place of Richard Hampden by 'John Savill, curate, William Wortley and John Trott, churchwardens, and the Worshipful Masters and others of the parish'. The salary had increased to seven shillings per quarter, and Forest remained in post until Nicholas Bedworth was 'nominated, elected and chosen' instead of him in 1588. Despite the Bishop's intervention on behalf of Forest, who had 'been detected of much lewdness', the appointment stood. Five years later the wardens gave Bedworth three shillings to apprentice his children, 'for Indentures and Bonds at ye bindinge of ye childerin', and when he died in September 1596 the formidable Forest tried to be re-appointed, unsuccessfully.

Parish Clerk is an ancient ecclesiastical office dating back to the time of St Augustine of Canterbury, and could be held by clergy or laity, but usually the latter.[4] In medieval England the Clerk had liturgical duties such as sprinkling the congregation with holy water to remind them of their baptism at the time of the absolution. After the Reformation he took general care of the building and made the responses to the prayers, and when triple-decker pulpits arrived he sat in the lower seat. The office was freehold, but since 1921 the appointment has been made by the incumbent and Parochial Church Council for a fixed term. After a lapse of over 100 years Chris Brooker was appointed to the post in 2004.

St Martin's Vestry minutes exist from 1574. Parishioners met together to decide local matters and one of their most important functions was to elect the two churchwardens. The Overseers, who collected the rates and gave donations to the poor, were responsible to them. Streets had to be kept clean – householders were responsible for the space in front of their house – and St Martin's possessed its own fire engine. In March 1585 the church and vicarage were robbed. Christopher Hayward, the vicar, lost a woollen cloak, cash and eight rings but fortunately the culprit, Oliver Taylor, was apprehended.

In 1596 a great deal of work was done to the structure of the building for the records show that stone piers and arches were taken down 'that the People may the better hear the preacher', two new great windows were installed and the pews 'where Mrs Dobbinson sitteth and the other where Mrs Child sitteth' were lengthened. Donors included the Bishop of Worcester, whose London house was presumably nearby, and Sir Walter Raleigh.

Until the time of Henry VIII St Martin's had over five hundred acres of common lands, but these were gradually enclosed, much to the parishioners' annoyance. They petitioned Lord Burghley, the High Steward of Westminster, who called together a committee of enquiry, but the local people decided to take matters into their own hands and forty men armed with shovels and pickaxes marched to Conduit Fields on 1 August 1592 and pulled down all the fences. The next day a larger party which included Mr Wells, the bailiff of Westminster, and Mr Cole, the previous High Constable of Westminster, went with constables and bailiffs to Enbery Farm and knocked down the fences there. Hardly a mob, they then returned quietly to their homes, but the farmers were furious and a trial ensued, after which the Lord Chamberlain sent several of the ringleaders to the Marshalsea Prison. Lands continued to be enclosed, and these enclosures were made legal by an Act of Parliament in 1785 so that today Green Park is probably all that is left of the common lands.

At this time each parish was expected to have a trained band of local men who would defend the area in emergencies, and in 1585 the wardens paid for 'gonnepowder' and six soldiers to go to the war with the Netherlands. Some of the parish armour was among the items stolen in 1585 – eight bombards (canons), a jerkin, two swords, two daggers and some flares went missing. St Martin's did not possess an armoury until 1614, so presumably the swords, corslettes, helmets and pikes mentioned in the 1598 Accounts were stored in the church. The men practised their skills in Military Street, now Gerrard Street, and in 1564 some of them were fined for having 'neglected to provide themselves with bows and arrows, and neglecting to practise archery'.

The 1599 Inventory of goods gives us a picture of what the furnishings and furniture of St Martin's were like. As well as bibles and books of homilies there were two chests with locks, a velvet pulpit cloth, green carpets in the sanctuary, a surplice for the vicar and silver vessels. There was also a red and green hearse cloth, a pair of trestles, cushions and a sanctus bell. The many leather buckets listed were presumably there as a fire precaution.

From the Accounts we learn that the sexes were segregated in church: in 1565 eleven pence was paid for 'lace and n'lls to dresse the jentillmens pewes'. Her Majesty obviously liked to hear the bells rung because there are 115 entries in the Accounts detailing payments to the ringers: 72 when her procession passed by; 19 marking her birthday on 7 September, and 24 celebrating her accession each year on 17 November. (At night the churchwardens had also to provide men holding torches at the side of the road to light her way.) Ten pence was usually paid for a peal of bells to mark Elizabeth's birthday and the same sum was paid for a peal to mark the execution of Mary, Queen of Scots. The last entry for torches was on 21 January 1602/3 when Elizabeth travelled from Whitehall to Richmond.[5] Two months later she was dead.

1600-1720

After the accession of James I in 1603 building was restricted in the parish as overcrowding could bring plague and pestilence; houses had to be built of brick and stone and not timber. The Scottish nobles who followed James southwards all settled in Charing Cross, which became known as New Edinburgh, and the Scots language was heard more than English. By now the church and graveyard were far too small for the number of parishioners so the King ordered that the building be enlarged. In 1607 a large spacious chancel and side aisles were added which meant that it doubled in size, but the medieval west tower was retained.[6] The King gave an acre of land – where the National Gallery now stands – and most of it was consecrated as a graveyard on 8 June 1608, Alice Stretting, a spinster, being interred that day. A small part of the land to the north had charity houses built on it, and some of it was let out – illegally – in plots. Later King Charles I forgave this on the understanding that any vacant land would be incorporated into the burial ground.[7]

With the new churchyard came a fixed scale of charges, but until 1792 no fee was ever demanded for pauper funerals. In that year Archdeacon Anthony Hamilton, the vicar, was told to pay the Poor Rate. He objected, pointing out that he had buried 4,544 bodies in 14 years, and enclosed a bill for £850 2s. 6d. The Vestry, however, insisted that he pay but agreed to give him one shilling per burial.

The rural character of the area is shown by a warrant of c.1608 for £100 'towards making a vault (or sewer) for draining etc. from St. Martin's Lane as far as St. Giles', so that the King's passage through those fields shall be both sweeter and more commodious'. In 1612 the Vestry ordered that the lane should be paved, but the 'water of the sewer' was still to be 'carried above the ground'.

Building on either side of the Lane was proscribed by Royal Proclamation but exceptions were clearly made. Whereas John Dunne, yeoman, was forbidden at the 18 January 1613/14 Middlesex Sessions from converting his newly erected stable into a dwelling house, the Earl of Salisbury, who had in 1608-9 bought four acres of ground on the west side of the Lane – around the present *Salisbury* pub – proceeded to build and lease houses on it. The Earl of Bedford was also erecting houses on the Lane's east side.[8]

The number of ratepayers in the parish increased from 164 in 1576 to 212 in 1594 then 307 in 1604.The 1603 Rate Book shows that 144 people living by the Thames, together with 150 living inland and 11 in 'Drewrie Lane', contributed a total of £80 6s. 3d. to the Poor Rate, and gifts from individuals including the Lord Chancellor added another £70 12s. 6d. Expenditure included weekly pensions to 41 men and women; Christmas gifts of bread and beef; burial costs of poor parishioners – 'a shrowde and herbs for Anne Myller, xv pence' – and various medical items including 'helping Margaret Bayley of the liver growne, and a six weeks diet and curing of Isabell Kinge and her childe'. In 1612 the wardens had still not paid for extending the building five years before and reported that the parish was in debt so, after taking legal advice, they levied a special rate – 'That for the coveringe of our Church and for the paying of the debts which the parish owe, we may Tax the parishioners, whether they be pleased or no.' The debt was cleared. Preachers in St Martin's have often caused a stir and Dr Everard, a Sunday Lecturer, was no exception. For some reason he took against the marriage of Prince Charles to the Roman Catholic Infanta of Spain. He was imprisoned so many times for his remarks that the dour James I ventured a rare joke, suggesting that his name be changed from Dr Ever-out to Dr Never-out.

Vestry meetings had to be held in the chancel until 1614 when a vestry, school house and armoury were built at a cost of £202 17s. 4d. The wardens, George Cade and James Howell, did not have sufficient funds to pay for this so they were empowered to borrow £100 from Jeremy Talcott, the King's bricklayer, and this was repaid with interest after six months thanks to the 3,258 communicants each paying a halfpenny. For this they were given a token which had to be presented before they could receive the sacrament in their pew. 'And the churchwardens shall take order where the pewes belong, to have every second pewe lefte emptie for the Minister to come the more conveniently.'

The building was now far too small, particularly since non-attendance had become a punishable offence. There was often an unseemly scramble for pews and Sir George Coppin, Clerk of the Crown in the Court of Chancery, who was one of the prime movers in the recent 'amplifying and beautifying the building', accused Ralph Dobbinson and some of the parishioners of annexing the 'highest and principal pews' to the deprivation of 'Earles, knightes and other bountiful benefactors'. This appropriation of pews was often discussed by the Vestry and in 1618 the wardens were ordered to see that parishioners could 'enjoye the liberty of their own pewes without being troubled with children or waiting women or others which have no Right to sitt in such pewes ... excepting the children of such honourable and worthy persons as the wardens ... shall think fitt'. Rails were now erected around the altar to stop people using it as a hat-stand. In 1621 the gallery on the north side was enlarged and that on the south side two years later. The parishioners petitioned the King to let them use the hall in Durham House for worship as St Martin's could not 'contain one half of those who would come to it'. The hall had been used in 1607/8 when the church was being renovated, but the King had other more pressing matters occupying him, so nothing was done.

The office of Lecturer was created at St Martin's early in the 17th century and the vicar, churchwardens and Vestry jealously guarded their right to appoint – having first heard the candidate preach. When King Charles I instructed William Laud, Bishop of London to appoint a Mr Peake in 1626 the parishioners resisted, and the royal mandate was revoked. Dr Mountforde, the vicar, and the Vestry then immediately appointed him as their choice. These rights were respected by the Committee for Plundered Ministers on 21 October 1641, who 'taking into consideracion the pietic abilitie and great desert of ffaithfull Dr Tate and his great sufferings in the Kingdom of Ireland for his good affeccon and constancie unto this parliament' recommended him to the parishioners as a lecturer, and he was appointed.[9] In 1646 the Vestry asked the vicar and 'Sabbath-day lecturer' to have public morning prayers daily at six in summer and seven in winter.

Civil war brought division and suffering to most places in England, and when King Charles marched on London with 15,000 men in 1642 the Trained Bands were called out. The churchwardens were ordered to keep a list of those who could provide carts, horses, boats etc. and who could shoot or cook. Parishioners had to help construct a rampart wall with batteries and redoubts which were near the present Charing Cross Road, Oxford Street and Wardour Street. The King reached Brentford to the west of the capital and 24,000 apprentices, citizens and soldiers went out to Turnham Green to stop any further advance. Large crowds of spectators who had ridden out of London to watch the battle were disappointed because the King, realising that he was heavily outnumbered, returned to Hampton Court.[10]

After the execution of King Charles I in Whitehall in 1649 religious gloom settled over England, and during the Commonwealth period the wardens' and Overseers' Accounts contain entries of fines for all manner of trivial offences committed on the Lord's Day. The Book of Sports, published by James I, which allowed dancing, archery, vaulting and other games after Divine Service on a Sunday, was publicly hung by the hangman. Dr White, a parishioner, was fined five shillings for 'keeping company' in his house on the Sabbath.[11]

Oliver Cromwell lived in the parish for some years in Long Acre, and on 11 November 1657 his daughter, the Lady Frances, married Sir Robert Rich of the parish of St Andrew's Holborn and a scion of old aristocratic stock. Registers were not signed then as now so her father's signature is not recorded. The Lord Protector caused great consternation by entering the building wearing spurs, so the choir boys claimed spur money, but there is no record of it being paid. Banns of marriage had to be called three times but not necessarily in church – those of Malcomb Craford and Katherin Williams married in July 1654 were called in the market place next to the parish church between the hours of eleven and two. Some incredible names are recorded – Samuel Euclid and May Hogsflesh, Joseph Squibb and Ann Physick, Samuel Dunce and Clara Pegg. Seventeenth-century baptisms included Prince Charles, later King Charles II, on 27 June 1630 and all of Sir Christopher Wren's children.

At the Restoration of King Charles II in 1660 the building was in a decayed state, but as funds were not available for a new church it was decided only to rebuild the tower and carry out urgent repairs, which were finished eight years later. Wren added a cupola in 1672. A small new gallery was built and Sir Edward Nicholas, one of the Secretaries of State, was given part of it, the fee being 'what his honour will be pleased to give for it'. According to Richard Baxter, the Puritan Divine, 40,000 people lived in the parish at this time, 'More than could find room in church, and neighbours lived here like Americans, without hearing a sermon for many years.'

The opening of St Anne, Soho and St James, Piccadilly helped relieve the situation, but it was still necessary to use a chapel in Oxendon Street from 1678 until 1726. This had been built in 1675 by Richard Baxter next to Coventry House the home of Henry Coventry, Secretary of State to King Charles II, who strongly disapproved of Baxter's views. When this pious and learned man, who had written many devotional books including *The Saints' Everlasting Rest*, climbed into the pulpit Mr Coventry would hurry into his garden and beat a drum loudly under the chapel window. Baxter went to see Dr William Lloyd at St Martin's, who advised a move and agreed to rent the building for £40 p.a. When the new St Martin's was built, the Oxendon Chapel was leased to the Church of Scotland, and after being sold to the Civil Service Stores was demolished.

The Vestry now needed land for their almshouses, and in 1677 they approached the Earl of St Albans about a vacant site on the west side of Hog Lane, now Charing Cross Road. Whilst negotiations were underway with the King, who was freeholder, the Bishop of London, Henry Compton, was asked for a chapel by the exiled Archbishop Joseph Georgines, who had fled to England to avoid persecution by the Turks. The Bishop persuaded St Martin's Vestry to let him have the centre of the site earmarked for the almshouses and a

4 *An extract from Morden and Lea's Map, 1682.*

building was erected, the Archbishop himself laying bricks to save expenditure. Unfortunately his English was not good, so when in 1681 it became apparent that the church was 'inconveniently situated' for his congregation he tried to sell it to some nonconformists for £626. William Lloyd was horrified and pointed out that the King was about to hand the freehold over to his Vestry, and the Archbishop had no lease. Compensation was offered and refused, so the matter went to court in 1682 and the Archbishop was evicted with no compensation. In July the building was let to a French Huguenot congregation and the new almshouses, which surrounded it, opened in 1686.

A generous benefactor and a well known parishioner was Sir Edmundbury Godfrey, who owned the wood yards on the Thames at Charing Cross. He was a local magistrate who in 1678 had taken the deposition of Titus Oates condemning the Roman Catholic Lord Stafford who was later executed. Shortly afterwards on 4 October, Sir Edmundbury was brutally strangled and his body dumped on Primrose Hill. The murder was thought to be part of a Popish plot and there was great indignation and anger, so when the body was brought from Bridewell Hospital for burial at St Martin's eight knights acted as pall bearers, and in the procession were City aldermen, 200 robed clergy and a huge crowd of people. The vicar, Dr William Lloyd, preached the sermon but for fear of assault asked two priests to stand with him.

Almost all the famous people who lived in St Martin's Lane in the 17th century lived on the west side, where there were large houses with stables and coach houses. Sir Theodore Mayerne, the royal physician whose memorial is in the crypt, lived here for 30 years; Sir Ralph Freeman, dramatist and Master of Requests, for seven years between 1631-8; and Abraham Vanderdoort, keeper of the pictures for Charles I, for nine years, 1630-9. During the Commonwealth period Sir Philip Stapleton was here from 1646-8, and Charles Fleetwood, who many thought Cromwell wanted to succeed him, from 1653 to 1670. The east side of the Lane seems to have been occupied mainly by artisans and traders.

Famous people who were buried in St Martin's in the 17th century included Nicholas Hilliard, artist, goldsmith, limner and the first English born miniaturist (1619, aged 82), and Sir Winston Churchill (1688), father of the first Duke of Marlborough. Robert Boyle, the natural philosopher and chemist who is known for his ideal Gas Law and was one of the founders of the Royal Society, was interred in 1691. John Evelyn, the diarist, established an annual lecture in his memory in the church which continued for over 200 years. George Farquhar, the Restoration dramatist and author of *The Recruiting Officer* and *The Beaux' Stratagem*, who died 'and left the house ringing with his jest', was buried in 1707.

Hungerford House, which stood on the site of the present Charing Cross station, was the home of Sir Edward Hungerford, one of Charles II's courtiers and a Member of Parliament for 33 years. At the Restoration he applied for a pew in the overcrowded St Martin's which was near his home. Known for his extreme extravagance and vanity he was addicted to gambling and lost his large fortune. Fire destroyed his house so he set up a market on the site to make money but the venture failed; he died in penury and was buried in St Martin's on 9 July 1711. The title was extinct but the name lives on in the footbridge over the Thames.

A wooden, movable tabernacle on wheels was constructed for King James II so that he could hear Mass whilst on manoeuvres with his troops without bothering local clergy who would not be in sympathy with his aim to make England a Roman Catholic country. It accompanied him to Hounslow Heath each summer until he fled into exile in 1688. The troops brought it to London where Dr Tenison was granted permission to put it on Conduit Fields at the top of Old Bond Street, close to the gardens of Burlington House, which was part of St Martin's parish.

Services were held there continually from 1691 when, on 18 July, John Evelyn heard Mr Stringfellow preach his first sermon, and was so impressed that he recommended him to Tenison. In 1716 it was demolished and a permanent chapel erected, 'a dull respectable looking barn'. Mayfair had several of these proprietary chapels, built by private persons as investments, and pandering to the fashionable piety of the wealthy who would pay for pews, so a powerful preacher was essential in these 'preaching boxes'. The freehold of the site was owned by the Corporation of the City of London which meant it was not possible for Dr Tenison to get a grant from the Commissioners who were erecting fifty new churches in the capital. Only part of its upkeep was derived from pew rents so the wardens made grants and paid for a new roof. In 1724 it passed into the new parish of St George, Hanover Square, and when the building was demolished and the site sold in 1877 St Martin's received one fifth of the proceeds.[12]

On Good Friday 1687 John Evelyn, who worshipped at St Martin's for 20 years from 1673, described the service at which Dr Tenison was preaching: 'A man came into near the middle of the church with his sword drawn with several others in that posture; in this zealous time it put the congregation into great confusion; but it appeared to be one who fled for sanctuary, being pursued by bailiffs.'

One bitterly cold night that November Tenison sat by the bedside of Nell Gwyn as she lay dying in her lodgings at 79 Pall Mall. Aged only 38 she was Charles II's most famous mistress and now, perhaps troubled by her past, she asked to be buried in the chancel of St Martin's. Dr Tenison interred her remains in his own vault despite much opposition. She left money to buy a decent pulpit cloth and cushion and £100 for 'clothes for the winter and such other necessaries as the Vicar shall think fit' for the poorest of his parishioners, and Roman Catholics were not to be excluded. A malicious parishioner told Queen Mary that the vicar's funeral sermon had praised Nell's pious end, but the Queen, who had already heard, said she was glad the poor unfortunate woman had died penitent.

The future Archbishop drew crowds to hear him preach – Evelyn reports that 'near 1,000 devout persons received communion' on 7 October 1688

– and when Tenison left to be Bishop of Lincoln in 1692 the Bishop of London appointed Dr William Lancaster. King William and Queen Mary said the patronage was theirs, however, and the King's Bench agreed with them, so Dr Nicholas Gouge was inducted. He died two years later so back came Lancaster, 'the petty schoolmaster from Westmoreland', who held the Archdeaconry of Middlesex in plurality. An interest in education also took him out of the parish to become the 30th Provost of Queen's College, Oxford and Chancellor of Oxford University. He died on 4 February 1717 and was buried at St Martin's, presumably in the vicar's vault.

Edmund Gibson, aged 29, was appointed Lecturer in 1698 when he was also domestic chaplain to Archbishop Tenison. Five years later he moved to be Rector of Lambeth, then in 1716 Bishop of Lincoln. A High Church Whig, he enjoyed ecclesiastical politics and tried to reconcile the clergy, mainly Tories, to the House of Hanover. He worked closely with the first minister, Robert Walpole, who rewarded him in 1723 with the Bishopric of London, but passed him over for Canterbury in 1737 probably because he had opposed the Bill to give relief to Quakers. In his 25 years in London Gibson ruled the diocese energetically and conscientiously, and he actively promoted the religious welfare of the American plantations still under the jurisdiction of the see of London.[13] When Archbishop Wake was ill – for a considerable time – Gibson was a sort of Archbishop Regent. He died in 1748.

Towards the end of the 17th century St Martin's Lane became crowded with coaches and other traffic, so Dr Barbon successfully petitioned Parliament to use some of its income from taxing hackney cabs to widen the Lane. But the southern part remained very narrow – two coaches could not pass and delays occurred.[14] Dr Lancaster and some parishioners asked Queen Anne if they could pull down the houses on the burial ground to the south of Hemming's Row and then give ten feet to widen the road. This was agreed and, by an Act of Parliament of 1702, the vicar and churchwardens were made a corporate body to hold the land originally given by James I, with the exception of Tenison's School and Library. On the south side of the Row a Girls' School and workhouse were built.

A quarrel arose between the vicar and his Vestry in 1707 when Dr William Lancaster nominated one of his servants to be sexton and the Vestry elected Richard Hussey. After debate it was decided to search for precedents and this was done. Records showed that when in 1588 Nicholas Bedworth had been made Parish Clerk instead of Robert Forest the appointment had not been by the incumbent alone and that on the same day a sexton had been elected in the same way. Vestries would now appoint sextons!

The best extant account of the old church is in Hatton's *A New View of London* of 1708:

> The roof is cover'd with Tile, the Walls of Brick and Stone with a Finishing; but the Tower is of fine Stone with strong Buttresses; the Roof within is a little arched and supported with Pillars, of the Tuscan and Modern Gothick Orders; and the Floor of the Chancel is 2 Steps above that of the Nave of the Church.

It is wainscoted about 6 Foot high with Oak, of which Timber are also the Pews and Pulpit, the latter having a square sound Board, with a Glory painted on the inside, and on the sides, 1 Cor 9 and 16.

There are galleries on the N, S, and W sides of the Church painted Deal; and at the entrance into the Chancel, the Aperture is adorned with 4 Columns, with their Entablature, of the Corinthian Order; above which are placed the Queen's Arms carved, and Enrichments of Cherubims, Figures of Plenty, &c., gilt with gold.

The Communion-Table is enclosed with Rail and Banister, and Foot-pace within is Marble; over the Table is a Window, which is betn the two Tables of the Commandments.

In 1710 a survey of the building by several master craftsmen revealed that all the walls were built of rubble and could no longer support the roof, which itself was defective. 'Wee are also of opinion that the said Church cannot be supported by repairing but must be rebuilt.' The Vestry agreed and the last services in the old St Martin's were held on 11 June 1721, the morning sermon being preached by the Bishop of Lincoln and the afternoon's by Dr Watson. Some of the monuments belonging to aristocratic or wealthy families were removed but most remained.

George Vertue, a well known artist and principal of a local school, who lived in St Martin's Lane, engraved three prints of the old building from which we learn that it was 84 feet long, 62 feet wide and had a steeple of 90 feet containing six bells. The west prospect shows the sun dial, the sculpture of a skeleton in a wall niche and the clock given in 1574 which cost a great deal to keep in good repair. The south view shows the staircase installed in 1597 when a gallery was added (see illustration nos 1 and 2, pp.4-5).

A gruesome account of the demolition reveals the parlous state of the old church:

> The Pews pale squares in their whole lengthened row
> Gave way, and opened a sad scene below!
> Beauty, youth, wealth, and power reduced to clay,
> Larded with bones, yet moist, unsheltered lay:
> Remnants of eyeless skulls, with hollow stare,
> Mocked the proud looks, which living charms wear.
> Coffins rose, broke, unfaithful to their trust!
> And flesh flew round me in unjointed dust.
> Scarce a short span beneath that opening floor,
> Where kneeling charmers prayed a week before.[15]

3

Present Building

Planning, architecture and consecration

An Act of Parliament of 1720 notes that, although the inhabitants of the parish of St Martin's have expended many and extraordinary sums of money to repair and support their church, it is now 'become decayed and ruinous ... so there is now great occasion for rebuilding'. Accordingly the vicar, Dr Thomas Green, and his wardens, Philip Davis and Giles Harris, together with the vestrymen and inhabitants were given permission to pull it down, erect a temporary tabernacle and vestry room, and then build a new church at a cost not exceeding £22,000. The poet, Aaron Hill, in 'To Celia in the Country. On the pulling down of St Martin's church', wrote a commemorative epitaph:

> Pensive, I view'd a sacred pile, of late
> Which falls, like man, to rise, in nobler state.
> The doors thrown wide, it seemed unveil'd to be
> And reverend ruin struck my startled eye.

'Rebuilding Commissioners' were appointed and told to present an estimate of the costs within 21 days of the Parliamentary session ending. They were also empowered to levy a rate of one pound on all the inhabitants to pay for this, landlords paying four-fifths and tenants one fifth. This could be increased if it proved insufficient. To create a larger site the Act also allowed the Dean and Chapter of Westminster to sell a parcel of land at the south-east corner of the churchyard which up till then had been leased to St Martin's for £2 11s. 10d. per annum and three good, sweet and fat capons which had to be delivered at the Abbey on the second Monday in Easter. The Act also provided for the owners of Northumberland House in the Strand, who had a pew in the old church's southern gallery, 5 feet 6 inches by 6 feet and a similar seat for servants below, to have an equal space in the new building.

On 23 June 1720 the Rebuilding Commissioners assembled in the Vestry Hall for their first meeting, Lord Carpenter taking the chair. The 41 members present, who included Sir Thomas Clarges, Generals Stewart and Evans, and Sir John Colbatch, elected Mr Phillips the Vestry Clerk as their clerk.[1] Six days later plans were submitted by Nicholas Dubois, George Sampson, John James, Sir James Thornhill and James Gibbs. In August Gibbs took the committee to view churches by his friend Sir Christopher Wren, such as St Andrew, Holborn and St James, Piccadilly, and on 24 November he was appointed as architect and surveyor. He had submitted other 'more capacious and convenient' designs, including one which had a domed rotunda entered through a temple front, presumably based on the Pantheon in Rome. Despite being approved by the Commissioners, this was rejected because of cost – the Grecian church of St Chad, Shrewsbury, built at the end of the 18th century, is a realisation of Gibbs' circular idea for St Martin's.

The Commissioners now needed some land to build a temporary tabernacle so they made a deal with Mrs Drayner to lease a piece of her ground at the top of Lancaster Court next to the churchyard for a rental of £5 per annum, two seats in the tabernacle and a private entrance from her house. Notices were inserted in the newspapers suggesting that monuments and memorials could be taken away by relatives and that the bodies themselves could be re-interred elsewhere if necessary. The body of Sir Amyas Pawlet with its alabaster monument was taken to Hinton St George and several others were removed. Those remaining were stored under the tabernacle and later transferred to the new crypt and are fully listed by McMaster.[2]

When the font, pews and organ had been removed into the tabernacle the building was cleared and offered for sale; it was bought by Christopher Cass for £300. In pulling it down one man suffered a cracked skull and another had his arm broken. They received £5 each, but a man who lost a finger was given £1 and another who had two broken ribs only 30 shillings. This compensation came from King George's gift of £105 which was also used for regular toasts to his health by the workmen. In digging the foundations they unearthed some buffalo heads and the bones of a man eight feet tall, probably one of the giants on show locally in the previous century. In his diary entry for August 1664 Pepys mentions that he went to Charing Cross and with his hat on walked under the arms of a Dutch giant. The most important find was a Roman brick arch with several ducts 14 feet below the present portico. Some stone coffins were also discovered containing various grave goods, and two glass 'palm cups' now in the British Museum.

Some of the parishioners who lived in the precincts of the royal palaces objected to the rate being levied to build the new church so on 15 December 1720 the Attorney General was asked for his advice. He ruled that all who were liable for Land Tax except the King and his household servants should pay, and polite demands were sent out. All had the desired effect except that sent to the Marlborough family, so silver plate had to be seized belonging to Sarah, Duchess of Marlborough, close friend of Queen Anne.[3]

The foundation stone of the new church was laid by the Bishop of Salisbury, the High Almoner, deputising for the King, on 19 March 1721. The old building was still standing so the stone was laid below ground and another laid above ground by a member of the Grand Lodge of the Free and Accepted Masons of England. A large crowd shouted and trumpets sounded as the Bishop, assisted by Sir Thomas Hewet, Principal Surveyor of the Royal Buildings, tapped three times with a mallet and laid the King's purse of a hundred guineas on the stone. Two months later Gibbs produced the master plan which was accepted by the Commissioners and a pine and mahogany model costing £71 10s. od. was made with a roof which lifted off to display the detail of the interior.

The present church is of Portland stone, rectangular, and entered through a commanding portico of huge Corinthian columns which support a pediment with the Royal Arms of George I carved on it. On the frieze is printed D. SACRAM AEDEM: Ṡ MARTINI PAROCHIANI EXTRUI FEC. A.D. MDCCXXVI, and over the centre bay on the architrave is inscribed IACOBI GIBBS ARCHITECTUS.

Gibbs employed as his master mason Christopher Cass, who had worked under Wren at Greenwich Hospital, and Benjamin Timbrell was the principal carpenter. An underground stream flowing below St Martin's Lane threatened the future stability of the portico, so to strengthen the foundations Gibbs had several hundred tombstones which had been taken from the old yard laid in the ground embedded in mortar. The result is the world famous temple front. When the National Gallery was built in the 1830s the architect, William Wilkins, was ordered to arrange it so that the St Martin's portico could be seen from Pall Mall. This proved to be a challenge as space was restricted, and the portico of the recently demolished Carlton House had to be used, but Wilkins achieved it.

To north and south the elevations are of seven bays divided by pilasters; each bay has two tiers of rusticated openings, the larger openings uppermost. The east end has a 'Venetian' triple window (with Ionic pillars), and in its pediment a Baroque cartouche design enclosed from below by the palm branches of Carlo Fontana. The balustrade running around the edge of the roof was to have had stone urns perched above each pilaster but these were not put in place, either because of expense or because one had recently fallen from the roof of St Mary-le-Strand and killed a man.

The tower was placed over the middle of the west end of the church behind the portico. The steeple, 192 feet high, wherein was hung 12 bells and a sanctus bell, resembles the City steeples of Wren, who died aged 90 during the rebuilding, on 25 February 1723. Steeples, said Gibbs, were 'of a Gothick extraction', but they had 'their beauties when their parts are well disposed'. All the six designs Gibbs made for St Martin's steeple were gracious creations, and the one erected, 'rising direct from the platform with the six-columned Corinthian portico before it is among London's loveliest creations in Portland stone. Its order is mixed Ionic and Corinthian, the clock stage has delightful little Baroque touches in its cornices and carving; in its turn the spire rises from a subdued Baroque cornice with concave sides.'[4] Its relation with the portico is, however, less happy – as Pevsner points out: 'Integration this procedure can hardly be called. The steeple is an excellent piece of design, the bell stage with coupled pilasters, the lantern recessed, octagonal, and with attached columns, and then a concave-sided entablature and a concave-sided obelisk spire with four tiers of circular openings. The treatment of the sides and the back is monumental too.'[5]

5 *Interior of St Martin's looking eastwards, 1751.*

Gibbs prepared a drawing for the railings of the portico but these were not installed until 1737. The joiner was Charles Griffith and they were supplied by the ironmonger, William Nind.

In his City of London churches and at St James, Piccadilly Wren had already adapted the conventional basilican interior to accommodate substantial galleries for large congregations to listen to sermons, whilst also lessening the emphasis on the eastern sanctuary. St Martin's interior, which owes much to Wren, has galleries around three sides. The chancel is narrower than the nave and on either side are the vestries and lobbies with stairs giving access to the galleries and boxes, the northern one of which was used as a royal pew (now a vestry) and the southern for the Admiralty (now an office). Gibbs himself designed the chairs for the royal pews. The Vestry Minutes record that the pews, all of which were in the galleries, should not be lined or have 'carpets, cloths or other ornaments hang down the front', except the pew of the Duke of Somerset. The churchwardens held the keys, and the pew-openers were instructed that unauthorised people should not be admitted. In March 1732 it was decided that some pews were for men and some for women only. It appears that keys were always being lost or stolen as there are a number of entries in the Accounts for cutting new keys.

With no pews in the body of the church and only plain glass in the windows there was a feeling of spaciousness in the new building. The pillars of five bays divide the nave from the aisles and support the galleries; the windows variegated with the 'rustication' blocks that were especially dear to Gibbs. The Corinthian columns stand on high panelled pedestals and today the interior is once again light and spacious as all the Victorian glass was blown out by the Luftwaffe's bombs and not replaced.

The decoration of the interior is exquisite. The blue-green ceiling is elliptical and divided into panels which, said Gibbs, 'I find by experience to be much better for the voice than the semi-circular, though not so beautiful.'[6] Two famous Italian artists, Giovanni Bagutti, 'The most proper Person to be Employed to Do the Fret Work and Gilding' and Giuseppe Artari, were invited to cover the ceiling with cherubim, clouds, shells and scrolls in a delicate, rococo design at a cost of £419 6s. od. An earlier design with plaques of Christ's life surrounding a gloria of putti was rejected. Gibbs often used the two men's services – they were also the stuccatori for St Peter, Vere Street and the Octagon Room which mercifully survived the destruction of Orleans House, Twickenham in 1926. At St Martin's they were assisted by Chrysostom Wilkens, who was paid considerably more (£593 4s. 4d.), presumably because he was responsible too for the less ambitious plastering of the whole building.

King George I's coat of arms is placed as part of the design on the ceiling above the chancel steps. The three lions of England, the single lion of Scotland and Ireland's harp join the fleur-de-lys of France. These lilies, witnessing to an ancient claim by English sovereigns to the throne of France, were only omitted in 1801. Because King George was still Elector of Hanover his German arms fill the lower right quarter. The design, which is also outside on the pediment of the portico, is shown within a Garter ribbon and is supported by the golden lion of England and the silver unicorn of Scotland. It was a great honour that the King agreed to be one of the churchwardens.

In 1722 His Majesty's Governor of South Carolina sent a gift of cedar wood and that November the Board elected the Hon. Andrew Drummond, the banker, as treasurer, replacing Mr Keat who had died. Drummond's Bank, which had been founded c.1712, stood at the Golden Eagle on the east side of Charing Cross and it financed the new church, instalments of the cost being paid against Gibbs' certificates.[7] A year later there were no funds to pay the accounts so on 20 January 1724 Lord Carpenter presented a petition to Parliament asking for further powers to raise funds to finish the building. This was granted and work was resumed. In April Gibbs presented some amended plans, presumably to save money. He had wanted the vestry and robing room to be in the crypt under the chancel and connected to the ground floor by a staircase at the south-eastern corner, but this had to be abandoned. By December the last stone of the steeple had been put in place and the interior decorations were well under way. The building was to seat 1,200 people and the construction work had taken four and a half years.

The oak pulpit, originally a three-decker with an elaborate sounding board, was set up on the north side of the nave. It is hexagonal and is supported on a hexagonal-shaped stem with a high base moulding. One of its panels bears the sacred monogram and the preacher today ascends a gracious and now rickety staircase to deliver the sermon.

Three Presbyterian ministers from Connecticut, Timothy Cutler, Samuel Johnson and Daniel Browne, arrived in London seeking ordination in the Church of England in 1723. Their baptisms were validated at St Sepulchre, Holborn on 20 March and two days later they were confirmed and deaconed in the new St Martin's, presumably by the Bishop of London who had responsibility for the Possessions, as America was still called. They were priested at 6 a.m. on 31 March by the Bishop of London and returned home, where Dr Cutler became the first Rector of the Old North Church, Boston and Dr Johnson the first President of what is now Columbia University.[8]

The Vestry had to decide a table of burial fees and in January 1726 adopted their subcommittee's recommendations:

> Under the new Church and portico for every burial, the sum of £3 10s., the pall to be used gratis.
> Under the vestry, £2.
> Under the tabernacle, £1.
> And 5s. to be charged for the use of the pall for any burial, and for the sixth bell.

The previous year Richard Miller, Esq., one of the gentlemen of the Vestry, had asked if he might have space for himself and his friends to be buried under the vestry room, and, as he had 'bestowed many great benefits on the parish', this was granted him on 14 February 1726. His fellow members requested that he sit for his portrait but instead he presented a marble bust of himself. At the same time the Vestry ordered the pews to be numbered and valued because a large crowd of fashionable people who could afford to pay for their seats were worshipping in the new building. 'London Spy' satirised this worldly congregation:

> The inhabitants are now supplied with a decent tabernacle, which can produce as handsome a show of white hands, diamond rings, pretty snuff boxes, and gilt prayer books as any cathedral whatever. Here the fair penitents pray in their patches, sue for pardon in their paint, and see their heaven in man.[9]

The church had been in use for some months when Dr Edmund Gibson, Bishop of London, returned to the parish where he had been Lecturer to consecrate the new building on 20 October 1726. The ceremony was in part a legal one as the new land purchased from the Dean and Chapter of Westminster Abbey had to be hallowed. A special liturgy was devised which contained prayers for those to be baptised, married and buried, and those who would receive communion. The Bishop went outside during the service and, standing by the west door of the Vestry Hall, he consecrated the burial ground, praying that those interred may rest in peace and reminding those present that in the midst of life we are in death. He returned to the church where the vicar, Dr Zachariah Pearce, preached a sermon before Holy Communion on Genesis 28 verse 18, which must have taken well over 30 minutes to deliver as it runs to 14 printed pages. Fortunately for the congregation he decided 'to shorten the discourse' by removing part of it to form a separate essay which ran to 20 pages.

When the final accounts were published the total cost was £33,661 16s. 7¾d., and items included:

Messrs Cass, Masons £15,147-1-4
Messrs With, Bricklayers £2,181-19-11
Messrs Sledge, Bricklayers. £1,213-19-0
Messrs Fincher & Slater, Plumbers £1,894-1-7
Messrs Timbrell & Phillips, Carpenters. £5,615-6-3
Messrs Griffiths, Joiners. £2,012-14-8
Messrs Young and Corner, Glaziers. £101-8-8
Messrs Hawkins, Watchman £6-10-6

In addition £1,264 18s. 3d. was paid to recast the bells, £1,109 2s. 10d. to alter the communion plate and £51 12s. 9d. for the copper weather-vane and ball. The fee paid to the Bishop's office for the service amounted to £21 14s. od.

Comments on the new building with its 'elegant and august' portico were varied. A Mr Ralph wrote, 'The east end is remarkably elegant, and very justly claims a particular applause ... if there is anything wanting in this fabric, it is a little more elevation; which is, I presume, apparently wanted within, and would create an additional beauty without. I cannot help thinking, too, that in complaisance to the galleries, the architect has reversed the order of the windows, it being always usual to have the larger ones nearer the eye, and the small, by way of attic, on the top.' Mr John Gwyn notes 'The absurd rustication of the windows and the heavy sills and trusses under them, are unpardonable blemishes, and very improperly introduced into the composition of the Corinthian order, as it takes away the delicacy which should be preserved in this kind of building.'

Mr Malton was more flattering about the exterior: 'It is the most successful attempt to unite the light and picturesque beauty of the modern steeple, to the sober grandeur and square solidity of the Grecian temple.'[10] The relationship between a classical portico and a Christian tower has always bothered some architectural pundits – 'The spire sits uneasily on the roof' (Hutton), and 'The incongruity of the temple-like church and the steeple which rushes up through the roof is undeniable' (Sir John Summerson).

Hogarth's 1729 painting *The Wedding of Stephen Beckingham and Mary Cox* gives us an idea of what the east end looked like, although the couple were actually married in St Benet, Paul's Wharf. Time is at the artist's command so he moved the ceremony to the grander St Martin's where, beneath the ornate ceiling, the bride's father leans on his stick, putti with their cornucopia hover overhead, a melancholy mother who had died two years earlier looks on and two urchins lean over the balcony of the Royal Box.[11]

The first years, 1730-1800

The area around the church was now crowded with people – 76 shops and over 3,000 houses – but the smell and sounds of the country were always present as sheep and cows were in Green Park, and fields, farms and woods lay between St Martin's and the village of Chelsea. A horse ferry crossed the Thames to the meadows of the south bank. Life was rarely dull in the new building. Watching the steeplejacks at work, a gentleman from Italy, Violante, asked if he might walk a tightrope from the weather-vane to the Royal Mews. Permission was granted. A large crowd cheered him on as a rope was stretched from the arches of the steeple to the Mews, and down this he descended head foremost. A few days later a Mr Cadman followed suit for a wager of £25 and on this occasion was successful, but he was not so lucky some years later in Shrewsbury when the rope snapped and he fell to his death.

On 10 September 1729 evening prayers were being said when Roger Campagnoll rushed in the main door and with two pistols fired at the of-

6   *Exterior of St Martin's, c.1770 showing the south churchyard, now Duncannon Street.*

ficiant, the Rev. Mr Taylor.[12] One bullet grazed his surplice and another seriously wounded Mr Williams, a farrier living in Bedfordbury, who was in the next pew to the priest. Pandemonium ensued and the congregation rushed outside. Someone restrained the maniac and it was later revealed in court that he was the son of the Governor of Brest and had been in London only seven months. His landlord in Seven Dials had cheated him of £138 so in a rage he had run into the church and fired at the first person he saw.

On 15 June 1729 the Prince of Wales received his communion before he was made Chancellor of the University of Dublin and Dr Zachariah Pearce, the vicar, preached an 'impressive sermon'. Many lawyers, including the Lord Chancellor himself, and professional men used St Martin's for this purpose as since the Test Act of 1673 anyone holding an official appointment had to get a certificate (costing a guinea) saying he was a communicant of the Church of England. He would come with two witnesses, receive communion, pay the fee and then be given the certificate signed by the incumbent and a warden.

Souvenir hunters caused problems and the members of the Vestry were told that the heavy gold tassels had been cut off the cushions on the communion table, reading desk and pulpit. Accordingly, on 1 October 1734 the Vestry ordered that the cushions out on display should no longer be made of expensive gold and silver thread.

The St Martin's watermen who plied their trade on the Thames, which was much closer to the church than it is today, asked if they could have a piece of the churchyard for their members to be buried in. A portion on the south side (now Duncannon Street) was given to them. Until 1759 there was only one bridge spanning the river, so they were important people to know as they waited for customers at the foot of the many steps leading from the Strand down to the Thames.

In 1737 galleries were installed to house charity children on each side of the organ at the west end of the church. Twenty years later temporary high pews were placed from the windows to the pillars. It is uncertain when fixed pews were installed, and chairs are seen in some early engravings. Gibbs preferred to follow the Italian churches, where only chairs were allowed on the main floor of the building, but he may have been ignored in the interests of income. John Dupre was appointed by the Vestry to collect pew rents and keep one shilling in the pound for himself, but he was dismissed shortly afterwards and another collector found. The best seats were in the front of the gallery – the 1st Earl of Northumberland paid £10 p.a. for his. An income of £600-700 was received each year until 1850 when it began to decline, so in 1877 pew rents were abolished and collections were taken at services. It seems, however, that many families kept 'their' pews and it took great courage for others to enter them. The position of the pulpit is uncertain: Gibbs' 1728 plan shows it in its present position; the engravings of 1738, 1751 and 1780 omit it entirely; and 19th-century prints have it on the north side. Behind the Holy Table were written the Creed, Ten Commandments and Lord's Prayer on the wall where the present mosaics are.

'The most shocking scene of murder imaginable' was how Horace Walpole described the event which took place on the evening of 15 July 1742. The St Martin's constables, who were all drunk, arrested 26 women who they found on the streets after dark. They put them in a small, airless room – the watch house to the west of the church – with no food or water and six died overnight.[13] No one was ever brought to trial or punished for this outrage but a large crowd of local people threw stones and bricks which damaged the small watch house, and on 27 July the churchwardens gave orders that 'a strong iron Padlock and Hasps be forthwith fixed to the Door of the said Watch-house and that the same be kept lockt up till Monday next'.

That autumn saw the interment in the churchyard of the famous 22-year-old highwayman, Jack Sheppard, whose execution on 16 November at Tyburn had been watched by 200,000 people. Graves being dug in the crypt now began to undermine the foundations of the church so in 1748 the sexton was ordered by the Vestry to seek permission before digging. This was obviously ignored and it was not until 7 April 1774 that a notice signed by the wardens, Thomas Adams and William Smith, was posted saying that no more graves could be dug, and that corpses interred in the crypt should now be in lead coffins.

Thomas Kynaston and Richard Smith, the churchwardens, decided to get tough in 1755, and on 20 September they published a warning to 'Tavern-keepers, Butchers, Fishmongers and other persons using any trade or business of buying and selling in the parish' that if they sold any flesh, fish or other things on a Sunday, or 'suffer any persons to sit tippling in any tavern', they would be prosecuted, fined and punished. Constables, beadles and other officers would visit shops and drinking houses to report misdemeanours. Householders were also told that from Michaelmas Day to Lady Day they should set lights in the street outside their houses until midnight. Failure to do so would mean a fine of two shillings.

7 *Old Slaughter's Coffee House, 74/75 St Martin's Lane, c.1750, demolished c.1843.*

Dr Erasmus Saunders was horrified when he arrived as vicar in 1756 to find that the famous Calvinist preacher, George Whitfield, had taken a lease on the Hanover Chapel recently built in the parish at the west end of Long Acre by the Mercers' Company. There is no record of harassment but Whitfield immediately moved out to found his tabernacle in Tottenham Court Road, and four years later Dr Saunders took a 31-year lease on the building at £80 p.a. to provide a chapel for the northern part of the parish.

8   *The Mews, 1794.*

St Martin's Lane, which was now a fashionable paved thoroughfare, was the home of London's artistic colony in the 18th century, and many painters, sculptors and craftsmen met in Old Slaughter's Coffee House which stood on the west side of the Lane at numbers 74 and 75, opposite Long Acre. Mark Girouard describes it as being to the mid-18th century what the Café Royal was to the 1890s. Established in 1692, it also provided a meeting place for players of whist, chess and various games of chance. One of the customers was Joshua Reynolds, now aged 21, who moved in 1744 into lodgings opposite May's Buildings, and returned to the Lane in 1753 when his sister Frances came from Devon to be his housekeeper. Later he moved to Leicester Square, and died in 1792 having been the first President of the Royal Academy. Another patron was the scientist and dilettante, Martin Folkes, President of the Society of Antiquaries, and in 1741 President of the Royal Society – his portrait by Hogarth 'hints at a bullying streak and an unruly private life'.[14] He was a friend of Sir Isaac Newton, who lived at 35 St Martin's Street from 1711 to 1727. Dr Burney, father of the novelist Fanny Burney, took the house in 1774 and enjoyed showing visitors the observatory built at the top of the house by Newton. The house was demolished in 1913 and Slaughter's was pulled down in 1843 to make way for Cranbourn Street.[15]

In the early 1740s Hogarth, who lived in Leicester Square, was at his most famous as a portrait painter and, as he had revived the St Martin's Lane Academy, he was surrounded at Slaughter's – where he was known as 'The King' – by his pupils. These included the American Benjamin West, who was married in the church in 1765. Hogarth's friends included Allan Ramsay, Francis Hayman and the engravers Nathaniel Smith, Hubert-Francois Gravelot and George Vertue, who described Slaughter's as 'a rendezvous of persons of all languages and Nations, Gentry, artists and others'.[16] David Garrick, who saw the publicity value of prints and portraits, enjoyed the place's atmosphere and it is possible that the precocious 13-year-old Thomas Gainsborough, who arrived in London in 1740, also drank coffee here.[17]

Louis Francois Roubiliac, who had been born in Lyons in 1695 and come to London in 1720, lived at 63 St Martin's Lane. He died there and was buried in St Martin's in 1762. Henry Fielding, the novelist, who enjoyed imitating the foreign accent of Roubiliac – much to everyone's amusement – nicknamed the head waiter 'Punch spiller' as he took a swig of wine before serving it and then said that he had spilt it.

Houses were first numbered in the 18th century so we know that Roubiliac's neighbour was young Thomas Chippendale, the master craftsman and furniture maker, who in 1753 had moved from Somerset Court, off the Strand, to 60-62 St Martin's Lane. Aged 35, he established his workshops and showroom there opposite Old Slaughter's, where he would meet other furniture makers such as John Channon, William Hallett, William Vile and John Cobb, who also lived in the Lane. In 1754 James Rannie, a wealthy Scottish merchant with money to invest, signed a joint lease with Chippendale on the property – which must have been sizeable as it was called 'The Cabinet and Upholstery

Warehouse'. The firm stayed there 60 years, and in 1776 Thomas handed the business over to his son, who was also a first-class craftsman. He died from consumption in 1779, and was buried in the church on 13 November, his son paying the £24 fee.

In Cecil Court the child Mozart lodged in 1764 at the house of 'Mr Couzin hare cutter'. Nearby lived many well-known members of the medical profession, including Gideon Harvey, Jean Misaubin – caricatured by Hogarth – and the entrepreneurial Sir John Colbatch who wrote 'The Treatment of Epilepsy by Mistletoe'. He claimed to have invented a powder that would stop heavy bleeding quickly but his fellow doctors were not impressed.

Magistrates were now meeting in the Vestry Hall and, somewhat surprisingly, they were making a great deal of noise, so on 1 April 1779 they were told that they could no longer transact business in the Hall during the time of Divine Service. Elections were also rather boisterous at this time, and in 1785 the wardens told their clerk to write to the Parliamentary Committee and ask them to repair the damage that had been done at one of their meetings.

An enraged, fanatical mob took over London for a week in June 1780, led by Lord George Gordon, an M.P. and son of the Duke of Gordon. A vain, bigoted man whose eccentricities verged on madness, he stirred up violent opposition to the Catholic Relief Act at a meeting of the London Protestant Association in St George's Fields in south London. The 50,000 people present went on the rampage, burning down chapels and houses of Roman Catholics and destroying prisons. After several days of appalling violence 12,000 troops were eventually called in, but by then over 700 people had died. The government levied a riot tax to pay for the damage, and St Martin's parishioners had to pay £1,762 15s. – a considerable sum, around £50,000 today.

The Vestry Minutes of 1 February 1793 record that two Lecturers, Mr Matthews and Mr Harrison, asked to be paid out of church funds as hitherto their stipends had been paid by voluntary contributions, but the Vestry refused. Twenty years later, on 6 December 1813, the same gentlemen made the same request and were successful. The churchwardens were ordered to pay each man £120 p.a. out of pew rents and burial fees, although the legality of this was questioned. Perhaps that is why the office of Lecturer was abolished at St Martin's in 1834. It was revived briefly in the 1950s when the distinguished scholar, Charles Raven, and Michael Wilson, a medical doctor and priest, were given the title.

A survey of the building was made in 1799 by 'Mr Cockle and Mr Craig' (probably S.P. Cockerell, the London Diocesan Surveyor, and Charles Craig) with a view to providing a new organ and carrying out repairs and improvements. The wardens, having received the recommendations and encouraged by counsel's opinion, levied a rate on parishioners of sixpence in the pound to pay for the work, which cost £4,165. The renovation was supervised by Prebendary Anthony Hamilton who stayed at St Martin's for a 36-year incumbency until his death in 1812 (he was at the same time Archdeacon of Colchester which was then part of the Diocese of London).

The nineteenth century

Scandal hit St Martin's in 1801 when Thomas Scott Smith walked into the church to find the curate, Mr Fell, indisposed, and offered to help as he himself was in Orders. He said he was the son of an eminent leather dealer in Crooked Lane, had an MA from Queens' College, Cambridge and was the nephew of Lord Eldon. His offer was accepted and over the next six months he administered the sacrament and conducted 16 weddings, 12 funerals and several baptisms. During this time he borrowed some clerical dress from a mercer's shop in Holywell Street, off the Strand, and ordered a set of canonicals to be made. The shopkeeper called at Lord Eldon's house to deliver the goods but was told by the steward that no such person existed. Mr Smith was arrested and at the court in Bow Street 'stared around him with an unmeaning eye, apparently indifferent to his situation'. A cartoon (below) shows that although the vicar, Prebendary Hamilton, and Mr Fell were angry some parishioners appreciated Mr Smith's administrations.[18] Two aggrieved couples shout abuse but another thinks differently, the groom shouting, 'Go along with you, I say this is the Parson for my Money.' The Registers reveal that Anthony Egan and Elizabeth Howell, married by Mr Smith on 10 August, were remarried on 11 October and eight couples followed suit. *The Times* wildly asserted that 'policies of insurance are opened at a house in Pall-mall, upon the hundred married couples so suddenly divorced by the discovery of the Sham-Parson'.[19] The report also said that he had been arrested for passing a 'forged draft on Messrs Smith, Payne and Smith' and the Queens' College Annual Register, 1801, states that he 'is under sentence of death'. The gentleman does not appear in the Newgate list of executions (perhaps he was transported?) and the Vestry Minutes ignore the affair.

9 *Ejection of Mr Thomas Scott Smith, the 'Sham-Parson', from St Martin's, 1802.*

By now the parish was a very busy one: there had been 858 baptisms in 1788, and weddings were numerous. Amongst them was a secret marriage on 2 October 1816 between the painter John Constable and Maria Bicknell, who lived in Spring Garden Terrace. Her godfather, the wealthy Dr Rhudde, was Rector of East Bergholt where they had met, but he thought that an impoverished painter was not a suitable choice.

The Rev. Joseph Pott was Archdeacon of London (1813-42) at the same time as being vicar (1812-24), and like nearly all incumbents of the time he was not bothered by being a pluralist, particularly as it brought in two salaries. Born in 1759, he had already been Archdeacon of St Albans and obviously enjoyed looking at down-pipes and guttering because he later became Archdeacon of Middlesex too. During his 12 years' incumbency he collected £1,309 13s. 3d. for the wounded and the families of the dead at the Battle of Waterloo. This was probably the first of many appeals made by a vicar of St Martin's for the needy. It was he who installed gas, supplied by the Equitable Gas Company, in the church which was thus one of the first to use gas. It worked out at half the cost of oil and candles which had been £80 per annum.

In 1820 the area in front of the church began to change completely as George IV moved his horses out of the Mews, and the 'vile houses' were demolished to make way for a scheme planned but not carried out by John Nash. The Commissioners of Woods and Forests were building a road to connect Pall Mall with the Strand and required a portion of St Martin's graveyard which later became Duncannon Street, named after the Chief Commissioner. Many bodies, some recently interred, were removed from the south churchyard and relatives were asked to decide whether the remains should be transferred to the church vaults, St Martin's cemetery, Pratt Street, Camden Town or another place.[20] The book containing details of all these re-interments in 1830, each signed by the vicar and wardens, is now lodged with Westminster City Archives.

An Act of Parliament of 1826 meant that the Mews and the surrounding houses were demolished and in 1832 the National Gallery was built. William Wilkins was told to place his building 50 feet northwards so that the view of St Martin's should not be obscured. Wilkins died before a decision could be made about the new square, so Sir Charles Barry took over, levelling and paving the central area, and laying out a terrace to the north. By then it had been decided that this should be a national memorial to Nelson and his victory at Trafalgar. Barry thought that the proposed column would dwarf the Gallery, but he was over-ruled and the 145ft Nelson Column designed by William Railton was erected. In November 1843 the 17ft high Craiglieth stone statue of the Admiral by E.H. Bailey was hoisted aloft to where it has remained ever since, although Hitler had a plan to remove it to Berlin after his invasion of England. 1867 saw the arrival of Sir Edwin Landseer's four lions, which Sir John Mortimer says look like aged and shifty politicians.

In return for the portion of graveyard the Commissioners were ordered to provide a space of equal dimensions underground to the north and east of the church for 3,300 burials, and to surround it with railings and gates. An expensive plan, it was implemented because underground burials would deter grave robbers and the beauty of the area would be enhanced. Railings were cast by the London iron founders, Cottam and Hallen, to match the original railings in the portico, and Nash specified that they should be 'painted four times in oil and coloured as bronze'. The consecration of the vaults took place on 7 June 1831 by Charles James Blomfield, Bishop of London. A tablet with the name of the vicar, Dr George Richards, and his wardens, John Gunter and James Aldridge, was placed on the entrance to the catacombs.

As burial fees were being lost the Commissioners had to pay £160 p.a. compensation for the next 11 years. The Vestry determined that interment would now cost:

> A parishioner £2-16-4
> Child parishioner £1-16-4
> Non-parishioner £7-0-10
> Child non-parishioner £4-10-10

Lead coffins should weigh six pounds to the foot. The first burial – on 5 September 1830, before the land was consecrated, – was of J.A Yates who had lived in the Strand. Two other burial grounds within the parish were also under the care of the wardens – Russell Court, Drury Lane which had 20,000 bodies interred over 50 years in 400 square yards, and the Tavistock paupers' cemetery in Drury Lane.

Dr George Richards, vicar 1834-44, realised that he could not accommodate all the parishioners who wanted to worship, so in 1833 at a cost of £6,000 he erected St Michael's, a Chapel of Ease, in Burleigh Street on the site of the old vicarage. At the same time he leased the Tavistock Chapel, Broad Court, Drury Lane, which had been built in 1763 by the 4th Duke of Bedford for the tenants of his estates. This meant, however, that the nearby Hanover (now St Mark's) Chapel had to be closed two years later and sold for £500. In 1855 the Tavistock became the separate parish of St John the Evangelist, Broad Court, and the wardens of St Martin's gave a lavish breakfast to celebrate. Their auditors objected to the £43 3s. 6d. spent but eventually relented.

In August 1853 an Order in Council forbade any more burials in the crypt. They had been causing a problem for some time, and in 1817 the wardens had paid £68 3s. 11d. to have the vaults cleaned, and again in 1841 the coffins had been re-stacked. Now they attempted another tidy-up and, as there were about 3,250 coffins in the crypt itself, the task was a huge one. An Order in Council authorised the clearance of the vaults, and churchwardens Benjamin Latchford and Charles H. Petter advertised in newspapers asking relatives to remove coffins before 1 February 1859. After that date the remains would either be taken to St Martin's Cemetery, Camden Town, or bricked up in three vaults in the south-eastern corner of the crypt under Adelaide Street and Duncannon Street, where they remained until 1938. In May Mr R.K. Burstall, the Vestry Surveyor, reported that approximately 1,857 coffins had been re-interred in the three new catacombs. All the bodies except 246 were listed by name and included a former vicar, Dr Richards, and his wife Hannah.[21]

Frank Buckland, a famous naturalist, spent 16 days trying to find the coffin of Dr John Hunter and has left us an account of his search: 'This crypt is supported by massive pillars, and the spaces between some of them are bricked up so as to form vaults, some large and some small. There are the rector's vault, the portico vault, and the steeple vault, as well as several smaller vaults taken by private families. The larger vaults were guarded by strong iron gates, through which the coffins could be seen from the outside. Mr Burstall having unlocked the ponderous oak door of the vault No.3, we threw the light of our bull's-eye lanterns into the vault, and then I beheld a sight I shall never forget. After our eyes had got accustomed to the light, we perceived that this vault was a good sized room, as full as it ever could hold with coffins, piled one over the other, from the very top to the very bottom. Many coffins were even piled up crosswise in front of the door, so that no entry could be obtained except by moving them and others were jammed up together in all possible positions, without the least attempt at order, reminding one much of books in a box to be sent away. To the left of this vault there began another, in which there was a great mass of wooden coffins of persons buried anterior to the Act which ordered that no person should be buried there except in lead. The faint and sickly effluvia which emanated from these was truly overpowering and poisonous.'[22]

One of the many projects initiated by Christians in London was the provision of bath-houses. Charles James Blomfield, Bishop of London, strongly backed the Bath and Wash Houses Act which permitted local boroughs to establish these on the rates. He did not, however, think that they should be free; there should be a charge of 2d. to discourage idle use. On 8 June 1846 he presented petitions, one of which was signed by 121 parochial clergy, to the government urging them to provide public baths for the poor. In getting the Act passed the Bishop was greatly helped by Sir Henry Dukinfield, vicar 1834-48, who persuaded the local authority to open a bath-house in Orange Street at a cost of £16,000. One of the first in London, it was opened by Mr Gladstone on 8 March 1849. It continued in use until 1911 when Westminster City Council felt that too few residents were using it to justify the extensive repairs needed.

Lewis's Topographical Dictionary, 1840, gives the population of the parish as 23,732. Those nearby which had been carved out of it also had large numbers which would soon decrease dramatically: St James, Piccadilly, 37,053; St Anne, Soho, 15,600; and St Paul, Covent Garden, 5,203. Victorian respectability demanded attendance at worship and a census taken in England on Sunday 30 March 1851, the evening of which was wet, revealed that out of a total population of 18 million people, 7,261,032 attended a service in church or chapel that day. At St Martin's, where the vicar was Dr Henry Mackenzie, later Suffragan Bishop of Nottingham, the figures were:

Morning: 1,500, Afternoon: 750, Evening: 1,300.

This was the second largest in London, some others being:

	Morn	Aft	Eve
West Hackney Parish Church:	1,750 +230 scholars	480	1,400
St Mary, Bryanston Square:	1,500+120	582+120	1,200
Holy Trinity, Marylebone:	1,443+133	582+7	1,305
St James, Piccadilly:	1,283+74	682+72	943
All Saints, West Ham:	743+289		600[23]

In 1855 began the 31-year incumbency of Prebendary William Humphry, a writer and scholar and a member of the committee which published the Revised Version of the New Testament. Extensive alterations were made to the building during his time: the choir had sat in the gallery near the organ, but now it was decided to seat them in the chancel, robed in surplices. It was closed so that some of the front pews could be removed, choir stalls could be erected in their present position on a marble pavement and new communion rails installed. These had been semi-circular but were now to be straight across, enclosing all the sanctuary.

The work was supervised by Thomas Hayter Lewis, Professor of Architecture at University College, London, 1865-81, and the architect of the incredible, Moorish-style Panopticon (1854) in Leicester Square. The pulpit lost its sounding-board and reading desks, and five mosaic panels, two on the flank walls and three behind the altar – replacing the Creed, Ten Commandments and Lord's Prayer – were installed in the sanctuary. A cream and gold redecoration took place and stained glass was put in the windows. The sanctuary and chancel floors were raised and paved with black and white tiles and three rows of choir stalls were added on each side of the chancel.

During this work the congregation worshipped in the small St Matthew's Chapel, 'a plain but convenient brick building' seating 300 and dating from 1731, which stood in Spring Gardens. Dr George Richards had taken it over in 1828 as a Chapel of Ease from the de Clifford family, whose private chapel it was. When extensions were planned to the nearby Admiralty in 1885 this was compulsorily purchased from St Martin's for £2,400 and eventually demolished in 1903.

Bedfordbury Mission Chapel, which was never consecrated, opened on 14 November 1861 and its services soon attracted more than local people. Mr Gladstone worshipped there occasionally, and in 1860 he and some of his friends including Sir William Harcourt, whom he made Home Secretary, had offered to build the chapel in the middle of Leicester Square. At that time the gardens of the Square were 'very ruinous and dilapidated', a playground 'for the unwashed Arabs of Westminster who disported themselves at their own will among the putrefying remains of dogs and cats'.[24] Mr Gladstone's plan would have cleaned the place up, and been a good long-term financial investment.

The site on the west side of Bedfordbury was small, only 60ft by 40ft, so Arthur Blomfield, the architect, placed the school above the chapel, which seated 240 people. As well as containing the staircase, the gabled tower had lavatories and two rooms in it. Named after the Good Shepherd because of the carving over the door, it soon became a centre of much parish social work thanks to curates like Pickering Clarke, who established clubs and gleefully reported in a letter of 17 June 1875 that 17 men in his Temperance Group had agreed not to tipple between meals for a month. The best efforts of the clergy and their workers did not, however, greatly improve social conditions in the area, and on 7 October 1875 John Skegg, the medical officer of the workhouse, reports:

> It is the black spot of this Royal Parish of Saint Martin in the Fields. Bedfordbury & the courts contiguous stand on a little over 3 acres and according to the last census of 1871 the population numbered 2,163. A long narrow street of 47 houses with courts leading out of it on either side. Some of these courts are blind & very narrow, thus rendering light and air difficult of access. These 47 houses are, with very few exceptions, so old and dilapidated that it is quite impossible to remodel so as to make them fit and proper habitations for the poor to live in.
>
> No. 37—33 people living in 6 rooms.
>
> No. 41—36 people in 9 rooms. In one room family of 6 & in another of 7. The banister rails broken, the treads of the stairs worn and dangerous when going up and down, especially for children; the closet dirty and frequently stopped up; the cistern which supplies the closet is also used for drinking purposes.
>
> I feel satisfied from the general condition of the houses in Bedfordbury that no amount of patching up can ever make them habitable places for the poor; therefore they should be pulled down and replaced by healthy homes.

At this time there were nine public houses in Bedfordbury; the only one remaining today is the *Lemon Tree*, which opened *c.*1737.[25] In 1880 the Peabody Trust and others cleared the area and built decent dwellings.

Prebendary Humphry attempted to make contact with the five common lodging houses in the parish by holding services in them on Sunday afternoons – although the men were forbidden to ask for cash. A clergyman would lead three hymns, say prayers and preach for ten minutes. During one winter the vicar entertained the men every Saturday evening in the recently vacated Quaker Meeting House to 'a substantial meat tea ... a screw of tobacco and a tankard of ale'. (Eyebrows were raised at the ale.) A concert followed.

An interesting wedding took place in St Martin's in June 1871 when Captain Martin Bates from Kentucky, a man well over seven feet tall, married a bride of equal height, Ann Swann of Nova Scotia. They had been on view at an exhibition in Willis's Rooms – as had their bridesmaids, Christine and Millie, who were Siamese twins.[26] Getting into the carriage after the service the groom put his foot through the floor.

The vicar died in the vicarage on 10 January 1886, to be succeeded by Prebendary Kitto who arrived with his eight children, cook and a large staff of servants. An extra floor had to be built on the vicarage to house them all. He kept his carriage in the vicarage mews, where his coachman lived. Amelia Purcell, who was a schoolgirl in the 1880s and lived in Peabody Buildings with her eight brothers and sisters, told Carolyn Scott what life was like at this time:

10 *The Bedfordbury Mission, 1861.*

St Martin's Lane was known as Dentists' Row. False teeth had just come in and you passed window after window of dentures. We were afraid they'd come and take our teeth and put them in the window.

Parents paid weekly to send children to the National School. It cost 2d. a week in the first year, 3d. in the second then 4d. and 6d. for the top class. They were church schools, and the teachers were employed by the Vicar. When people were very poor, he helped them. Children had a lot of illnesses then. It was quite ordinary to hear them calling out, 'Here's the fever cart!' Then you'd see a little child being carried down in a blanket.

We didn't often go to St. Martin's; I remember school prize-givings there. The pews were all locked in those days. They were kept for the rich people from Carlton House Terrace and St. James's Square. They were family pews and each had a number and we couldn't go into them. But we could walk down each side or sit on the rush chairs in the middle. I remember sitting on the rush chairs when I was little. The verger had a cane to keep us quiet. It was a very fashionable church and the rich people came in their carriages with their coachmen and footmen. There were mothers' meetings and the Band of Hope, needlework classes for coster women and classes for the flower women who sold buttonholes, and the step-women who cleaned the shops. The vicars were always very attentive to the poor people.[27]

It was obviously a time of great upheaval for the parish. The appeal which had been launched to meet the considerable cost of the improvements to the building had not raised sufficient money, but Queen Victoria, unwittingly, came to the rescue. It was announced that as part of her Golden Jubilee celebrations she would drive in an open carriage with a huge procession to a Service of Thanksgiving in St Paul's Cathedral. The route included Duncannon Street, so with permission from the Faculty Office the entrepreneurial vicar and wardens advertised to see if anyone would care to erect stands on the churchyard. Harrods paid £4,000 for the privilege and all money worries evaporated.[28] Fortunately a precedent had been set and further large sums were received at the Diamond Jubilee and later coronations.

Sir Arthur Blomfield, son of the great reforming Bishop of London, was now the architect appointed to supervise the necessary work, which included repairs to the steeple and the external stonework. In 1887 a large choir vestry was created in the crypt and a new staircase was installed at the north-east corner of the church to enable choristers to reach the clergy vestry. Pews were slightly altered and their doors removed. A shelf wide enough to take a top hat was provided, on which sat a Bible, prayer book and hymn book for each worshipper. The pulpit crossed the aisle to its present position at this time. New fittings for electricity were installed in 1888, and a few years later an Electrophone was installed so that those unable to attend could hear the service in their homes.

The plain glass in all the windows was not to the taste of the mid-Victorians so in June 1867 the three panels of the east window were filled with stained glass depicting the Ascension of Christ by Messrs Clayton and Bell. Gabriel Parry of *The Times* said, 'it is a very grand window … the most impossible of all subjects for painted glass is treated magnificently'. The cost of £654 2s. was met by subscribers who included the Lords of the Admiralty and Mr Gladstone. In 1888 the congregation filled one of the upper south side windows with stained glass as a memorial to Prebendary Humphry and all the windows were filled over the next 18 years, finishing with a Nativity design in a lower window in memory of Prebendary Kitto in 1906.

The Diamond Jubilee celebrations of 1897 included a Princess of Wales dinner for the poor of London, organised by St Martin's and held in various venues including the Town Hall, in which most of the cooking took place, local schools and the Orange Street Chapel. Tickets were issued to the poor, who could collect meat, plum pudding, bread, tea, sugar and tobacco at 9a.m. to take home if they wished. The large number of guests, who were entertained by a boys' band and music hall artists, consumed amongst other things 1,000lbs of meat, 500lbs of ham, five cwt of potatoes and 750lbs of plum pudding.[29] Three thousand people watched the procession from the stands.

Charles Booth, the business man and pioneer in social research whose 17-volume *Life and Labour of the People in London* was written between 1886 and 1903, interviewed Mr Kitto on 27 May 1898 and was not impressed, perhaps because he was only given an hour:

Though with a not unkindly expression he is exceedingly ugly ... sallow parchment expression, small eyes peering through a narrow slit, strange protruding lips ... He is small, awkward and ungainly. The parish contains literally every class, 'from the Queen to the crossing sweeper'. Speaking of his wealthy parishioners generally Mr K said that they had 'no souls, only purses'. If you call on them they always assume that you want money and to their credit be it said that they pay up well ... but beyond this their support to the church is very lax. The parish is becoming non-residential ... There is however a considerable working class population left, probably some 3 or 4,000, mostly of a poor class, and in Turner's Court very rough.

Mr K says that the population is one peculiarly difficult to work among as it lives in 'the centre of pleasure-seeking.

11 *The Rev. Prebendary John Kitto, vicar, 1886-1903.*

Many of them find their living in the theatres, the children act in pantomimes and all have a tendency to be stage struck. It is too exciting to be good ... the district is saturated with drink and prostitution.' Mr K declined to give figures for attendance on a Sunday but late morning and evening especially in winter the church is well filled or even full. 'As to my congregation, with a few exceptions of people who have pews allotted to them, I can't tell who they are: they are constantly shifting and changing'. Mr K claims, however, that a very large number of the poorer parishioners are occasional if not habitual worshippers.[30]

Booth borrowed some of the parish visiting books and discovered that, of the occupants of 91 tenements, 32 had a worshipper at St Martin's – usually the wife. He was impressed that all homes were visited several times a year but notes that 'there is a good deal of badgering to attend services and meetings'. He lists many extracts from the books including:

Peabody Bldgs
D2 Boston. French Polisher. Bad tempered man: there are twins: Wife extremely under influence of All Saints Sisters. Mrs Boston promised to go to Evening Services. 3rd visit. Visitor saw Mr Boston alone ... would try to attend Men's Services.
D4 Motley. Man in bad health. Woman monthly nurse: large family: rather inclined to beg: would be church or chapel whichever paid best.

Bedfordbury
Collier. Man lame: keeps cat meat barrow. Mrs C promised to go to Mission Sunday, worked hard and too tired week days. Mr C would not promise even Sundays ... 3 girls, 16, 12 and 7 do not go SS: eldest out with her father and barrow Sunday morning: next girl cooks dinner. 3rd visit Mrs C promised girls for SS.

Smith. Postman: very devout and eccentric, peculiar views: wife the same: children not baptised.
24 Top back. Widow O'Hara son, actor, supported her. Very strange, talks to herself about murder.
5 First front. Cosford. Wife seldom sober, low people, 4 children.
8 Second floor, front. Alfred Beresford. All the Bs are idle and begging.[31]

Booth noted that Mrs Kitto, a very sweet looking lady, had a quiet influence for good in the parish and though her husband had no great personal attraction he had a thorough grip on his parish – 'Though that side of his character did not come out in our conversation he is probably a man of genuine piety.'

1900-1914

A proposal to remove the front steps was made in 1900 because the huge volume of traffic was causing congestion in the tiny road to the west of St Martin's and more space was needed. This act of vandalism was averted because the vicar and wardens agreed to take away the wide steps and replace them with new steps with no wide ledge in the centre. This added five feet to the highway and was paid for by the new Westminster City Council. The year before, when the tube line was being constructed under the church and school, a sum of £1,200 was paid by the Charing Cross, Euston and Hampstead Tube Railway as compensation for the inconvenience caused.

When plans for King George V's coronation were under way the wardens began to panic as the Chancellor of the diocese Dr Tristam, who had to issue the Faculty to erect the lucrative stands, was ill. Prebendary Shelford, vicar 1903-1914, and Churchwarden John McMaster drove to the Chancellor's home in Hampton where the court was held in his bedroom.[32] Messrs Keith, Prowse took the licence as they had done for King Edward's coronation, and the income was used to paint the interior, adjust the bells and repair the railings. £800 of the £1,850 profit was used to restore the organ. The stands were also used a few days later when the King and Queen drove to St Paul's. This time Keith, Prowse and Co. invited 4,000 local schoolchildren and their teachers to watch the procession and wardens Rudderforth and McMaster made sure that they were filled with food and drink.

By the end of the century the population of the parish was decreasing rapidly – it had gone down a third in 15 years to around 9,000 in 1902. The Daily News did a census of churchgoing in Westminster on 11 January 1903 and discovered that in St Martin's 888 attended the Morning Service and 448 the Evening Service. The attendances at the two services in the Bedfordbury Mission Chapel totalled 178. The Registers show that during the previous year 3,044 made their communion, a drop of a sixth since 1897.

Dr Kitto was now having a quarrel with Westminster City Council, who claimed unsuccessfully that it owned all the portraits of previous incumbents in the Vestry Hall because they were civil as well as ecclesiastical functionaries. They were probably angry that the vicar had criticised them for keeping their

12 *The Coronation Procession passes the stands outside St Martin's, 1902.*

bath-houses open and employing men to clean the streets and lay paving stones on the Sabbath. Towards the end of the year he fell ill and the doctors told him he was worn out by his work. On Easter Monday 1903 he died in the vicarage. Before being appointed he had spent nearly all his ministry in the East End as incumbent of three important, large parishes, St Matthias, Poplar, St Mary, Whitechapel and St Dunstan, Stepney. George Lansbury, the famous pacifist Labour politician, said that as a boy he had been greatly influenced by him in the Whitechapel Sunday School, although his mother would take him afterwards to the Primitive Methodists in Banner Lane 'to hear about Hell'. George was prepared for confirmation and later married to Bessie in 1880 by Kitto, 'who entered into our lives, teaching us mainly by example'.[33]

Bearded, formidable and looking like an Old Testament prophet, the new vicar Leonard Shelford was 67, and according to the Bishop of London had 'the ripe experience of a man, the enthusiasm of a youth and the heart of a child'. An enthusiastic optimist, he had served with distinction in East London parishes where he had trained 17 curates over 43 years. He refused to be bullied by Westminster City Council, which was now claiming that it owned the Vestry Hall, citing the Local Government Act of 1899 as their authority. The case was heard in the Chancery Court before Mr Justice Joyce in November 1906 and lasted seven days. On 30 November judgement was given in favour of the vicar and wardens; the judge commenting that this had not been 'a very generous action' on Westminster's part. The Council had to pay costs.

As the residential population was declining Mr Shelford decided to close St Michael's, Burleigh Street. It was demolished in 1905, the valuable site was sold, and the proceeds used to build St Michael, Chiswick which was given the font, pulpit, choir stalls, plate, organ and bells. Patronage was placed in the hands of the vicar of St Martin's where it still rests. Mr Shelford was deeply hurt by the criticisms he received when he appointed his son, telling the *Messenger* that as he had held curacies in the diocese for 12 years he deserved the living.

Gymnastic classes for girls organised by the Misses Buck and a Slate Club enabling 100 members to save sixpence a week were among the many parish organisations in 1908. The fifth annual dinner for the over 60s was attended by 70 parishioners who listened afterwards to 'pleasant songs' from the Misses Fleming and Miss Zoller. The latter had also sung at a ham tea for the Mothers' Meeting when Mr Ernest James gave 'some capital recitations' according to the vicar, who sent each guest home with a ticket for a hundredweight of coal. The Band of Hope, the Men's Club, the Choral and Literary Societies and the Girls Friendly Society met weekly and there were 329 children in the Sunday school. An energetic body of nearly 100 volunteers and paid staff enabled all this to happen.

Parish life was obviously lively and on Easter Day 1908 there were 160 communicants and 27 at the Bedfordbury Chapel. During the year there were 57 baptisms, 58 weddings and 43 churchings. The Good Friday Evening Service was particularly popular, possibly because it was held in the Garrick Theatre and then, for three years running, in the Pavilion Music Hall. By 1911 the parish population had fallen to 7,682 because many homes were being replaced by offices and shops, but attendance remained stable and communicants on Easter Day rose to 246 in the parish church with 124 in Bedfordbury.

A bomb hidden under a pew in the south aisle exploded on the evening of Palm Sunday, 5 April 1914. Fortunately no one was injured but it cracked several of the stained glass windows. The tin canister wrapped in suffragette literature had a clockwork device which exploded it at 10.28p.m., and within five minutes a crowd of 1,000 people had gathered outside.[34] McMaster was acidic:

> Saint Martin's church contains one of the surest and simplest examples of women's ability to work on public boards, viz., the windows erected in the church by Mrs M. M. Evans, with the titles of the offices held by her in St. Martin's parish at the time, e.g., overseer, vestrywoman and a guardian of the poor, surely a more effective argument for the vote than placing infernal machines in any place of worship, which is more likely to retard than advance the cause.[35]

The following month, on 29 May, Dr Shelford died aged 77, and was buried at Walthamstow. Hamilton Rose, one of his assistant priests, said in a tribute that he was 'thoroughly human and never acquired clerical mannerisms or narrowness of outlook'.

On 4 August war was declared on Germany.

4

Dick and Pat

The Rev. Canon H.R.L.Sheppard, Vicar 1914-26
The Rev. Canon W.P.G. McCormick, Vicar 1927-40

The two famous incumbents of St Martin's in the early 20th century were known simply as Dick and Pat – somewhat surprising in an age of ecclesiastical stuffiness. Both men were decidedly unstuffy and created an informal atmosphere in and around the church which has lasted until today. They had known one another since birth and their lives crossed and re-crossed. Dick's father, Canon Edgar Sheppard, was Sub Dean of the Chapels Royal at St James's Palace when Pat's father was Rector of St James, Piccadilly. Dick always said that he had been brought to ordination by a sermon preached by Canon McCormick, who was a big man in every way. Six feet and three inches and 17 stone, he was a great oarsman and athlete who had once bowled out W.G.Grace. Pat was the fourth of McCormick's eight children.

Dick, born in 1880, was only three years younger than Pat so together they decided to volunteer to serve in the Boer War at the turn of the century, but on his way to the station Dick was thrown out of his cab when one of the horses fell. A cab shaft went through his leg, which left him with a permanent limp. While he convalesced, Pat arrived in South Africa. But the war had ended while he was on board ship, and the Bishop asked him to become chaplain to the gold mines in Cleveland. The miners gave him a rough time but like his father he was well over six feet and being a keen rugby player could look after himself. In Cleveland he met Miriam Shelton, sister-in-law to one of the managers, and when, in 1910, he was given a parish in Johannesburg, they were married.[1]

Whilst Pat was in Africa Dick graduated in 1904 from Trinity Hall, Cambridge where he told everyone that study had not been a priority. He became a member of the Bad Eating Club by eating jelly through his nose. During vacations he did voluntary work at Oxford House, Bethnal Green, which then as now served the most deprived in East London. There he met another student, William Temple, who later became Archbishop of Canterbury, and the two men became great friends. Dick found academic work dull and tiresome for, as Dean Matthews said later, 'Knowledge divorced from activity had little interest for him.'

Central London Recruiting Depot,
Whitehall, S.W.,
8th August, 1914.

To WHOM IT MAY CONCERN.

The Schools situated in St. Martin's Lane, W.C.,

being required as a Recruiting Office, YOU ARE

HEREBY DIRECTED TO HAND THE SAME OVER

WITHOUT DELAY TO THE BEARER OF THIS

WARRANT. *together with such arm. y.*
S. Martin, Churchyard and as may be considered *

For His Majesty's Secretary of State for War,

Captain,
Recruiting Staff Officer.

* *essential with the undertaking which*
I give hereby that the consecrated nature
of the ground shall be duly respected

13 The school building is requisitioned, 1914.

Whilst at Oxford House he was spotted by another soon-to-be Archbishop, Cosmo Gordon Lang, Bishop of Stepney. Always on the lookout for talented, handsome young men, Lang invited him to be his secretary at 2 Amen Court and later said, 'He delighted me with his wilful wayward whimsical ways'. The older brother relationship blossomed – there were only 15 years between the two men – and when Dick decided to be ordained he went to 'the holy hill' at Cuddesdon, Lang's beloved alma mater near Oxford. On leaving London he told his replacement, 'You'll find him clean about the house'. Like many he found Cuddesdon an infuriatingly snobbish place but grew to love its ordered life and Catholic worship.

On 6 October 1907 he was made deacon in St Paul's Cathedral and went to work not in a parish but at Oxford House as chaplain. His boxing and cricketing skills proved to be more useful than his intellect and he built up large men's and boys' clubs. The poverty of the area appalled him – the police patrolled in pairs and he stayed late in the pubs to try to discourage his men from getting drunk. Often there were fights: 'If there were only two or three I took them on, if there were more I cleared out.'[2] One of the local women described him as 'a small, kindly man always laughing … he had a very very deep religious belief, as if he lived so close to God that it brushed off on you.' However, his health suffered and after three years Lang secured him a job in the West-End parish of St George, Hanover Square. The men did not forget him: 25 years later a homeless man was found dead on the Embankment, his only possession a letter from Dick.

Four years later, on the outbreak of the Great War, Pat returned to England. He and Dick wanted to enlist but only Pat was accepted and he left immediately for France as a chaplain. Despite opposition from the King, Dick was allowed to spend three months in the trenches before arriving at St Martin's and the experience changed his life. In September a badly mutilated German soldier refused an injection in the English hospital thinking he was about to be killed so Dick was sent for. He told him, 'I am trying to represent Jesus Christ whom you know about in this world that is beside itself. Supposing I return with a crucifix and a syringe of morphine will you please trust me to serve you in the name of Jesus?' The man agreed. Dick celebrated his 34th birthday kneeling by a dying soldier:

> As I bent to catch his painfully-spoken words, I discovered that he had little need of my ministry. He was thinking of a life that was still unborn. His wife was expecting a baby at Christmas, and he died thanking God that if the child was a boy, he would never have to go through the hell of a war. That man believed what he had been told – that he was fighting in the war to end war. Innumerable others also believed it and died, as he did, at least happy in the thought that their sons would be spared Calvary.[3]

Dick's Incumbency

Dick had been offered St Martin's on 14 July 1914. Now 34, he had been in the ministry only seven years and so, slightly apprehensive, he went to look. 'I did not find the atmosphere stimulating. The church struck me as cold and rather depressing ... as for the high pulpit – well! If I ever got into it, I should be as remote as Nelson in the Square.' His second visit the following Sunday was even less encouraging.

> The service was conducted by a little man with an amazingly powerful voice ... He roared at us as if he were a sergeant-major shouting against the wind. The sermon – the longest I think I have ever sat through – seemed to urge us to give all we possessed to a certain church society ... for which I had a peculiar dislike. In the gallery were a few children very insufficiently policed, and one small boy created great diversion by popping his head up over the pew near the preacher, to make faces at a friend below, and then with incredible speed racing round to repeat his antics on the opposite side of the gallery.

He visited the hospital, walked round the parish and sat on a bench all night talking to the homeless. 'That night's impressions persuaded me that no square mile could provide a more thrilling or adventurous pitch.'

During his summer in the trenches he had written down his hopes,

> I saw a great church standing in the greatest square in the greatest city of the world ... There passed me into its warm inside hundreds and hundreds of all sorts of people, going up to the temple of their Lord, with all their difficulties, trials and sorrows ... And I said to them, 'Where are you going?' And they said only one thing, 'This is our home. This is where we are going to learn of the love of Jesus Christ'.[4]

Some have suggested that there were only 11 people present at the Induction in November 1914 and that attendance was low, but this was not so. The parish records show that Easter communicants totalled 238 in 1913; 2,393 made their communion during that year and there were 40 confirmation candidates. Dick found that the building and its organ were in good shape and the parish organisations were flourishing, including a Mothers' Meeting with a membership of 100, a large Sunday school of 234 and a gymnastics class led by Miss Queenie Buck whose star pupils amongst the 90 girls were Elsie Nutty and Babs Fitt.[5]

Dick obviously did not enjoy the Induction – 'The whole Service was almost the unhappiest recollection I have' he wrote later – but the *Messenger* noted that a large congregation attended the service. The two churchwardens gave him a cool welcome: they were John McMaster, a local shop-owner who would later write the first history of St Martin's, and a gentleman who told him that he was too busy as a publican to attend Sunday worship. No doubt they were apprehensive about the changes which soon became evident. Sunday services were re-arranged so that Morning Prayer was detached from the Communion which became the main choral service, and the new vicar appealed for 150 people to form a voluntary choir to sing at the new 8p.m. People's Service. A side chapel at the east end of the south aisle, designed by Sir Arthur Blomfield, was created for smaller weekday services. Parishioners were asked to pay two pence for the monthly *Messenger*.

The Parochial Church Council were persuaded to abolish reserved seats, much to the horror of an old lady who had installed all sorts of comforts in 'her' pew including an umbrella stand.[6] Reserved cards had caused chaos when Archbishop Lang came to preach. The two elementary schools in Adelaide Street with 430 pupils, the Northern Schools with 350 in Castle Street and Archbishop Tenison's Boys School in Leicester Square all took up much of the new incumbent's time, as did the nearby Charing Cross Hospital.

After five months Dick became unwell and his doctors ordered him to rest for four months. During this time he married Alison Carver, a good-looking, tall, blond woman, in her parish church in Cheshire. There had been two broken engagements with women who soon realised he was wedded to his job but Alison took up the challenge. She had once told a friend that she was easily bored. This was not to be a problem over the next few years.

By now the war was raging in France with a horrific number of dead and wounded on both sides. Recruiting took place at St Martin's and Captain Annesley, the officer in charge, and his team based in the Vestry Hall and vicarage stables sent hundreds of men to the various regiments. People would often come to lay flowers near the altar since they could not visit graves in France. Charing Cross station was the point of arrival and departure for many of the troops. Dick opened the church and crypt all day and night so that men arriving in the early hours found a warm place to shelter and receive food. He was often there to greet them himself. A red lamp, which in France had other connotations, was installed over the west door to welcome everyone. Some of the congregation thought all sorts of bugs and diseases would be brought into the building and one old lady was heard to say, 'What with air raids outside the church and you inside there seems nothing but explosions'.

An Electrophone had been installed in the pulpit for some time which permitted the sick or elderly at home who subscribed to the owners of the company to listen to theatre productions and church services. Dick thought this was great fun and would occasionally whisper to someone a message which the congregation could not hear, such as 'switch off now, Nellie' to an old lady who didn't like his socialist views. While the band played he once sent a message to his wife saying: 'Don't get up tonight, Alison,' and later received a letter from another Alison expressing deep wonder at his insight as she had been told by her doctor to get up, but now wouldn't!

By 1916 Easter communicants had doubled to 561 which included 99 in the hospital where a full-time chaplain, the Rev. W.G. Rudd, was now appointed, thus allowing the St Martin's clergy to devote more time to the parish. A clutch of complaints followed the changes to Morning Prayer, which the vicar said had not been 'a converting or sustaining Service ... It is not conducive to a realised contact with God'. Open-air Lent Services were held in various parts of the parish: 'We spoke mainly to heads behind windows at the top of the buildings and the wall opposite.' In December it was announced that thanks to the generosity of Lady Wantage the northern vaults under the passage would be converted into a new hall.

By the beginning of 1917 the church was attracting a great deal of attention. 'It is a challenge in stone,' wrote John Garrett Leigh, 'with its lectures, services, pageants etc ... it is to become a kind of Sorbonne, a little University, a place which helps ordinary people to understand religion ... There is no realm of human life which is not to be brought to the touchstone of the Cross.' New ideas were welcomed and sermons tackled subjects like democracy, economics and human interdependence. A Guild of Fellowship was started and a first parish conference discussed the life and liturgy of the church. By now 1,200 were attending Sunday services.

In February a Sunday afternoon service was started for those in the Armed Forces with one of the Guards' Bands playing and the wounded seated in the front pews. These were immediately popular and 1,300 attended the second one. There were plenty of well-known hymns and always a rousing sermon from the vicar. In October the King and Queen attended. Somewhat

14 *The First World War: soldiers pray in St Martin's before leaving from Charing Cross for the trenches.*

flustered, Dick prepared a note to remind himself to welcome the Royals but by mistake left it in the royal pew: 'Loyal and sincere gratitude to His Majesty, but no soap.'[7] To begin with the services were only for men but after a while he allowed lady guests. Women would wait outside and link hands with a soldier to get in. Some of the men had only just arrived at Charing Cross so, worn and weary, they would sleep in the back pews. Dick said they must not be disturbed which led to a newspaper headline, 'Broad minded Vicar advocates sleeping during Service'. In November over 4,000 came to the Patronal Festival Services.

The beginning of 1918 brought local tragedy when a bomb fell on a large printing works near the church where many men and women were sheltering, including the much loved vicar of St Paul's, Covent Garden, the Rev. E.H. Mosse, who was killed instantly. A young boy rescued four children but was killed as he brought out a little girl on his back. The horror of the trenches had come nearer home and 4,000 attended the Memorial Service. On St Martin's Day, 11 November, came the end of the war. 'The maroons went off on Monday and we went mad,' wrote Dick, 'and the rest of the week we got rather violent in the Square every evening at sunset.' Hundreds came to pray, 'some looking so gloriously happy and some so unutterably sad.' The following Sunday there were huge congregations at all services with queues stretching down Adelaide Street to Duncannon Street.

The area around the building was now giving cause for concern, with many adults and children begging. Prostitution and illegal trading were so rife that an Association was formed which employed two policewomen to try to make contact with girls on the streets. The YMCA provided a place where they and the drunken soldiers found in the gutter could be taken. The Church Army and a further four policewomen were called in to help, patrolling until 4 a.m. Seventy-four women asked for help and some returned home but others, lured by the large sums of cash on offer, returned to the streets. Dick despaired that so little help was available. The Charing Cross Association, led by him, naively put on a service for prostitutes and their clients 'with the object of raising their moral standards and bringing them a message of hope'. Six policewomen, 30 girls and no clients attended, and the venture was not repeated.

The end of the war resulted in thousands of troops flooding back to England to be demobbed; all carried with them horrendous memories of the trenches which would remain for ever. Cynicism and contempt for authority allied to an embittered resentment for the needless slaughter they had witnessed caused many to turn away from religion. Where was God in all this? The padres returned with similar feelings and many believed they no longer fitted into the comfortable structures of the Church of England. One of them, Tubby Clayton, the founder of Toc H, who had named his chapel at Poperinghe after St Martin's, was greatly helped by Dick to find a house in London to be the headquarters of his 4,000 local branches; two parishioners gave him £10,000.

Another padre, G.A. Studdert Kennedy, 36, vicar of St Paul's, Worcester, returned to London to put his life together. In March 1919 he walked into

15 *The Rev. Canon Dick Sheppard, Vicar 1914-27, welcomes King George V and Queen Mary to St Martin's, October 1917.*

Dick's study and much to the latter's astonishment treated him to a lecture on the person of Jesus. The vicar observed 'An ugly little man, with wonderful eyes, wearing an immense collar using strange and strong language.' Woodbine Willie, as he had been known in the trenches (where his asthma had been severely aggravated by gas), had been a famous padre in France but was now dogged by self-doubt and depression. Awarded the MC, he had been made a royal chaplain by King George V so Dick looked at him with curiosity. Could they work together? They did for several months. Even after leaving his temporary job at St Martin's, he returned many times to preach at the Sunday afternoon services, helping the men there turn their rage and self-pity into something positive. The teachings of Jesus provided a possible answer. 'That chap must have been on the dole,' said one ex-soldier, 'or he could never talk like that.' His poetry and sermons expressed his feelings:

> Waste of Blood and waste of Tears
> Waste of youth's most precious years,
> Waste of ways the Saints have trod
> Waste of Glory, Waste of God –
> War![8]

Fortunately an Irish sense of humour lightened his sermons and, like Dick, he could have his audience laughing and crying in a short space of time. The two men spent hours talking together and there was never a trace of jealousy or envy. In 1921 Studdert was invited to preach at the Good Friday Service held in the Strand theatre, and the *Morning Post* reported, 'On the stage throughout the whole of the time stood the priest, burning with nervous zeal. Men – there were hundreds of them – and women sat as if hypnotised, moved often to tears.' However, the man was a maverick and in October the *Review* commented, 'The Revd G.A. Studdert Kennedy is now officially on the staff though we have not the slightest idea where he is or where he is living.'

The following year he became Rector of St Edmund the King in the City of London which gave him a base for his work as Missioner for the Industrial Christian Fellowship. His long-suffering wife saw little of him as he travelled to every part of the country and in 1929, aged only 46, he was dead, physically and emotionally worn out. In the *Review* Dick tried to sum up his feelings: 'For some his language in the pulpit was too colloquial but it was sincere, intelligent, human preaching ... he walked around whilst talking, tears often falling down. A mystic and a poet. The Irish accent made his speech irresistible. Perhaps there was too much intellectual meat in his sermons, perhaps they were a little long but he was the biggest little man of our day.' William Temple referred to Studdert's 'Great Illumination', which was that God in Christ is personally involved in our sufferings – only that helped him to face the horror of the trenches.[9] Faith is a gamble and he was willing to bet his life upon God's side in life's Great War but the cost to him was enormous.

It was now decided to close the Bedfordbury Chapel which had served that area for over 50 years. The organ, font, reredos and two stained glass windows were sold for £20 and a 14-year lease of the building from Lady Day 1919 was granted to Messrs Harrisons.[10]

The year 1920 began with many hundreds being turned away from the Watch Night Service. Lady Margot Asquith, wife of the former Prime Minister, wrote to the vicar, 'Is it possible to get into your church? I stood from 11.00 to 11.30 last Sunday, and then sat on a hassock.' The situation was getting impossible and a note appeared in the *Review* from Dick: 'I am afraid it is increasingly difficult at times for those who live in the parish to get a seat at the 11.30am and 6.15pm Sunday Services. Any parishioner arriving before the Service begins will be given a good seat if they approach the wardens.' Collections soared from £265 in January to £541 in October and 5,000 people worshipped on Harvest Festival Sunday.

The congregation was a good cross-section of society with all classes represented. Dick loved to tell the story of a Dowager apologising for not being at church, 'My daughter has just come out.' 'Yes, so has my son,' said her neighbour, 'How long did your daughter get?' One morning an Admiral, 'all gold braid and temperament', pranced up the aisle about as calm as a centre of a cyclone, saying, 'What sort of pilot do you want?' Dick trying to be funny said, 'A sky pilot.' He was then told that the flag on the church flagstaff said the ship urgently needed a pilot. The nearby Admiralty enjoyed the joke, and agreed the building could be an honorary ship.

Nurse Edith Cavell's Memorial Service had been held at St Martin's six days after her execution in 1915 and the Bishop of London, Winnington Ingram, who enjoyed wearing khaki and preaching anti-German rhetoric, said there would be no further need of recruiting campaigns because her death would inspire young men to fight. In 1920 a statue of her by Sir George Frampton was erected in the middle of the road outside the vicarage. Dick crept out after dark to inspect it, and a policeman surprised to see the tarpaulin billowing went to investigate. Dick thought it an artistic abomination, and began a campaign to have her final words inscribed on the plinth. Cavell, the daughter of a Norfolk parson, had for five years been a governess to a Belgian family before returning home to care for her father. In 1907 she was asked to become Matron of Belgium's first nurses' training school. On the outbreak of war she stayed there, nursing soldiers and helping them to escape. An informer infiltrated the resistance

16 'Woodbine Willie', the Rev. G.A. Studdert Kennedy, an honorary member of staff at St Martin's after the First World War.

movement, of which she was part, and she was arrested in St Gilles, and found guilty of treason. At dawn on 12 October 1915 she was shot. She faced death with serenity and, having received communion, said the words which it took Dick four years to have written below her statue:

> Patriotism is not enough.
> I must have no hatred or bitterness
> For anyone.

The following year a Pageant was held for five evenings in the Great Hall (now demolished) of Church Hall, Westminster to commemorate the 200th anniversary of the consecration of St Martin's. Alison produced it, Dick played the beggar, Gustav Holst conducted the choir and Morley College provided the orchestra. Laurence Housman, 'romantically agnostic, conservative and radical', an admirer of Christianity but not the Church, wrote the script. Afterwards Dick, worn out, had to go into a nursing home for several weeks but the Pageant was repeated the following year in the Lyceum theatre on five Sunday evenings, the last attracting an audience of three thousand.

The *Review* was now fast becoming an important theological journal and bestseller; monthly sales rose from 1,500 in 1919 to nearly 6,000 in 1924. It also had other uses: police investigating a robbery in central London discovered a jemmy wrapped up in it. In November 1925 15,000 copies were sold including 4,000 to postal subscribers. Lord Astor wrote on the liquor trade, Hilaire Belloc on Germany, and provocative articles included 'Is Life Insurance Gambling?' and 'The Dictatorship of Newspaper Owners'. The institution of the Church often came in for an editorial lambasting from the vicar: 'In the War we saw the tasks in their true proportions but the Church is now becoming timid and safe. The nation needs a prophet but receives a chaplain who says grace. The Establishment must go.' Bertine Buxton, 21, assisted by her dog, was the business manager and Jef Francis, who owned the antiquated Athenaeum Press, was the printer. There were soon subscribers in 40 countries: 'We are delighted to announce that in one of the islands in the Pacific fifty per cent of the white population take the Review,' wrote Dick, going on to say there were only two on the island! His request for a piece from George Bernard Shaw resulted in a postcard, 'I shall not send an article for your bloody Review GBS.' He replied, 'Dear Mr Shaw, thank you so much for your postcard which will be printed in full in the next number.' An article came by return.

Between 1922 and 1924 over £12,000 was spent restoring and redecorating the church, which also needed new lighting. Edward Maufe, the architect, reported that the walls would be painted oyster white and a cerulean blue, as in the cathedral at Pisa, and that he had decided the pews and panelling would remain black. The Vestry Hall was repaired, and a rostrum, bandstand and coffee stall were placed in the yard as a service to the neighbourhood. A plaque in the present crypt records that all this was paid for by voluntary contributions.

In 1924 the British Isles became St Martin's parish when Mr J.C. (later Lord) Reith, Managing Director of the BBC, asked Dick to broadcast a Monthly Service from the church, believing that there must be a connection between broadcasting and the Christian religion. The first was held at 6.15 p.m. on 6 January. Amongst the 1,000 letters which poured in was one from a scandalised priest who was worried that it might be heard by a man in a public house with his hat on, and the Rev. A.G. Edwards, vicar of St Stephen, Norbury wrote, 'You have set on foot a practice of having a kind of entertainment (for it can be called nothing else) during the time of Evening Service. If it is necessary to provide a Service for Invalids by the Wireless surely it could be done at a time when other churches are not holding their Services.'

Listeners included people in Algiers, Switzerland and Estonia and the crew of a ship in the Suez Canal sent a fan letter. A Dutchman said the sound was 'As of hundreds of kettles with boiling water and thousands of singing birds'. Later technical developments fortunately improved the quality of the sound and the service was moved to 8.15 p.m. on the second Sunday of every month. Many housebound said how much they appreciated it all. A Wiltshire correspondent wrote, 'Next door to me is living an old blind lady. In the summer I used to put my loud speaker in the garden under her bedroom window and your Services were a great joy to her.' A schoolboy told Dick, 'Your sermon on kindliness had such an effect upon our Head Master he actually commended us on our good work. A very unusual occurrence.' A listener in Australia offered to donate five milking goats and one stud billy that would graze in the Fields and supply milk to the poor.

Listeners were invited to the Albert Hall to hear an entertainment by the Mayfair Singers, the Master of the Music leading songs and Dick giving an Address. Ten thousand applied for tickets and Reith said that it was the first time the owner of the voice met the owner of the ears. All this attention resulted in huge numbers looking to St Martin's for spiritual leadership and the electoral roll of regular worshippers now numbered 1,394. Services were held once again in the church – not the crypt – with the walls now re-painted, the organ cleaned, bells re-hung and the tower and roof repaired at a cost of £12,500.

In Vancouver, Canada the Rev. Lloyd Keating died and bequeathed a large sum of money so that a new building could replace a brown shingle church in Victoria where he had been a curate in the early years of the century and be named St Martin-in-the-Fields. This was built and opened in 1926. Several gifts, including a piece of stone engraved with the saint on it, crossed the Atlantic and later money was sent to build a belfry.

By now Dick was once again physically and spiritually worn out, so just before Christmas he went away to Italy and Australia for six months. His mother had died and, as had been the case with his father, he felt guilty that he had drifted away from them. His family always came second: Alison rarely went to church and his daughters saw little of him. One said, 'He was special and removed and I adored him … He was always ill. Growing up was the sound of coughing and gasping for breath behind closed doors. We were always being kept away from him.' Early in the new year he wrote from Ceylon to say that his asthma was much worse but he returned to work in May 1925, opening a hostel in Grosvenor Road for homeless men.

In the autumn he was horrified to discover that a Ball was to be held on Armistice Day in the Albert Hall so, working quickly, he persuaded the organisers to withdraw and himself arranged a huge Service of Remembrance for 4,000 people, including the King and Queen, which continues every year to this day. Shortly after this he offered to resign and a shocked PCC, after adjourning for a fortnight, suggested he work for six months each year, allowing the Rev. C.H. Ritchie as his deputy to look after everything. Full of frustration, he agreed and he and Alison left for Egypt and then Capri. He returned in time for the General Strike the following May, when mass meetings were held in Trafalgar Square and the crypt was full to overflowing each night, but he was confined to his bed for seven weeks with asthma which was no doubt aggravated by the 50 cigarettes he smoked each day.

Alison found all this impossible to cope with and went away on her own. In October he announced he would leave after Christmas with no job to go to. Fortunately, as an American admirer had bequeathed £100,000 to St Martin's and £20,000 to him, there would be no financial hardship and he was able to move to 2 Holland Road in Kensington. Enormous sadness surrounded his departure but people realised that ill health had defeated him. He had been away for 18 months during his 12-year incumbency.

In May 1929 he accepted the Deanery of Canterbury. One of the choristers observed that he was like a bomb falling on the cloisters and Housman, hearing he refused to wear the correct garb, wrote,

> Dick says that wearing gaiters
> His legs are in a pen
> They act as separators
> 'Twixt him and other men.[11]

Pat had been to see the Prime Minister, who lobbied hard to get him the job, but it only lasted two years and after a spell in a nursing home he moved to a house near Guildford. Pat urged him to return to London, and a room was made available in the vicarage. A canonry at St Paul's Cathedral was eventually offered to him and the family moved to 1 Amen Court where like so many before and after him he complained that the Cathedral had no soul – 'They crush all that is human in the place.'[12] In January 1935 the wardens asked Dick to leave the Cathedral and be Assistant to the Vicar, but he declined. He threw himself with gusto into the new Movement for Peace; 100,000 people pledged their support and he travelled all over England preaching and teaching. His ardent pacifism fitted well into the appeasement movement of the 1930s so detested by Churchill, and some have suggested that it strengthened Hitler's view that the British would never fight. Dick had many critics: the *Church Times* said his theology was 'mischievous and dangerous', and to a despairing Lang it was 'tiresome and unhelpful'. Sydney Dark told the *Review*: 'It is sentimental modernism backed by a tremendous enthusiasm for service and good works.'[13]

By now Alison had begun a new relationship, and eventually left Dick after 22 years of marriage. She had found it difficult to cope with his need to work every minute of the day, and his deep personal unhappiness was showing itself in periods of intense gloom. He may have been a manic-depressive, but it is impossible to diagnose after such a long period of time. She became absorbed in her loneliness and sought comfort in another man. Great unhappiness lurked beneath the surface of the marriage, carefully concealed from everyone. The end came unexpectedly in May 1937 when Dick, aged only 57, was found dead in his bedroom at Amen Court by Pat and Miriam.

A portrait of him in his black – not scarlet – cassock wearing the Companion of Honour decoration was painted by Sir Gerald Kelly, PRA, and Cosmo Gordon Lang in a revealing moment said that it looked at him and said, 'You hypocrite'.

17   *The Rev. Canon Pat McCormick, Vicar 1927-40.*

Pat's Incumbency

McCormick was 37 when war began and the next four years stretched him to his limits. Within a month he was in action as a chaplain and medical orderly in charge of eight motor ambulances, the first to be used. Many more were needed so he wrote to *The Times* and raised £250,000 for further vehicles.[14] Each Sunday he had to take nine services for his various units and at one of them he had to preach to 5,000 men and so would jump on to a water wagon to be seen by everyone. At the Battle of Ypres he heard that some wounded Germans were alone in a nearby village nursed by only two nuns, a Belgian girl and an old cook so with three volunteer doctors he took a fleet of ambulances to bring them to an English hospital. It meant a drive of three days and nights through front-line shelling.

He was appalled by the huge losses all around him: one battalion of 1,000 men had only 200 survivors. In 1915 he joined the Brigade of Guards, where he encountered the Prince of Wales and taught him to play badminton. During the Battle of Loos he worked in a dressing station continually under fire, the wounded arriving in huge numbers, the heat stifling and stench appalling. Working non-stop for 36 hours, he did dressings, made tea and took funerals – once he had to jump into a grave to avoid a shell. This was interspersed with months of chronic boredom, but when he was appointed Senior Chaplain he found himself supervising and caring for the younger chaplains. He was awarded the DSO and was mentioned in dispatches four times.

18   *Pat McCormick with a parishioner, HM Queen Mary, during one of her many visits.*

After the war Pat accepted one of the most prestigious livings in the Canterbury diocese, Croydon, where he held services for the unemployed and invited them to speak. In 1925 he asked Studdert Kennedy to lead a Mission and the church was packed each night with people queuing till midnight to talk to the missioners. When Sheppard decided to leave St Martin's he wrote to the Bishop of London who was in China suggesting he appoint Pat, and after a short delay a telegram arrived 'Appoint McCormick'. The two men were as lightning and steel, having the same vision but different gifts with which to implement it. Dick, like his ancestor Napoleon, made swift moves and unexpected conquests such as opening the church during the war and allowing soldiers to sleep there, and his preaching was racy and exciting. Pat considered his actions more and only moved if he could take people with him. Above all, he did not feel threatened or over-awed by his famous predecessor, immediately invited him to be an honorary member of staff so that he could preach and broadcast, and was delighted when he agreed to be Associate Editor of the *Review*. Not many clergy would have been so gracious. In return Dick was supportive and affectionate, and in 1934 when illness forced Pat to go away for four months he found on his return that Dick had taken the Albert Hall for a two-night welcome-back rally. Thirty thousand people applied for tickets and Pat was so moved that he offered to resign and become Dick's curate.

Pat was inducted on 1 March 1927 and decided not to change the direction of the work but he did put the relief work on a firmer footing and appointed a committee to oversee it. A hostel for 25 men opened at Forest Hill, the Christmas and Holiday Funds were properly supervised and a vacation home was purchased in Herne Bay – 116 children and adults stayed there during its first summer. Thousands of people continued to pour into the building for help and in 1931 the vicar reported that 16,838 men, 2,541 women and 12 children had found shelter in the crypt in three months.

Pat enjoyed broadcasting and his distinctive voice made him very well known. His published sermons had a huge sale and he made several gramophone records. He was the first parson to be televised – following the King on Christmas Day 1937. No notes were allowed for the broadcast and after four minutes the camera man tapped his watch to show there was one minute left. Pat reported that the make-up lady thought he was too rubicund of countenance so powdered him well, and noted that the 'man in the next chair' was the 'Mad Hatter'.

The vicarage was now used as an open house for meetings and social gatherings and Miriam entertained hundreds of friends and parishioners to meals. The folding doors between the drawing room and nursery on the first floor would be thrown open for parties and dancing. Pat's daughter Patricia Frank remembers that meals were never taken alone and he liked everyone around him when he wrote his sermons in his front room study. A diminutive gentleman lived among the coal stores in the basement, where warmth was provided by the kitchen and pantry which were also down there. A cook and a maid lived on the fourth floor.

Amplifiers were installed in the crypt so that a 1,000 extra people could hear the service in St Martin's under the Fields, and in 1928 plans were drawn up to modernise the whole area beneath the church. Much merriment was caused at this time by a poster outside advertising a course of sermons

The Man that England loves – The Vicar
The Man that won the war – The Vicar
England's God – The Vicar

On Whit Mondays and August Bank Holidays an all-day beàno was now held which attracted up to 20,000 people to concerts, dances, sports, services, etc., and *Paris Soir* noted that the church, 'Longtemps fameuse pour ses emissions radiophoniques', had a fete which terminated 'par un dancing avec un orchestre de choix'. The fun included a Punch and Judy stall which was an appropriate entertainment because in 1667 the St Martin's Vestry had charged Punchillo, the Italian puppet player, £3 to erect his booth at Charing Cross.

Pat began a Nativity Play called 'The Christmas Story' which ran twice nightly from the beginning of December every year from 1928-38. It was written and often narrated by him and usually had a cast of sixty. Sir Oswald Stoll always lent the stage and a curtain. It usually ended with Gabriel balanced precariously on the window sill behind the altar, before which the Holy Family were seated on a stage with angels peering down from the royal box. It became immensely

19   *100,000 people file past Dick Sheppard's coffin.*

popular. In 1937 the Queen brought her daughters Elizabeth and Margaret Rose. They sat with the vicar in the gallery next to the organ. The future Queen commented, 'What a pity there is no donkey'.

Both Dick and Pat were royal chaplains who wore scarlet cassocks and were soon dubbed 'bloody lobsters' by soldiers on leave. Laurence Housman wrote to Dick, 'Here have you been rampaging unpatriotically against the war and breaking most of the 39 Articles of our modern social belief and the King goes and makes you one of his chaplains. Is he a stealthy pacifist, or is it only his Charlie Chaplin he intends you to be?' Cheques regularly arrived from Buckingham Palace for the work of the crypt and both men were often asked to preach at various royal chapels. In 1919 Pat was told to wear uniform but eight years later Clive Wigram, the Private Secretary, wrote from Sandringham, 'You had better bring morning dress and a top hat but there is no necessity for you to travel in these. On Sunday afternoon the King generally goes round the stud and farm and this is rather a cold operation so I should advise a good coat and a soft hat.'[15] He also asked if Pat would be accompanied by a servant. Pat was shocked by the King's bad language and even more by Queen Mary's, but always obeyed their order to bring a fund of funny stories to lighten the sermon and entertain them after dinner. Wearing knee breeches, he watched his wife and daughters being presented at Court on various occasions, and Patricia remembers curtseying 'wearing a window box', a white dress with silk net across her bosom, stuffed with artificial flowers!

On 2 January 1927 the Prince of Wales wrote to offer his congratulations on Pat's appointment to St Martin's: 'I haven't any doubt that you won't find any difficulty following Dick and carrying on his good work.'[16] The friendship begun in the war continued but was strained by Edward's friendship with Mrs Simpson, and Stanley Baldwin, the Prime Minister, once took Pat for a walk round the cricket pitch at Lord's urging him to persuade the Prince to end it. Edward abdicated and married but had great difficulty in finding an Anglican priest to officiate. Before choosing anyone the Prince's solicitors had written to a member of Pat's staff asking if he would take the service, but Pat advised against. On 26 May 1937, a few days before the ceremony, he wrote to the former King:

My dear Prince

As Mr Lasham has asked my advice about the request put by your solicitors to him, I feel I ought to let you know that being a curate, through having had to resign his living on account of debts, he is not independent, and would be most unlikely to get a living if he did what has been asked. I am sorry, but I am sure you would be the last to wish to jeopardise his future. I took him on here because he could not get a job, and had great difficulty in getting the Bishop of London to allow it. I hope very much later on to get him a living, as he has done good work here, but even that will not be easy.

I wish for old time's sake that I could have advised him otherwise because I know that religion means more to you than some people seem to think.

May I be allowed to say that I shall think much of you on Thursday next, and pray God that He will bless and guide you in your new life, and enable you to be of use to Him and to all those who come within your influence.

Forgive, Sir, please, this poor expression of what my heart feels, and the wish I have to help you at this time.

I have the honour to be Your Royal Highness's obedient and humble servant
Pat McCormick[17]

From France the Prince replied in his own hand thanking Pat for his good wishes, and adding, 'Although I was disappointed at the time I understood the reasons for the advice you gave Mr Lasham.'[18] As a reward Pat was, in May 1938, able to secure a living in Penzance for Joseph Lasham. Meanwhile the Prince persuaded the Rev. J.A. Jardine, a turbulent Darlington priest, who was described by Archbishop Lang as 'a seeker of notoriety' to take the service. Walter Monckton considered that he had 'a marked weakness for self-advertisement' which was proved correct when he later embarked on a lecture tour of the United States delighting audiences with inside stories of the Windsor wedding.[19]

In September 1937 Pat and his eldest daughter had a few weeks' health rest in Canada where Patricia, another daughter, now lived with her husband John, a former curate. A stone was to be sent to St Martin-in-the-Fields, Winnipeg where, with a wooden cross, it is still to be seen near the pulpit. Back in England they were summoned early in the morning of 1 November to go to Amen Court. Having persuaded a policeman to break down Dick's bedroom door they found him slumped over a table dead. Later Pat had to tell a stunned congregation the news and then arrange that the body rest in St Martin's – 'He is in his home again.' Members of the staff and congregation kept watch and 100,000 people filed passed the coffin. Crowds four deep lined the Strand when the cortege made its way to St Paul's for the funeral and Dean Matthews, who had asked Alison not to attend, in the Eulogy called him a primitive Christian and a fool for Christ's sake. George Lansbury said, 'His whole life radiated realism', and Dr L.P. Jacks called him a 'Living proof of the existence of God'. His priesthood, he would tell everyone, made him the happiest man in Europe but divine discontent had made him rebellious and often contemptuous of the Church. Rose Macaulay said that the world's temperature dropped when he died: 'He worked himself to death.'

'Simply a mass of skulls and bones' was how the Chancellor of the Diocese of London, Dr F.H.L. Errington, described part of St Martin's crypt in July 1938 when he was asked for permission to clear six vaults to create offices and rooms for the church's social work. Five thousand people were now asking for help each year and more room was needed to welcome them properly. The Consistory Court gave permission for around 3,000 lead coffins and a large quantity of human remains to be cleared from the vaults and taken to Brookwood cemetery in Surrey. The transfer was done at night to avoid distress to passers-by. This new space became extremely valuable when war broke out because it was used as an air-raid shelter. To begin with, up to 2,000 people came each night from as far away as Poplar and Bow in East London – one lady arriving and asking what time the next air raid would be – but soon the authorities limited it to 550 with dormitories of 100 each. By 7 p.m. the place was full; songs were being sung around the ancient, out-of-tune piano and the canteen was busy. The senior curate, George Davey, slept there every night and the vicar would say prayers at 9 p.m.

Broadcasts continued during the war, which meant that Pat's voice was known worldwide. A monthly 9.30 a.m. Sunday Service went out at different times to different countries, and at 8 p.m. there were Evening Services broadcast every second Sunday in the month. Things had changed since a technician noted, 'Minister blasting badly, congregation faint'. Other churches were also now broadcasting and one listener tuned in to a rival channel which featured a tub-thumping nonconformist divine, who asked, 'Where shall salvation be found?' Bored and baffled, the listener twiddled the knob on the radio and the next thing she heard was, 'it can be purchased from the Vicar of St Martin-in-the-Fields, price one and nine pence.'

20 *People paying their respects to a much-loved priest and broadcaster, November 1937.*

In the first two years of the war crowded services were held in Trafalgar Square and in the Coliseum, and Pat's magnificent tenor voice, presence and warmth greatly enhanced these occasions. Several years running the Bishop of London asked him to write his Lent Book.

On 15 October 1940 he was greatly distressed to hear that his old home at St James, Piccadilly had been bombed the previous night and Miriam reported that half the vicarage had fallen into the road. The Carlton and Travellers clubs and theatres in the Haymarket were also hit. The day before he had shown an Admiral round the crypt pointing out the bunk-beds for mothers and babies, and then said prayers before returning home exhausted. On the same day Pat, in a letter to his daughter Patricia, said, 'We are all well and cheery, however things have been a bit hectic round here the last few nights ... nothing nearer than Shaftesbury Avenue where fires were started early in the evening which gives the blighters a good target. ... I am in bed ... my bronchial tubes have been playing tunes.' Bombs were falling most nights and a cinema in Leicester Square was destroyed and Mr Bryant, the churchwarden, and his wife were killed.

During the Blitz the ground floor of Number 6 was busy day and night – when Pat, George Davey the curate and Tom Harrison, who had been bombed out, slept in the rear dining room and Miriam, Joyce Hollins the Churchwarden and Mogie (Mabel Hart, Pat's secretary for 25 years) in the front study. Early on Wednesday 16 October at 5.30 a.m. as the bombs were falling outside, Pat, who had been unwell the previous day, woke with a coughing fit and Miriam came to the room to give him his medicine. She asked a nurse to come from the crypt and she thought his pulse was steady. He fell asleep so Miriam went to make tea, but on her return she found him unconscious and in a few minutes he was dead. Fortunately the others, including William Ainsley the verger, who had been Dick's valet, and old Mr Ambler the odd job man were there to comfort her.

21   *Soldiers view the portrait of Dick Sheppard by Sir Gerald Kelly (1879-1972).*

The congregation now had to face another sudden bereavement and Pat's death affected thousands of people. Tributes poured in from all over England and beyond. He had left clear instructions for his funeral – no lying-in-state or fuss – but on 18 October a simple Memorial Service was held in a packed St Martin's for this gentle, unassuming, family man whose many gifts had enabled the church to move triumphantly forward after Dick's departure.

5

Sixty Changeful Years

Following in Pat McCormick's footsteps would obviously not be easy, but on 1 March 1941 Eric and Wendy Loveday arrived in London from Bristol where he had done a magnificent job as Rector of St Peter, building up a large lively congregation who had to move to another church when theirs was destroyed in the first blitz on the city. They found that during the interregnum the St Martin's vicarage had been commandeered by the Canadian Army who were using it as a club, so with their housekeeper Amelia they went to live in a flat near Victoria. Their home became a place of great hospitality and they frequently had refugees from Nazi Germany to stay including Pastor Hilderbrandt. Eric's secretary, Freda Champion, moved with them to London, much to her parents' consternation as the Blitz was at its height. She was joined in the office which was situated above the Vestry Hall by three German girls who had fled to England.

Lean, wiry and good looking, Eric, now 36, was an accomplished poet, painter and singer. He was a good team player – unusual at a time when clergy were trained to be independent – and he soon surrounded himself with a very talented group of clergy. Three or four were usually full-time and an equal number were honorary; these he called 'Spare wheels'. Amongst the latter were Roy Lee, who worked at the BBC, Charles Claxton, formerly Bishop of Blackburn who called St Martin's his retirement home, David Say, General Secretary of the Church of England Youth Council and later a much loved Bishop of Rochester, and Lloyd Griffiths, chaplain at St George's Hospital, Hyde Park Corner. (One of his many gifts was conjuring!) As soon as the new vicar was inducted he invited the Rev. F.D.U. (Dudley) Narborough to be full time Lecturer. Formerly a Canon Residentiary at Bristol Cathedral and now Provost of Southwark, he had a very fine intellect, and it is a great tribute to Eric that he did not feel threatened by such a distinguished man, older than himself, on his staff.

In 1941 there were 1,568 people on the electoral roll, some living in the parish but most not. One parishioner, Queen Mary, the Queen Mother, worshipped occasionally in St Martin's when she was in London at Marlborough House, and three months after his arrival Eric welcomed Queen Elizabeth, who toured the crypt for an hour speaking to civilians who were preparing to bed down for

22 *The Rev. Eric Loveday, Vicar 1941-8, welcomes HM Queen Elizabeth, 1941.*

the night, soldiers in the canteen and the mothers and babies sheltering in the area beneath the church steps. The 'Silver Lady' canteen, run by the mother of actress Fay Compton, continued to work at full capacity for the duration of the war and Helen Roberts now took charge of the welfare centre. A skilled leader, she made the work more professional and went on to be Secretary of the World YMCA in Geneva.

The windows of the church, many of which had been seriously damaged by a land mine which exploded in Duncannon Street on the evening of 6 November 1940, were now boarded up and the atmosphere inside the building was dark and gloomy. The services, however, were full of colour and music. The new vicar had a splendid, deep bass voice and, being a born communicator, his carefully prepared sermons, written out in full, were inspiring, thoughtful and easy to understand. 'Every sermon was itself a poem', someone remarked.[1] The Sunday congregations, 2,000 in the morning and the same in the evening, came from miles around and often included many high-ranking officers and top civil servants who had slept in their offices because of the bombs. They appreciated Eric's thoughtful, relevant sermons and his conduct of worship, and he always greeted them afterwards on the steps.

The Blitz continued and although two other bombs fell only yards away in 1940 the church was saved. (One exploded between the National Portrait

Gallery and the Cavell statue on 16 November, and one caused severe damage in William IV Street on 29 December.) Each night firewatchers were precariously perched on the roofs. Three men – Albert Perry, Sidney Ambler and Tom Gaston – took charge of the fire-watching arrangements and had no difficulty in getting eight volunteers each night (6p.m.-6a.m.) from a list of 60 people. After a sausage and mash supper, boiler suits and tin helmets were donned to inspect the church and offices and then go aloft to the rat-run and the roof. One of the Monday team was Elizabeth England, who had joined the congregation in 1933 and was to be closely connected for 70 years. Teaching in Plaistow and living nearby in Russell Court, she had trained as a Red Cross nurse and each evening ministered to the people sleeping on the tube station platforms. On a Monday, however, she would report in the crypt after a full day's teaching and check that the pumps and First Aid materials were in order before having her off-ration supper. She and the other volunteers then said Compline, and later received four shillings and sixpence for their night's work. On quiet nights it was possible to creep into a bunk, but she had to be away at 6a.m. to get to school on time.

23 *Bomb damage to the east of St Martin's following the air raids of November/December 1940.*

24 *A broadcast from St Martin's, 1944. The BBC engineer is in his cubby hole beneath the stairs.*

The Tuesday team of firewatchers were a musical lot and Eric founded the St Martin's Singers from amongst them. They sang every week, stirrup pumps and sand buckets to hand, dashing up to the roof if there was an air raid. In 1943 a young priest, the Rev. W.D. Kennedy-Bell (KB), sang as a stop-gap tenor for the group, and a year later became a full-time member of staff. Of his vicar he said, 'He widened my horizons so much that I grew dizzy with turning from side to side.' When Eric went to visit Australia he told KB, 'You sit in the middle and conduct until I come back.' KB was to conduct the Singers for many years even after he took charge of the BBC's overseas religious broadcasts in 1948 and they owed their fine standard to him. He kept in contact after retirement and until the mid-1990s took the early Sunday service every week. He died in 2001 aged 86.

The main Sunday services were crowded and often every seat was taken long before they began. One side of the nave was reserved for members of the Armed Services, all of whom wanted to worship in 'The parish church of the Empire'. Eric was well aware that some London clergy felt he was poaching parishioners so suggested that people should return to their own parishes having been nourished and inspired. There were several young pacifists in the congregation and he made sure they were welcomed and affirmed. Some were hoping to be ordained after the war so he began a New Testament Greek class for them. Broadcasts continued – once every three months on the Home Service and monthly on the BBC's short wave services – which meant St Martin's became even better known at home and abroad. The war also meant that many heartbreaking Memorial Services were held which caused great stress to those officiating at them. When the 'doodlebugs' (unmanned flying bombs) began Dudley Narborough refused to allow the organ to be played so that everyone would hear when the engine cut out. After one very bad attack in June 1944 people went to sleep in St James Park for safety, but some were hurt when the Guards' Chapel was destroyed. Irene Say's life was saved by someone pulling her under a bush. In the building itself 121 were killed and many injured.

Just before his untimely death in 1944 William Temple, the Archbishop of Canterbury, was asked to conduct a Quiet Day for American padres in the Vestry Hall. Great preparations went into the event and on the day itself the St Martin's staff, whose ration books rarely allowed treats, were astounded at the huge amount of delicious food provided for lunch. That Christmas the church received a great vote of confidence as a record amount was donated to the vicar's broadcast appeal – £15,526, a fifty per cent rise on the previous year.

VE (Victory in Europe) Day on 8 May 1945 brought scenes of great rejoicing to all parts of the country, and in London huge crowds gathered in The Mall and Trafalgar Square. The BBC used the building as an observation point for one of their commentaries, and Eric reported that 25,000 people attended the services held hourly from 8 a.m. to 9 p.m. Nearly the same number were in church the next day. The wardens, Albert Perry and Joyce Hollins, thanked the members of the congregation who marshalled the queues and thus missed seeing the sights themselves. Everyone was profoundly thankful that there had been no serious damage and the boards were now removed from the windows. The Troops' Canteen closed in August, and Eric reported that the income raised by using the crypt as an air-raid shelter would, of course, cease.

Bells were now allowed to be rung again throughout the land and keen St Martin's members rang the bells before the weekday service. Dame Myra Hess, who was in the middle of a concert in the National Gallery, was not pleased at the competition and afterwards she tackled Eric who promised it would not happen again. Unfortunately communications were not of the best and the following day Bill Rowett on his lunch break from the War Office rang the bells. The parish secretaries were told that an angry Dame was crossing the road. Courage failed Dudley Narborough, who fled into the crypt, but the staff were astounded when Dame Myra arrived with a bag of cherries and another gentle request that the bells be silenced. Bill remained in the congregation as a lay reader and, after a distinguished 33-year career in the Army, ending as Brigadier, he trained for the priesthood and joined the staff as a curate.

25 *Second World War: sleeping bunks in the crypt air-raid shelters.*

In 1946 another young man was invited to be a spare wheel: Austen Williams, who was on the staff of Toc H. Eric told his secretary, Freda, that he had two reservations (which were

26   *The staff meeting, 1945. Left to right: The vicar's secretary, Freda Newall (later Champion), vicar Eric Loveday, assistant clergy Lloyd Griffith, David Say, Roy Lee, James Ashworth and Lecturer Dudley Narborough.*

soon overcome) about the appointment – all the women in the congregation would fall in love with this handsome man, and he might not be able to get over his horrendous wartime prison-camp experiences. In fact, those four and a half years were the crucible in which his faith had been refined, and he later said, 'The people you didn't like were always round you, and there was no evasion. There was no privacy. You just had to learn to live with yourself and your inadequacies. In that situation Christ made sense. He understood.' Another member of staff – but only for six months – was Martin Sullivan from New Zealand, who said the experience was worth twenty years. Later when he became Dean of St Paul's he said that he wanted to make it into 'A massive St Martin's'.

A Brains Trust starring the clergy took place every Friday lunchtime and the large audience was allowed to answer back! Some were distressed that the clergy often disagreed, but one of the vicar's many gifts was to choose and preside over a very talented team of clergy from different backgrounds. Disagreements and tensions could be held within a loving fellowship. David Say recalls that Eric's staff meetings were exciting occasions and that he never attempted to dominate proceedings: 'He was often very diffident about his own views. Indeed, he was sometimes looking over his shoulder at alternative jobs he might do.' Most clergy would deal with differences of opinion combatively but Eric preferred partnership to authority. His style was attractive so huge crowds came to hear him preach and he began to think that the church was too small, particularly when someone complained bitterly that three times he had been turned away because the building was full. He reminded the congregation that they should consider returning to their local parishes, thus making St Martin's 'a school for Christians'. Pews were now reserved on Sunday for parishioners.

The following summer Eric and Wendy went for a holiday in Australia. A preaching tour had been arranged to follow it, ending in New Zealand. On Sunday 6 July 1,500 people assembled to hear Eric preach in St Paul's Cathedral, Melbourne and the following Wednesday he spoke to the clergy in the Chapter House, reminding them that new pictures and patterns of thought were now needed to help the outsider understand the Christian faith. The Archbishop commented on the rich voice talking of the life to come. 'We soon forgot the man and heard a voice which was not of earth but of heaven. We are not likely to forget that we are humble and unworthy instruments for God's great Purposing.' The following morning, whilst asleep, a heart seizure took Eric unexpectedly to his death. Six years earlier Dr Geoffrey Fisher, Bishop of London, in his Induction sermon had said that two incumbents had already been killed; there must not be a third.[2] Now there was. A large crowd surrounded the stunned widow at the funeral the following day. The Bishop of Geelong in his address talked of a burning and shining light, the 'tremendous total effect of the spirit of Eric Loveday'. A young university student commented that his friends had run from one talk to another 'with growing exhilaration. I think that meeting him has done more to increase our desire to learn to pray than anything else could possibly do. No one has done any work; in spite of the times he told us that a second class degree was the mark of a second class Christian!' The next year, on 4 December, a memorial plaque to him was placed near the pulpit in Melbourne Cathedral where he preached his last sermon.

1948-1955

After Eric's death three members of staff including Austen travelled to Newark to see the man whom the Bishop of London had suggested as his replacement. They liked what they saw and on 17 January Mervyn Charles-Edwards was instituted into the living by Bishop William Wand of London. The King was represented by the Dean of Westminster, and the Mayor of Westminster and representatives of the Dominions were present. At this time St Martin's was running a high temperature, and the pace of life was feverish as the congregation had not recovered from the shock of their vicar's death. Post-war restrictions and rationing brought their own challenges, and the problem of rebuilding London seemed immense. What had the Christian faith to contribute? In some ways the parish had not been a large enough canvas for Eric, with his interest in ecumenism and the worldwide Anglican Communion (which made his death in Australia somehow appropriate), but now St Martin's received as its vicar a genial, kind countryman who approached life in a slow, unhurried way. There

27 *The Rev. Mervyn Charles-Edwards, Vicar 1948-56, Bishop of Worcester 1956-70.*

would be no revolution or confrontation, as he preferred not to hurry or impose change but open out what was already there. The vicarage, having had a year-long refurbishment after the men had returned to Newfoundland, was ready to receive its new occupants. The vicar's family moved into the first and second floors, curates on the ground floor and vergers in the basement and top floor. Conscious that so many of his predecessors had died from over-work, Mervyn (who fortunately was fit – he played football and hockey and had rowed for his college at Oxford) was determined to cherish his family life and spend time with them. Later his successor commented, 'He and Louise formed a partnership of love which sustained their own family and St Martin's through many vicissitudes.' From this secure base he started work.

The congregation soon realised that their new vicar was prepared to spend time with them and, as David Say has pointed out, was very much at home in the domestic and local life of St Martin's. His sermons, which came out of his own experience and prayer, were refreshing, and he had an endless supply of anecdotes. He could be understood and his monthly broadcasts on the World Service were much appreciated. Kennedy-Bell, who was now in charge of these at the BBC, remained as a part-time member of Mervyn's staff, which also now included Austen as a full-time deputy vicar. At Christmas 1950 St Martin's was the first church to give a televised service, and two years later on the death of King George VI the televised Memorial Service came from here.

In 1950 John Bullock, who had a distinguished war record in Italy and Greece before being ordained, was appointed senior curate, and Joyce Hollins retired after ten hectic years as Churchwarden. The new wardens were Sir G.A.Titman and P. Brock. Brigadier Harwood was appointed Administrator in 1951 and for the next four years supervised the repair of war damage and controlled all ecclesiastical business, leaving the clergy free to do their pastoral work. Mervyn told him that he was grateful for his help because the Church tends to be more like a rabble than an army on the march. There was plenty to do as there were over 700 on the Electoral Roll, and an average Sunday saw 3-4,000 worshippers attending services. Queen Mary liked to take her place in the Royal Box, and was not amused when the vicar suggested that the stairs to it were rather steep so perhaps she might like to sit in a chair with a reading desk in front of the pews. 'I come to worship the Almighty,' she said, 'not to be stared at.' To get a seat many people would arrive an hour early and sit and chatter in the pews, so the vicar arranged for the organ to play loudly. John Churchill, Organist and Master of the Music since 1949, thought that sixty per cent of these congregations changed every Sunday, so the services, led by different choirs, had to have well-known hymns and psalms. Hundreds of people also came to seek help and advice, and in 1951 3,000 men and women were interviewed in the newly named St Martin's Social Service Unit. These included the unemployed, women deserted by their husbands, alcoholics, discharged prisoners, drug addicts and those quaintly called homoerotics. The Welfare Office had been transferred to 5 St Martin's Place and so its old room was in July 1954 consecrated as the Dick Sheppard Memorial Chapel. Down steps on the south side of the church it still provides a quiet place for meditation and prayer.

After a year on the staff John Bullock suggested that an Association of Friends be formed, and in the May 1951 *Review* asked all those interested in being linked by a bond of fellowship and work to contact him. They should be prepared to pay 2s. 6d. to enrol, and a 2s. 6d. annual subscription to receive a November newsletter and invitations to various events. Cards were left in the pews and 800 people expressed an interest, and the following year a pilgrimage to Canterbury was arranged to visit the Cathedral, lay a wreath on Dick Sheppard's grave and attend Evensong in the little church of St Martin. Mervyn now wanted some Vice Presidents so wrote to the Great and the Good. Sir Anthony Eden, the Foreign Secretary, Lord Kilmuir, the Lord Chancellor, Laurence Olivier, John Mills and assorted politicians and theatre impresarios all agreed to serve. Royal patronage was sought and the Duke of Edinburgh was approached. Back came the reply via his Private Secretary, 'I think this is the sort of thing that might be of interest to the Queen Mother, but for Heaven's sake don't say that I suggested it.' So began a happy relationship of fifty years with this much-loved parishioner who visited often and occasionally asked her chef, Michael Sealy, to provide a course for the Festival lunch. This meant that the organiser, Sibyl Allen, had to visit Clarence House to discuss the menu over a gin and tonic.

Membership of the Friends peaked at around 900 in 1965, and in 2003 there were just over 400 in all parts of the world except Antarctica. Over the years they have generously supported many good causes including the Cala Sona project in Lanarkshire, which was a centre for refugee families, and they 'adopted' a number of children at the Kumi Leprosy Centre in Uganda. At home the Friends have paid for various projects including the restoration of the Stuart Coat of Arms, and cleaning Francesco Solimena's painting *St Martin and the Beggar*. The pattern of their annual Festival in June was established early on: worship, lunch, outing, tea then Evensong. Usually, visits to interesting places are made each year.

It took four years to prepare for the Festival of Britain in 1951 and it provided some relief from the austerity and gloom which still stalked the country. The government, which depended on a majority of eight, asked Herbert Morrison (Lord Festival according to a dubious press) to organise it, and as well as providing an Exhibition and Fun Fair on the South Bank he asked every organisation in the British Isles to take part. The congregation took up the challenge by arranging an exhibition in the crypt showing the church's work and it drew 100,000 visitors during the summer. Mervyn arranged five Sunday afternoon open-air services in Trafalgar Square, and also invited his friend, Dr Austin Pardue, Bishop of Pittsburgh to lead a week's Mission in July, speaking every day at 1.15 and 8p.m. On one afternoon the Bishop went to watch tennis at Wimbledon and told the American finalists, Shirley Fry and Doris Hart, that as he had come to see them he expected them to come to hear him. Much to his surprise they came, and afterwards lunched at the vicarage.

In 1954 the staff was greatly enhanced by the arrival as Lecturer of Canon Charles Raven, Vice Chancellor of Cambridge University, who was one of the most powerful preachers in England. A philosopher of religion and science and a pacifist (during the war he had been forbidden to broadcast), he was a fiery, charismatic man whose radical views did not please everyone. No accommodation was offered except a camp bed in the vicar's study! Until his death on 8 July 1964 St Martin's benefited greatly from his explosive sermons and lectures.

Mrs Williams, the manageress, and her volunteers established a lunch club in the crypt for local business people, and soon there were 300 members who each paid a subscription of two shillings a year. The canteen remained open until 9 p.m. and was used by the congregation after services. Mervyn also began negotiations with Felix Aylmer of Equity to see if a club could be started in the crypt for actors and actresses from the nine local theatres who were between performances, or who were 'resting'. They could meet one another, obtain refreshments and make telephone calls. On 6 February 1956 the new Nell Gwynne Club was opened by Dame Edith Evans in the Francis Room of the crypt. David Savill, the curate, was deputed to take responsibility for it, and a 'permanent hostess', Miss Elsie Day, was to be in charge and open the club 10.30-5 every weekday. Seven years later membership had grown to 470 and the monthly lunchtime talks given by stars such as Peggy Ashcroft, Michael Redgrave, Flora Robson and Harry Secombe drew large audiences. Sybil Thorndike was elected President after speaking at a meeting when she strode around, emphasising her points with gusto – 'Read Shakespeare, read Browning.' She told every one that her father, Canon Thorndike, had the next door parish to Laurence Olivier's father. 'I saw him act aged eight – I knew he'd be great.'[3] St Martin's was at this time the home of the Actors' Church Union, and at one of their annual services Gerald Ellison, Bishop of Chester, reminded them that their lives are news, and that their example could sustain and uplift the moral and spiritual standards of everyone. Shortly afterwards the saint's name had to be added to the club's title because a Nell Gwynne strip club opened in Soho. The St Martin's club closed in 1967.

28 *Eileen Joyce plays for the Darby and Joan Club, in the crypt 1951. Where are the Darbies?*

During his seven-year incumbency the vicar went to the United States three times on a preaching/lecturing tour, and in 1955 took with him a stone salvaged from the bomb damage to be the corner stone of the new St Martin-in-the-Fields, Severna Park, Maryland, where the Rev. Lewis Heck was the vicar. Three years later a plaque and piece of stone from St Martin's were built into the wall of the south porch of the new St Martin-in-the-Fields in Forest Acres, Columbia, South Carolina. An American writing in *Here's England* pointed out that the building in Trafalgar Square was obviously 'the handsome stone model for half the little wooden churches in New England. Were the builders homesick?'

When Independent Television began in September 1955 Mervyn, who was Religious Advisor to Associated Rediffusion Ltd, deputed the job to his curate, Geoffrey Holland, who realised the potential of the religious programmes which at this time usually had an audience of around 600,000.

In December 1955 Mervyn was appointed Bishop of Worcester, and someone said that the stagnancy of this ecclesiastical backwater would now soon disappear. Urban and noisy Trafalgar Square had, perhaps, not been an ideal place for such a gentle countryman, but he had been a superb pastor to his congregation, 'inaccessible to none'. Someone once told him that he had a Peter Pan quality which appealed to the boy in men and the mother in women.

1956-1984

It is very rare in the Church of England for a former curate to return as incumbent, but William Wand, the Bishop of London since 1945, had seen the quality of Austen's work, and so it was probably he who made the recommendation to the Queen (when an incumbent is made a bishop the Crown has patronage). Austen was vicar of St Alban, Bristol so he and Daphne travelled to the House of Lords and Downing Street to be interviewed. He wanted to be back in Bristol that evening as his 'Demon King' was needed at the rehearsal for the parish pantomime. A prophetic parishioner admiring his black tights had suggested his legs would look good in gaiters. In fact he had also been offered the Deanery of Liverpool (as in 1931 had Dick Sheppard, who declined it), and

29 *The Rev. Prebendary Austen Williams, Vicar 1956-84.*

someone had foolishly told him to accept it as anyone could be vicar of St Martin's. It was a no-contest because, as Daphne recalls, he only had one ambition – to be vicar of St Martin's. So he accepted the offer. Mervyn was delighted at the news as the two men were close friends, and five years earlier he had paid him a fulsome tribute in the *Review* – 'Since 1914 St Martin's has owed much of its greatness to the genius of three men ... I personally would put A.W.'s name first.'[4] This was said before Austen's thrilling 28 years as vicar!

The family moved into the vicarage and allowed the vergers to live in the basement and top floor. They were surprised how many people had keys to the house including the window cleaner; the milkman and grocer would let themselves in to stock up the kitchen.

Two years after his arrival Austen appointed George Fearon as Public Relations Officer, and he has recounted his adventures in *You owe me 5 Farthins* (1961). This was not to boost the church, or to publicise the clergy (Fearon, although an admirer of Austen, thought him too shy to be newsworthy), but to give an accurate picture of events. He was told, 'We have to live in the modern world, and not clown around in the Victorian Age.'[5] It was an inspired appointment as Fearon knew the press, and helped the staff to treat them courteously and give them something to write about. Austen knew that his forceful views would bring controversy, but the first two battles of Trafalgar were with the local authorities. The 1899 lamp posts in the area were now thought to be too small and unsafe and so Westminster City Council proposed to replace them with part steel/part cast-iron ones which would have WCC on them instead of the St Martin's badge. There was lots of press attention and famous people agreed with the *Review* (which was now selling around 2,500 copies each month) that this was 'an act of philistinism for which there is no justification'. The battle was lost but the smart new posts erected in 2003 bear the saint's name.

The second battle concerned Austen's request in May 1959 to place a crib beside the Norwegian Christmas tree in the Square as part of World Refugee Year. Mr T.L. Jones of the Ministry of Works wrote to say that he sympathised, but had to refuse as it would make it more difficult for the police to control the crowds and might provoke controversy and disorder. *The Sunday Times* wondered why the police would have more trouble with people looking at a Christian symbol than at an illuminated conifer, a modern revival of a pagan custom: 'Let us not foreswear our Faith.' *The Times*' report was headlined 'No Room in the Square.' Austen went to see Hugh Molson, the Minister of Works, who told him he could have his crib. The stable with its life-size figures created by Josephina de Vasconcellos, was made and erected by boys from a borstal in Surrey. The Protestant Truth Society was refused permission to hold a protest rally in the Square.[6]

'The parish church of the Commonwealth' now drew people of many colours and races to Trafalgar Square, mainly because they had heard broadcasts from St Martin's before coming to this country. Once here they often experienced prejudice in congregations as few English people had seen or got to know non-whites. St Martin's opened its doors to them and in March 1959 Fr Trevor Huddleston preached at the Ghana Day Service commemorating the second anniversary of this new country's independence. 'The peace of the world depends on what happens in Africa now. The victory of fear over faith will have dire consequences,' the future Archbishop told them. A year later the Service was held during the normal Sunday Eucharist and 2,000 people, including the High Commissioner, filled the building. Behind the altar Josephina de Vasconcellos erected a six-foot high reredos showing Simon of Cyrene carrying the Cross, and a bewildered African boy, watching.

On the first Sunday of the 1960s Austen reminded the congregation that St Martin's is no longer 'our church'. 'It is,' he said, 'the church of Africans, West Indians and Asians,' and two weeks later he invited the members of the Kenya Constitutional Conference, meeting at Lancaster House, to worship on Sunday morning. Half of that black and white group came and were able to pray before the bitter arguments began. The previous year there had been 27 weddings of overseas people (and of 33 native Londoners) which meant that calling banns was a tongue-twisting exercise. One couple did not recognise their name when it was read out, and Austen received a round of applause for correctly reading the name of Mr Wekerereoyenemisa Wakama. The congregation gave money for a new village church in the Kumi Leprosy Settlement at Ongino in Uganda, and when it was consecrated in July 1959 it was dedicated to Martin.

Mrs Pandit, then High Commissioner for India, opened the International Week in the summer of 1960, when dances, concerts and an exhibition were

30 *Mrs V.L. Pandit, High Commissioner for India, opens the International Fair, 25 June 1960.*

held. She spoke of her frequent visits to St Martin's 'in search of peace and inner harmony'. Unfortunately there was not much peace in the church as part of the ceiling had collapsed. The manager of the Garrick theatre offered his auditorium for the Festival Service, but it was decided to use the courtyard, where a tent covered the altar. All Sunday services were held there that summer and weekday events were transferred to St Paul, Covent Garden. After a while the congregation was allowed back inside but the organ was banned in case it brought more ceiling down. During the repairs the workmen discovered a collection of documents which included receipts and accounts dated 1777/8 and an indenture signed by Tenison.

'Pray and Protest' was the slogan at St Martin's following the shootings at Sharpeville in South Africa. Early in the morning of 21 March 1960 the police had opened fire on a crowd of 10,000 people who were waiting quietly to hear a statement on the pass laws. 700 shots were fired and 180 were wounded and 69 killed, many in the back as they ran away. 'This isn't a private affair in one particular place,' said Austen. 'In Algeria, in Nyasaland, in Kenya, in the whole of Africa, Christian values and Christian integrity are on trial. And we're all involved.' A thousand people came to hear Fr Huddleston preach at a lunchtime service, and Austen afterwards declared war on apartheid: 'The shootings bear final witness to the blindness, wickedness and invincible stupidity which was certainly its cause ... Apartheid can only be continued at the point of a gun. We in England are partly to blame ... We are on trial in Africa and here.'

The plight of refugees was a special concern of the congregation and in December 1958, to prepare for World Refugee Year which began the following month, a charity matinée in the Theatre Royal, Drury Lane raised £4,000. The Rev. Lloyd Griffith, who had been one of Dick Sheppard's curates, suggested it and Prince Littler offered his theatre free of charge; over the next few years this became an important, annual event in parish life. Austen mobilised the congregation to help, and a box office was opened in the courtyard. The shape of the afternoon was always the same – the first part was a Nativity Play, for which Ralph Vaughan Williams wrote the music in 1958 and Malcolm Arnold in early January 1960. St Martin's Concert Orchestra played with a full choir. After the interval came variety acts by, in 1958, Bea Lillie (then in *Auntie Mame*), Norman Wisdom and Max Bygraves, and in 1960 the Tiller Girls, Peter Sellers and Dickie Henderson. Nadia Nerina and David Blair of the Royal Ballet danced. Proceedings ended with carols played by the Band of the Coldstream Guards, and a columnist in the *Daily Telegraph* said that he

31 *The Tiller Girls performing after the Nativity Play at the St Martin's Christmas Charity Matinée, Theatre Royal, Drury Lane, December 1960.*

hoped they did not all get mixed up. That year the profit of £2,500 went to child refugees in Germany. A refugee appeal office opened in the crypt and in May a replica of a refugee camp was built in the courtyard. In August 1959 Sir Alexander Grantham opened a full-scale replica of a street with squatters' huts in Hong Kong, of which he had been Governor. The hundreds who visited it over three weeks donated £6,000.

Six other Christmas matinées were held, and in December 1960 the Queen Mother watched Lynne Seymour, Desmond Doyle and John Gilpin dance following a Nativity Play arranged by Malcolm Arnold and Christopher Hassall. In 1962 the Coldstream Guards Band marched from Trafalgar Square to the theatre, where Margot Fonteyn danced and Constance Shacklock climbed the highest mountain in excerpts from *The Sound of Music*. Julie Andrews withdrew as her contract forbade her to appear anywhere except in *My Fair Lady*. The last matinée was in December 1965, when a live donkey, who mercifully behaved himself, appeared in the Nativity Play. These performances had created a great deal of work for the congregation but huge sums of money had been raised for refugee charities. The brochures on sale were always superbly produced and contained articles, drawings and cartoons sent in by the famous.

The population of the parish had dropped to 1,800 by 1964, but the area remained as colourful as ever with its 12 theatres, 50 pubs and 60 restaurants. There was now an international flavour to the place – the Friends of St Martin's, founded in 1951, now had 800 members, 140 living overseas. The Rev. S.Y. Lee arrived to care for the Chinese congregation, which now included Baptists, Congregationalists and Roman Catholics as well as Anglicans. Austen enjoyed visiting other countries – in 1963 he spent Holy Week in Nashville, Tennessee giving a series of addresses – and he and Daphne returned from their tour of the West Indies more determined than ever to welcome those who had come to live here from overseas. There were now 700 on the electoral roll and services, especially Sunday Evening Prayer, were well attended. But how was it possible to keep in touch with everyone? Ken Gibbons, one of the curates, and the Home Committee decided that some parish visiting should be done, so in September 70 men and women received training in the Vestry Hall and then set out in twos to visit people on the roll in places like Hounslow, Haringey and Hampstead. The intrepid visitors were daunted by huge houses with lots of bells, so occasionally pressed them all with disastrous results. Each pair had 30 addresses, and when they met again in October they reported that some had moved but others were delighted to be visited, although some regulars were surprised at not being instantly recognised by the callers.

Trevor Beeson, who later became Dean of Winchester and is the author of several books, joined the staff in 1965, although he remembers visiting the church twenty years earlier whilst in the RAF and being astonished that he had to join a queue stretching to the Strand to get into the service to hear one of Loveday's elegant sermons. In his first days as a curate he was taking an early communion service when half way through a man emerged from beneath the altar where he had been sleeping all night. He returned shortly afterwards to

32 *'You said it was the Sound of Music!' Cartoon donated by Carl Giles for the programme of the 1962 Christmas Matinée.*

retrieve his cap. Beeson feels that Austen found it difficult to address many of the 'Whitehall issues', so attempted himself to call the congregation to the barricades, 'but soon gave up when I realised that most of them were on crutches of one kind or another'.[7]

Furore followed the Commonwealth Day Act of Witness in St Martin's on 11 June 1966. Television cameras came to record representatives of the Hindu, Moslem, Buddhist, Christian and Jewish faiths come together in a Christian place of worship with the Queen and Prince Philip sitting in front of the huge congregation. Austen was horrified at the virulent criticisms he received from his fellow Christians, and he was told in no uncertain terms by the Bishop of London that he should not host the event again. It sparked off discussions on inter-faith services in the Church Assembly and the British Council of Churches, and the majority view was that they lead to religious syncretism, compromised the uniqueness of Jesus as Saviour and would weaken the Christian Missionary task overseas. Serious doubts were also expressed as to whether it was appropriate to hold such events in a Christian building. So great was the confusion and debate that no Act of Witness took place the following year. The vicar was unrepentant:

> To those who believe this kind of venture is wrong in the first place there's no obvious reply. To those who say that the time is not yet ripe for this sort of thing one can only say that St Martin's has handled a good deal of very unripe

fruit before now. The purpose of the Act is clear enough. It is certainly not to pretend to any kind of religious unity which does not exist, nor is it in any way to suggest an agreed common faith at the expense of what is unique or precious to any one religious community. It is rather that, on truly common ground, as peoples bound together under the Queen in a Commonwealth of Nations which recognises, respects, and delights in our diversity, we should bear emphatic witness to our shared faith in certain fundamental things – the sovereignty of God, the dignity and value of every man irrespective of nationality, race, or capacity, the supremacy of love, and the brotherhood of men revealed most truly in service and sacrifice for the common good.

Two years later the Act was held on 8 June 1968 in the City of London's Guildhall, where Roman Catholics, Greek Orthodox, Anglicans and members of the Free Churches joined with non-Christians in prayers and readings in the presence of their monarch. 'In spite of the splendour of the Guildhall,' Austen wrote afterwards, 'I still feel very strongly that it should have been allowed in church; that the embargo is a sad and disturbing thing. It is precisely there that people realise that faith is not after all, what so many believe it to be, just one more of those many things which divide us.' Soon afterwards his wish was granted because the Act moved to Westminster Abbey. When in 1993 the House of Bishops advised that a non-religious building is the best place to hold such a service the Dean of Westminster told the *Church Times,* 'The point is that as a royal peculiar the Abbey comes directly under the Queen, and it is her desire that this should happen here.' Austen's concern for these issues was partly prompted by his overseas tours and partly by his experiences in the crypt where the East-West Club, under the care of his curate Patrick Brock, now had over 600 members which included people of all faiths and none. This met monthly, and the Overseas Club, which had many Nigerian and West Indian members, met weekly on a Friday evening – the monthly Overseas broadcast meant that many men and women came as soon as they arrived in London.

The 1970s began with the exterior being scrubbed, which made someone comment, 'I wish they hadn't cleaned it – it now seems to lack experience'. Over the next ten years the interior was redecorated and re-lit, the balustrade on the roof renovated or replaced and the clock, made by John Leroux of Charing Cross in 1759, electrified. (Till then someone had to climb the tower stairs every day to wind it.) The redecoration offered a puzzling challenge as no one knew what the original colours were, although Hogarth's painting, now in the Metropolitan Museum, New York, of the marriage of Stephen Beckenham and Mary Cox offered some clues, and recently the dominant colour had been deep blue. Sir Trenchard Cox, churchwarden and former Director of the Victoria and Albert Museum, told the *Review*: 'Now the effect is one of discreet simplicity, the gold has been reduced to a minimum, and the walls and ceiling are painted in subtle tones of pinkish grey.' It was to last for thirty years. On 10 July 1975 Austen conducted a service on the roof, saying, 'The church is much lighter and strangely looks and feels much larger'.

On 12 June 1973 the Duke of Edinburgh officially opened the Centre for Young People in the old school which had been completely renovated. There was now a ground-floor coffee bar offering inexpensive food, an information unit giving housing/employment advice, and a large first-floor open space with TV and games but also suitable for meetings of up to 250 people. On the top floor were more meeting rooms, offices and a flat for the new Director, Louis Alexander. He had studied law at London University then spent eight years in a Roman Catholic missionary order in Holland, Belgium and India. Austen had always wanted an advice centre for the many rootless and friendless young people in the area and the Inner London Education Authority agreed to provide staff and charitable trusts gave money. By 1977 there were over 100 people aged 16-25 in the Centre each evening. Two years later Tony Leach took charge of the work.

Congregations in England continued to decline at this time and this accelerated as the century continued. The galleries were no longer needed at St Martin's except for carol services and memorial services for people like Duke Ellington, Vivien Leigh, Peter Sellers and Terence Rattigan. In 1975 Dr Celia Swan took a look at the three Sunday congregations and discovered that 75 per cent of those at 9.45 a.m. worshipped more than once a month, and 22 per cent were new. Sixty-eight per cent of the 6.30p.m. congregation came more than once a month, and 13 per cent were new. This was the largest congregation, with many enquirers who might after a while move on to their local church. The service was short but the sermon, connecting Christian faith with current issues, usually lasted 30 minutes, and about fifty of the 200-300 young people who came to the 8 p.m. Folk Club would be there. This was organised in the crypt by curates Hugh Maddox and then Ron Swan, who reported that half the membership (whose average age was 23) were working in London and a quarter were students. It was run on very professional lines, the equipment was good, the singers were paid a proper fee and because of this the Club was self-supporting. One of its best features was the liquid light provided by Ron Henderson, an American artist, who used projectors to spill the most vivid light on to the arches of the crypt, ever moving globules of mauve, green and blue. Several famous singers and instrumentalists performed and Billy Connolly told some almost clean jokes.

Wendy Loveday, Eric's widow and the 'Mother' of the St Martin's Singers for over thirty years, died in June 1976. After Eric's tragically early death she had trained as a hospital almoner and joined the staff of St Thomas's Hospital, and then from 1968 until her death worked for the Friends of the Elderly. She had kept in touch with many of the refugees from Nazi Germany whom Eric and she had helped and did voluntary visiting at Charing Cross Hospital. The Singers owed their fine standard of singing to KB, but it was Wendy's organising ability, toughness and care which made it not just a choir but a living, warm fellowship. Today they continue to give concerts in St Martin's and other venues and still rehearse once a week.

The 250th Anniversary of the present building was kept in 1976, when over 20,000 people visited the Festival Exhibition in the crypt which had been planned by Kay Gordon-Ewen. Miss Mangold, Headmistress of the St Martin's High School, with her girls supervised by Miss Marjorie Austin-Reeve of the Art Department, had prepared drawings, photographs and models illustrating the history and work of the church. In another area of the crypt Heather Flowerdew and Patricia Dawes helped assemble all the items which had been lent, and three weeks before opening began to panic. Rapid mounting of photographs began – 'If we cut off Pat Brock's chest there will be more room for Austen's head ... Tell K I've lost the American Ambassador AGAIN.' Heather was heard telephoning the photographer, 'Can you blow up the Vicar in two days?' Afterwards they discovered a few mistakes: Dick Sheppard lay in state for three years, two South African countries transposed and the Middle East crisis almost solved by re-drawing boundaries.

The Festival Service was a grand affair and the music was arranged by Robert Vincent, who after nine years as Master of the Music was leaving to be organist of Manchester Cathedral. He said that it was the first time he felt he had the vicar under control! The anniversary was also commemorated by parties, poetry readings, concerts and by a production in the crypt of the newly formed drama group's *Martin*.

Dr Ronald Keay, Secretary of the Royal Society and one of the churchwardens, gives in the October 1981 *Review* a description of a typical week at St Martin's 25 years after Austen arrived as vicar, and it shows that the pace had not slowed. On Saturday evening the Scrub Club founded 24 years earlier by Joyce Carlisle and now led by Jane Whitley would send some of its 24 members to clean the church ready for Sunday morning when, after the early services, Ben Duke and his ringers would peal the bells to herald the 9.45 Sung Eucharist. David Hardwick would marshal some of his 35 stewards to welcome the congregation, and Head Verger Chris Woods and his staff, who were on duty 12 hours a day, 7 days a week, would have prepared the vestments and communion vessels. The organ was played by Christopher Stokes, Master of the Music, and the children would go to the crypt for part of the service, supervised by Peter Szalay and Margaret Ainsworth. Afterwards Joan Keay and her helpers would provide tea in the canteen, and the *Review*, edited by Daphne Williams, would be sold by Elizabeth England – she sold them for 50 years! Lunch was provided one Sunday a month and arranged by Sibyl Allen. The soup kitchen would be open in the Undercroft. The Centre in the old school building now had a new Director, John Stott, and this was open for those aged 16-25 every weekday from 5 to 11p.m.

The Chinese Service at 3p.m. would usually attract a congregation of about 200 people, including 90 children, and twice a month at 4.15 a choir from King's College, London or the Musical Society would sing Choral Evensong. Evensong at 6.30 was well attended and on the third Sunday of the month it was recorded for broadcast by BBC World Service the following Sunday. Each Sunday evening one to two hundred young people came to the Folk Club in the crypt.

33 *Perched precariously on the roof, Austen Williams publicises the appeal for the Church Building Restoration Fund, 1984.*

Music and dancing also had their place as the Monday and Tuesday lunchtime concerts often had an audience of 600 in the summer. The Chamber Choir and Orchestra would perform at Christmas and Easter. The St Martin's Singers, who were about to mark their 40th anniversary, rehearsed weekly and gave 12 concerts a year. The two dance groups were the St Martin's Morris Dancers, who met every Thursday evening, and the Cedar Dance Theatre which on Monday evenings had classes on dance and worship.

Weekly clubs were still numerous: a Tuesday midday group was for office workers, Jenny French arranged the weekly Tuesday Party for 30 retired people, and a branch of the Girls Friendly Society met every Wednesday. The Darby and Joan Club had nearly 100 members, and the International Club for men and women from overseas met every Saturday afternoon and evening. There were also several discussion groups and cell groups for prayer and study.

Sadly, it was now discovered that much more needed to be done to the building, and so on 23 February 1983 an appeal was launched for £350,000 to repair the tower and the northern steps to the portico, re-hang the bells, waterproof the crypt and provide a new kitchen and lavatories. The organ needed attention and the flooring beneath the pews was in a deplorable condition. Viscount Caldercote, chairman of the Delta Metal Group, and his committee, ably served by Eunice Davies the Administrator, were so successful that they reached the half-way mark in a few months. After 18 months the target had risen to £400,000 as the cost of re-wiring the church, crypt and Vestry Hall had massively increased. The target was reached in September 1985. The year before £17,000 had been raised on 1 November at a splendid

Royal Gala performance at the Coliseum of *Madame Butterfly* attended by the Queen Mother.

Austen kept his distance from ecclesiastical politics, and although courteous to local clergy felt that they would never support a plan for working together in central London. He received a prebendal stall in St Paul's and a C.V.O. but no preferment came his way in England – he declined the bishopric of the Bahamas. He had very little interest in synods or diocesan committees, reserving all his energy for the parish. In Lent one year his curate, Ron Swan, noticed how grey and tired he looked, so asked if all was well. 'I always look like this in Lent,' he replied, 'don't worry. There's nothing St Martin's likes more than a dying vicar, but they are not going to get me.' When asked how he had survived he said, 'when I get exhausted Daphne stands at the top of the stairs, and tells people to go away for three days'. There is no doubt that everyone owed a huge debt to her; someone once perceptively remarked, 'Daphne is the lady who enables Austen to behave like a saint!'

Like his predecessors, he enjoyed employing a talented staff of curates who included Bruce Reed, founder of the Grubb Institute of Behavioural Studies, and Michael Wilson, priest and doctor who pioneered the teaching of pastoral studies at Birmingham University. The part-time members would try to attend the lively weekly staff meetings when, after a Daphne breakfast, Austen would preside (opening his post) whilst plans and policies were discussed. He gave his staff a huge amount of freedom but always knew what was going on, mainly because he liked to get out of his office and walk around the building most days. He was, however, at his desk late afternoon to see a procession of callers, some of whom came frequently, perhaps too frequently. He kept up a correspondence with listeners to his broadcasts and would get up very early each day to answer letters from all over the world. In 1977 the hundreds of letters received came from 81 countries and Colin Semper, Head of BBC Religious Broadcasting Overseas, said that 'he communicates in an intensely personal way to his listeners'. He and Daphne certainly enjoyed their overseas visits, and in West Africa went out of their way to call on a regular correspondent. A small boy answered the door. 'I am Austen Williams from St Martin's. Is your daddy in?' The boy turned and shouted, 'Dad, the vicar's here.'

Usually wearing a tie, Austen had a clip-on dog collar in the vestry for services, usually arriving with minutes to go. He disliked proceedings to be too well choreographed because he thought that the Holy Spirit was deadened by order, so in a procession he would break off to greet someone or suddenly dash back to the vestry to get a book. He liked to preach himself, and his sermons, laced with poetry and humour, were down to earth and practical. His intercessions were memorable, touching on the issues of the day but also bringing to God the needs of the people kneeling in the pews. Like many clergy he was a rather shy introvert, and so had to force himself to be a showman, but he told one of his curates that he was saved from exploiting his role by his personal sense of insecurity. His broadcasts were always well received, even by the technicians to whom he once said, 'If you give me a green light, I'll give you a blessing.' He had always been more interested in people than buildings and told Daphne of a recurring nightmare where he was responsible for the tower and spire sliding into St Martin's Lane. Fortunately he was able to keep everything in good repair, and one of the favourite photographs of him was on the roof, arms outstretched, celebrating the end of his fabric appeal.

The Very Rev. David Edwards, on Austen's staff 1958-66 and later Dean of Norwich and then Provost of Southwark Cathedral, has paid this tribute:

> Although St Martin's in his time continued to welcome an extraordinarily wide range of humanity, the variety was increased when he agreed to be the vicar of a curate who was both a Fellow of All Souls College in Oxford and a very immature and nervous young priest. (At the first I was part-time on the staff then honorary. My main job was as a theological publisher, as editor of the S.C.M. Press.) But he immediately and consistently showed that he was no more anti-intellectual than he was anti-anyone else. Amid the almost incessant demands on his time he read and thought a lot and that helped him to avoid being sentimental about any subject; he was not even sentimental about the people who looked to him for sensitive love. His sharp-minded wife Daphne helped too.
>
> I think that the way he treated me was typical although I was so odd. He talked about books and ideas, and asked me to preach and lecture after which he praised me. So he got alongside and inside me. But gently he encouraged me to become interested in other individuals and to go out to them as he had gone out to me. Years later when I wrote a kind of autobiography a reviewer spotted that this was the spiritual experience which a priest is supposed to have and which I had lacked before, and this was a fair comment. St Martin's gave me something which no book could give; it was teeming with contemporary life whereas I had been trained as a historian; it was full of human problems but also of the presence of Christ; it gave me glimpses of a God more real than the God who before had been for me an intellectual problem.
>
> At this distance from the events it might be right to add that he took my wedding and when that marriage came unstuck, more than twenty years later he took my second wedding and, more than anyone apart from my new wife, healed me.[8]

Austen had now been at St Martin's as curate and vicar for a third of a century – longer than his three predecessors put together – so it was inevitable that his retirement would bring massive bereavement to the congregation, the majority of whom had never known another incumbent. They realised, as he did, that the time had come for retirement, particularly as he had suffered two heart attacks. In July 1984 after many farewell parties and services he and Daphne moved to south London where they spent 17 happy years together. He died on 9 December 2001 aged 89 and at his Memorial Service the Bishop of Leicester, the Rt Rev. Tim Stevens who was married at St Martin's, reminded everyone that Austen's sermons often took the form: 'This is where I am on my spiritual pilgrimage. Come with me if you are brave enough, but if you can't at least make one small step in the right direction.'[9]

1984-1995

To provide short-term continuity Charles Hedley, who had been on the staff for five years and was later to become Rector of St James, Piccadilly, was licensed by the Bishop as Priest in Charge for one year. He was the most practical curate ever because when he arrived at the vicarage for interview he saw water cascading down the stairs from a burst pipe. Whilst the other curate held his arms up in horror (or prayer) Charles went into the cellar and turned the stopcock off. He soon became an expert on the intimate secrets of the church's ancient heating system, and was not afraid to throw a ladder across a yawning abyss in the roof to inspect any defect. Soon the catchphrase of the year was 'Where's Charles?' He attempted to get the congregation to look forward not back – 'This is not St Austen's.' He and the other curate, Fred Stevens, together with the five sub-committees of the P.C.C. (Hospitality, Finance, Appeal, International and Lay Training), kept the pastoral and preaching work going until the arrival of the new incumbent, Canon Geoffrey Brown, who was inducted on 1 May 1985. Graham Leonard, Bishop of London preached a deeply theological sermon which scarcely mentioned the occasion, but the day was saved by a warm welcome to Geoffrey and Jane from Frank Harvey, Archdeacon of London, who once described himself as 'A thug who says his prayers'. St Martin's suffered greatly by his sudden death the following year.

Geoffrey had been a Team Rector in Grimsby for 12 years so had experience of working collaboratively with clergy and laity – although he felt that new curates should be like kittens, not allowed out too early. On a walk in the Lincolnshire Wolds he and his wife, Jane, had decided that the only place they definitely would not move to was London, but the interviews in No.6 changed all that. Having accepted the incumbency he went on a business management course to prepare himself for the days ahead. It was obvious to everyone that the parish finances needed addressing because, as Austen had pointed out, they survived only because of the Angel of Death. Legacies and the huge sum recently raised for the building could not finance everything over the next decade. Bankruptcy loomed unless something drastic was done – the newly formed St Martin's Players presented *Doomsday*, which must have sent a chill down the congregational spine. Geoffrey, however, noted that 1986 was Industry Year and John Garnett, the Director of the Industrial Society, told him that a church was needed in central London that would stand for the centrality of the world of work in people's lives. Geoffrey agreed and in his usual prophetic way said, 'If we could make people who work in industry feel that they are as much valued by spiritual people as are teachers, preachers, doctors and social workers there would be more chance of encouraging those who work in the wheeling and dealing atmosphere of the market place to take the world of the spirit more seriously. They feel that they have been branded as second class citizens so their response is to stay outside the churches.'

What better way for the Church to do this than itself plunging into the world of business? Geoffrey's wide-ranging report, *Into the 1990s*, of 26 January

34 *Former members of staff and friends celebrate the 60th anniversary of Austen Williams'
ordination, 1997. Left to right: Hugh Maddox, Hilary Dereham, Chris Walker, Andrew
Couch, ?, David Say, Daphne and Austen Williams, Charles Hedley, ?, Ron Swan, Derek
Spottiswood, David Edwards, Nick Holtam, Tim Stevens, ?, Fred Stevens and Sybil Eccles.*

1986 suggested this amongst many other things, and everybody was invited to
comment on all the recommendations. A residential P.C.C. conference was
held the following December in a somewhat seedy hotel off the Gloucester
Road to discuss it. The congregation gradually realised that the church had the
capacity to earn its own living, and had a duty to do so using all the resources
it possessed. Too many religious people and projects expect to be supported
financially by handouts from those who work for a living; would it not be better
for a congregation to engage in honest commerce itself, creating new jobs and
making a profit? Geoffrey and Ronald Keay began to rationalise the 23 parish
accounts and later appointed trustees for the Vicar's General Fund which had
attracted large gifts since Dick Sheppard's day. The 13 members of the P.C.C.
met regularly, often late into the night, and with courageous thinking and
careful planning the St Martin-in-the-Fields Enterprise Ltd was born.

A large loan was negotiated and the Enterprise was launched on 1 December
1987, when the newly appointed managers described to the press what they
would be doing. Sarah Hardingham took visitors to see the new 200-seat crypt
restaurant which would be open from 10a.m. to midnight; Fr Basil Youdell
explained how the bookshop would sell a wide range of literature, icons,

records and cards; Faith Arnold and Glynis Carpenter, both silversmith gradu-
ates, showed off the new outside market with its 46 stalls, and Susan Wilkin
described the function of the new Visitors' Centre and exhibition space. The
brass rubbing centre, recently moved from St James, Piccadilly, was staffed by
Andrew and Patricia Dodwell. A champagne brunch was held for celebrities
like Dickie Davies, ITV Sports commentator, actors Tom Conti and Michael
Palin and other guests.

Former Head Verger Trevor Critchlow became the first General Manager,
and when he departed for theological college in June 1988 he handed over to
Caroline Graham-Brown. Disaster loomed when considerable losses were made in
the first few months, and later Geoffrey said that the Enterprise would not have
survived without this forceful, committed woman. Sometimes abrasive, always
serious and conscientious, she knew what was wanted and made it happen. 'She
stripped away many of my delusions,' he told the *Review*, 'and taught me a lot
about strategic planning. Most of all she turned the business round.'[10]

Not all the congregation were impressed by these daring decisions, believing
that the homeless had been marginalised by the new venture. Some wanted a
revitalised church but on the old, much-loved model. Was there now a Berlin
Wall between the rich in the café and the poor in the Unit? The loss of the
regular broadcasts also brought criticism to which Matthew Portal, one of
the wardens, replied in the *Review*. St Martin's could not expect permanent
influence over BBC policy, and the Enterprise was a practical necessity because
the congregation would not survive financially without it. Some objected on
religious grounds to Sunday trading and a few wondered how events like the
annual Fair could survive if the restaurant took up most of the crypt.

The Church of England's response to the rapacious Britain of Margaret
Thatcher, with its mantra 'greed is good', was mainly concentrated on Archbishop
Runcie's *Faith in the City* report (1985), which was provoked by Canon Eric James
and led to the setting up of the Church Urban Fund. Geoffrey's stance, which
was also theological and pragmatic, has been overlooked. In a conversation
with Kenneth Adams, Comino Fellow at the Royal Society of Arts, he explored
the significance of Martin's cloak. On the one hand was the commerce which
brought it into being (sheep rearing, dyeing, weaving, distributing, etc.) which
enabled it to be cut in two (mining, refining, forging, sword-making, distributing,
etc.), and on the other hand the beggar needed to be clothed. 'What I wanted
to do was to bring the two into balance,' said Geoffrey, 'and would have loved
two chapels (the word itself derives from the *capella* or cloak of St Martin),
one for the half cloak kept by Martin symbolising utility and reminding us of
its origin, and the other dedicated to the proper use of wealth in the service
of others and reminding us of our obligations to those in need.'

Many other issues received the P.C.C.'s attention including the old school in
Adelaide Street, which had opened its doors to 16-24-year-olds for 15 years as an
alternative to local pubs and clubs. Recently it had been making a loss and the
building and its furniture were in a dilapidated condition, so the Centre joined
with two other organisations to form The London Connection, and the newly

restored and furnished premises were opened by Prince Edward on 2 November 1988. On the ground floor was the No Room Café; the cellars had interview rooms and a launderette and the first floor had large meeting rooms; the top floor housed the former Soho Project which offered counselling and advice on jobs, accommodation, etc. The building was open from 8 a.m. to 9.30 p.m. and was used as a permanent address by youngsters looking for a job. In the heart of London, it provided a much needed service to homeless young men and women who had come to the capital for work and been disappointed.

The improvements to the church, crypt and courtyard meant that many negotiations had to be held with diocesan officials but relationships with these were at a low ebb. In August 1988 Geoffrey joined what became known as the Angry Vicars' Group formed by five central London parishes.[11] The incumbents felt that their imaginative plans were being hindered and not helped by a Bishop who rarely answered letters or telephone calls, a litigious, new Archdeacon who had summoned all five to a Consistory Court for various Faculty irregularities, and a Diocesan Advisory Council which was secretive and obstructive. St Martin's felt particularly aggrieved with the D.A.C. because a large number of faculties were needed quickly and the saga of the roof walkway to the flagpole was a good example of the problems they faced – it had been agreed by Archdeacon Harvey on 16 October 1986 and been erected three months later at a cost in excess of £1,000, but the D.A.C. ordered it to be removed on 8 April 1988.

After many discussions the incumbents, each with a Warden, went to London House to see Bishop Leonard and Archdeacon Cassidy on 13 July 1989 and presented their suggestions for change: diocesan administration should be more efficient, an area bishop should be appointed to give better pastoral care to the four central London deaneries, and improvements requiring a Faculty should be discussed informally with the Archdeacon and D.A.C. at a much earlier stage to avoid confrontation. Very little was done, but the Bishop decided there should be an Episcopal Visitation at St Martin's; the Diocese was apprehensive that if the church went into liquidation it might be held financially responsible. Three wise men – a priest and two laymen – were appointed to do this and, after a careful study of accounts and a full enquiry into all other matters, they gave St Martin's a clean bill of health and said that the new plans should be supported and affirmed.

In November 1989 it was reported that the Enterprise was now making a profit but that the bank loan would not be discharged until 1992. Until then the parish would receive a licence fee – £82,000 in 1989. It was estimated that without this funding all the assets would be gone by 1995. Some worshippers needed to be reminded that profits are not wicked and, as Richard Rouse, chairman of the Enterprise pointed out, God loves the poor but He also loves accountants, stock brokers and the stinking rich. In 1993 the music recitals were integrated with the Enterprise and now they too were expected to make a profit. Around 200 were attending the midday concerts, 300-400 came in the evenings and occasionally a full house of 750 was achieved.

Parish life continued during all these dramas; there were 400 on the electoral roll and the work of the Unit continued to grow. Special services continued in the church, including one to mark the 70th anniversary of the Peoples Dispensary for Sick Animals at which Gladstone, the vicar's secretary's dog who kept everyone sane in troubled times and would do anything for food, shared the pulpit with Geoffrey. Various four-footed friends filled the pews including a Shetland pony and an assortment of cats.

Geoffrey wanted the ministry at St Martin's to be holistic and arranged Sunday evening services on various themes and began an annual residential weekend. New bells were hung in 1988 and a new organ installed and paid for in 1990. Mark Stringer, the organist, and he were determined to improve the quality of the choral music so, with the help of the Enterprise and Mohan Solomon, choral scholars were recruited and services and broadcasts have benefited ever since. Geoffrey had a keen interest in liturgy and the service books he devised with prayers and readings for private use on one side of the page were immensely helpful. With the help of John Pridmore, later rector of Hackney, he wrote a Prayer for the World which is now used regularly in church and on the BBC World Service:

O God our Heavenly Father,
Give us a vision of our world as your love would make it;
A world where the weak are protected and none go hungry or poor;
A world where the benefits of civilised life are shared, and everyone can enjoy them;
A world where different races, nations and cultures live in tolerance and mutual
  respect;
A world where peace is built with justice, and justice is guided by love;
And give us the inspiration and courage to build it,
Through Jesus Christ our Lord. Amen.

On 4 June 1995 Geoffrey's imaginative and realistic ministry ended with his retirement. Looking back he said, 'St Martin's is a temple where doors are open to the world and within which dogmatic and ecclesiastical edges are nicely blunted by the variety of people who come.'

1995-2004

Nicholas Holtam's Induction was a noisy, fun affair on 13 September, young Chinese drumming enthusiastically as an 8ft-tall lion leapt around in front of the procession moving up the nave. For seven years Nick had been vicar of the Isle of Dogs where the local community was coming to terms with the huge Canary Wharf business development. Disillusionment, poverty and unemployment in the area meant that it was a breeding ground for violence and extreme right-wing politics. He showed great courage in standing up to the British National Party and working with others to bring reconciliation and justice to his parishioners. Now he and his wife Helen, who is a teacher with degrees in computing and maths, moved into the top floors of No.6 with their four children, David, Tim, Sarah and Philip.

35 *The choir visit to South Africa, 2000.*

In June 1996 the P.C.C. held a congregational meeting after morning service, uncharacteristically closing the doors, to discuss future plans. The electoral roll now numbered 250, 30 per cent of whom were Chinese; the building was looking down-at-heel; the congregation had many tourists in it, and the elderly outnumbered the young. Members were relying too much on the profits of the Enterprise so the conclusion of the meeting was 'build up the congregation' then challenge everyone to take a full part in parish affairs. 'St Martin's is the Martha of the Church of England', Nick wrote. 'Not for us the moral probing of St James, Piccadilly; the material self confidence of All Souls, Langham Place and never the emotional outpourings of Holy Trinity, Brompton; we are glad to be the Anglican worker bees.'[12]

Broadcasts began again in 1996 after Nick had met with the Head of BBC Religious Broadcasting and the Head of World Service Religious Broadcasting. After Austen left it was decided to have a break but now services were heard once again at home and abroad, and this coincided with the Academy taking its place again in St Martin's life.

Because of the ordination of women to the priesthood in 1994 the shrill statements of Evangelical and Catholic extremists in the Church of England had been receiving too much attention, so Nick was now determined that St Martin's should express a central Anglican position based clearly and firmly on the three authorities of Scripture, Tradition and Reason. A Mission Action Plan was drawn up and an educational programme put in place for people to explore their faith. Probably the most exciting component of this was the 1997 Lent Course when 140 people made a special 'Way of the Cross' tour around the National Gallery at the invitation of its Director, Neil MacGregor. A very confident communicator, he attended two of the sessions and described some of

36 *HRH Prince Charles visits St Martin's and discusses the new plans with the vicar, 25 March 2004.*

the religious paintings whilst Nick gave a theological comment. This was one of a series of events that tested the Gallery's plans for their magnificent millennium exhibition 'Seeing Salvation'. Neil and his successor, Charles Saumarez-Smith, have been very encouraging neighbours.

Clare Herbert, a skilled educator and spiritual director, became the first woman priest to work with the English-speaking congregation at St Martin's when she joined the staff in 1996. She left two years later to be the first woman incumbent in the London Diocese – at St Anne, Soho. Only very few of the congregation found it hard to accept her priesthood but, as she pointed out, 'our bodies are only scaffolding for the spirit'. She was followed by Rosemary Lain-Priestley, associate vicar, Liz Russell and Liz Griffiths.

In three minutes today the vicar can collect £411,000, which must be a record! The amount raised by the annual Christmas broadcast appeal which began in 1927 has grown amazingly over the years, even allowing for inflation. £16,297 was donated in 1956, £50,371 in 1978 and £164,202 in 1987. Since 2000 the church has been given an extra 15-minute slot by the BBC called 'Received with Thanks' at 9.45 a.m., which explains how the money is used, and this is repeated twice during the day. The Vicar's Relief Fund receives nearly half the sum for its work with individuals and families nationwide, and over 2,000 letters pour in each year from voluntary and statutory agencies telling stories of people who for one reason or another fall through the safety net of the benefit system. These can be helped speedily and efficiently. The rest of the amount is given to the Connection at St Martin's for their work. On the day of the appeal volunteers wait by the phone from before the 7.55 a.m. broadcast until the evening in order to list credit card donations. On Monday morning Sibyl Allen and her volunteers begin to open the sacks of letters and suitably labelled shoeboxes receive the cheques and cash. This goes on well into the New Year because whatever the size of the gift the donor is thanked and a computer records the details.

The St Martin's Fair is another annual event and Dorothy Cone has helped with all of these since they started in 1953; she told the *Review* recently that in its heyday there were over 30 stalls as well as sideshows. Once Beryl Reid flew down from Scotland to open it and other famous openers have included Anna Neagle, Judi Dench, Paul Eddington and Derek Nimmo, who had his car towed away![12] In 1981 Harry Secombe made Austen laugh so much that he fell off the stage. Apart from fund raising – around £4,000 is taken today – the Fair is also an excellent opportunity for St Martin's many friends to meet and talk.

Regular consultations were now being held with the congregation, the staff of the Enterprise and others to see how the buildings could be improved and renewed. The damp Dickensian vaults used by the Social Care Unit particularly shocked many visitors. Plans were discussed then discarded, but on 12 May 2003 the P.C.C. adopted a conservation plan commissioned from Alan Baxter and Associates and prepared by Robert Thorne assisted by Frank Kelsall and Neil Burton. A huge affirmation for the new plans came that July when the Heritage Lottery Fund gave approval in principle to a gift of £14.67 million, and fund raising led by the Campaign Director Julia Chadwick continued in earnest to reach the target of £34m.

In 15 years the Enterprise, which now employs 70 full- and part-time staff aged 17-82, has made a profit of £3m. The café won the Les Routiers London Café of the Year award in 2003. Allyson Hargreaves, who began as the café

37   *Architect's visualisation of the proposed entrance pavilion and widened Church Path.*

manager in 1987, is now the Business Operations Manager of the company formed in 2004 (St Martin-in-the-Fields Ltd) and is proud that the catering is not contracted out. 'It is part of the St Martin's team and serves 260,000 meals a year. We have a licence for private parties till 2a.m. and were once raided by the police who had to apologise when they saw the licence. Each of us has given our advice about the new developments so all our grumbles about blocked drains, no lift, etc. will soon be over!'

Hugh Player holds the important post of Chief Executive of the company and as he has experience of the tourist and commercial worlds he realises the complexities of the job. 'The vicar is the ultimate chairman and I have to understand his priorities and position the business behind those priorities.' The immediate challenge is to adapt everything around a building site. 'The biggest pleasure will be when the last hoarding goes down and the church is restored. I know it will be stunningly beautiful.'

2005/6 Development

So the most exciting and ambitious development in St Martin's 800-year history will begin in 2005 when the unique mix of church, care and commerce will be given rooms, structures and spaces fit for the 21st century. Eric Parry Architects has created a contemporary design that grows out of the historic setting and will make many areas fully accessible for the first time. Modern, flexible care facilities for the Connection at St Martin's will be provided in the buildings to the north; a new entrance pavilion and foyer below the present market will welcome visitors; and new rehearsal rooms will be given to visiting choirs

38 *At the east end of Church Path a lightwell will mirror the west end's entrance pavilion and bring light to the underground spaces.*

39   *The Café in the Crypt, which serves over a quarter-million meals each year and hosts many private functions.*

and musicians in the present damp east vault. Gibbs' church will be totally redecorated and restored to its original glory, and a sequence of beautiful, practical and inspirational spaces will provide meeting and exhibition areas which will be easily accessible by stairs and lifts. A new lightwell will enable the underground rooms to be bright and airy. Anglicans desperately need such a place in central London which is available for people of all faiths and none. St Martin's tradition of worship, music-making, social care, hospitality and outreach will receive the buildings and spaces it deserves.

6

The Parish – People

Thomas Tenison (1636-1715)

Tenison lived at a time of huge upheaval in England when civil war and religious wrangling divided the nation. He kept his head – literally – and refused to be a Vicar of Bray who would change his ideas to suit the times. Instead he was a key figure in devising a strategy to enable the Church of England to recover its influence on the nation. Unfairly branded a Whig Latitudinarian who wanted to destroy the authority of the institution and its clergy, he came into conflict with Tory politicians and priests, and when Anne ascended the throne she made no secret of her dislike for him, choosing John Sharp, the Archbishop of York as her spiritual adviser. During her reign he had very little influence at Court, particularly on appointments. Perhaps things may have been different if his personality had been more open and outgoing for, as Canon Gary Bennett pointed out, 'His depth of feeling and pastoral concern were often hidden from all but his closest friends. In an age of witty and expressive letter-writers he wrote terse notes in an almost illegible hand. Gossip, social scandal or personal revelation were wholly foreign to his nature and his presence on public occasions was invariably severe.'

Born in 1636, he was a teenager when King Charles went to the scaffold. It was not advisable to be an Anglican under Cromwell and so Thomas studied medicine at Corpus Christi College, Cambridge and then switched to divinity but was not ordained until the Restoration in 1660. No doubt his parents, 'good and reputable folk' in Norfolk, were proud of him. Five years later the Great Plague hit England and Tenison, by now vicar of St Andrew the Great in Cambridge, acquitted himself well as a pastor. He had obviously learnt his trade by watching his father who was rector of Mundesley in Norfolk. Fortunately his wife, Anne, brought him a considerable fortune which he proceeded to give away for the rest of his life.

By 1680 he was a Doctor of Divinity and chaplain to the Merry Monarch, Charles II, who probably secured for him the living of St Martin-in-the-Fields, 'The greatest cure in England'. John Evelyn in his diary called him, 'One of the most profitable preachers in the Church of England being also of a most holy conversation, very learned and ingenious. The pains he takes and care of his parish will, I fear, wear him out, which would be an inexpressible loss.' Late one

40 *Thomas Tenison, Vicar 1680-91 and Archbishop of Canterbury 1694-1715.*

night Tenison was called out to minister to a dying man in Gardner's Lane. The man, who died before he got there, turned out to be the King's masked executioner who wanted absolution. He had told his friends who were with him that night that he had been in the troop of Cromwell's Army ordered to find someone to behead Charles. No one would do it, so they cast lots and the lot fell on him. Afterwards he slipped into the crowd and carried a sense of guilt with him henceforth which is why he wanted Tenison at his death bed.

Thomas persuaded Evelyn to help him found a public library, which was designed by Christopher Wren and built in Castle Street, off Leicester Square. Under the same roof he opened a school which was to be named after him and still thrives today in Vauxhall. Tenison was obviously good at his job and the saintly Bishop Ken wrote of him, 'God prospers his labours. He gives the Age so great an Example of a good parish priest that I cannot but have a particular reverence for him.' The parish included the royal palaces and grand houses but also slums, brothels and squalid tenements. The death rate and particularly infant mortality was appalling, but the rich came to church in great numbers, John Evelyn reporting regular congregations of a thousand people. On a Sacrament Sunday, when office holders had to get a certificate of attendance because of the 1673 Test Act, vast quantities of bread and wine were consumed at communion. Dainty sips were unknown. Hearty swigs led to chalices having to be re-filled from huge silver flagons.

Tenison used the gifts of the rich to set up a programme of relief work, and donated large sums from his annual stipend of £1,000. He set up 'societies' of laymen, 'middling sort of people', businessmen, craftsmen and their apprentices, to undertake this work. They prayed together and then went out to provide food and clothing for the destitute. They visited prisons and much of their time was spent giving Christian instruction, particularly to children. Later, when he became Archbishop, he encouraged lay people to set up societies not under clerical control to do the work of the Gospel, the two most famous being the Society for Promoting Christian Knowledge (SPCK) and the Society for the Propagation of the Gospel (now USPG). Both are still thriving today.

The death of Charles II in 1685 brought a sea change in English life because his successor was a Roman Catholic. Tenison thought that Roman Catholicism was un-English and incompatible with constitutional monarchy, and said so firmly from the pulpit. James II ordered a Declaration of Toleration to be read in churches and Tenison refused. Seven bishops also refused and he drew up their defence. After trial they were acquitted and when James fled to Europe in 1688 Tenison was rewarded with the Archdeaconry of London. He had, with others, been in touch with William of Orange so was delighted when he shared the monarchy with Mary. Two years later he became Bishop of Lincoln and then in 1694, at the age of 58, he was made Archbishop of Canterbury – the first to be enthroned in person since the Reformation. Macaulay in his *History* says, 'The new Primate was not pre-eminently distinguished by eloquence or learning ... but he was honest, prudent, laborious and benevolent.' His task was to quiet a 'discontented and distracted Church'. Jonathan Swift unkindly described him as 'hot and heavy like a tailor's goose'. Tories agreed and Thomas Hearne, expressing his disgust in his *Remarks and Collections*, quotes a contemporary rhymester:

> Tho' his old solid Grace was preferr'd cross the water
> For tacking the Tyde, and well trimming the matter,
> Yet does it not follow that the Church of St. Martin
> Makes her Rectors all Prelates for being uncertain.[1]

Tenison immediately held his primary visitation in the diocese of Canterbury and during it confirmed 3,674 people. The clergy soon realised that he would tolerate no abuses when he drew up a number of injunctions concerned with the practical ordering of the Church's life – ordination, conduct of services, obedience to the canons and so on.

The Archbishop worked hard to support Protestant refugees who had fled to England, raising funds for their support and attempting with no success to form closer links with Protestants in Germany. He was largely responsible for the religious clauses of the Act of Union of 1707, which recognised the Presbyterian Church in Scotland, and this brought him criticism from high churchmen. 'He believed the Church of Scotland to be as true a Protestant Church as the Church of England, though he could not say it was so perfect.'[2]

Tenison's last act was to crown George I, which must have given him immense satisfaction since Queen Anne, George's predecessor, had made it clear she disliked her Archbishop for his Low Church, Whig views and for his support for the Hanoverians. He had regularly corresponded with the Electress Sophia who died in 1713 and constantly supported her interests, so her son's coronation brought him 'peculiar joy'. He died in 1715 not quite reaching his 80th birthday. Swift, in his usual barbed way, described him as 'a very dull man who had a horror of anything like levity in his clergy, especially of whist.' A comment like this shows how much hatred was stirred up by this serious and sincere man whose views remained steadfast during turbulent times. Edward Carpenter comments: 'The archiepiscopate of Thomas Tenison, perhaps even more than that of Sancroft, marks the end of an era. Up to the beginning of the 18th century, it is almost impossible to tell the story of the developing life of the English people without reference to Church and Archbishop. These days were now to cease.'[3]

James Gibbs, Architect (1682-1754)

When the commission for the re-building of St Martin's met in June 1720 they received plans and estimates from Nicholas Dubois, George Sampson, John James, Sir James Thornhill and James Gibbs, who submitted three designs for the church and six designs for the steeple.[4] In November he was chosen as architect and surveyor and £632 was eventually paid to this extremely busy man who was at the time working on St Peter, Vere Street, the Senate House in Cambridge, All Hallows, Derby (now the cathedral) and other smaller commissions. He was also writing books on architecture which would later influence ecclesiastical buildings on both sides of the Atlantic profoundly. (Gibbs' first idea for St Martin's, a round church, was later built in Connecticut in 1755.) Many churches built over the next hundred years in the eastern seaboard states were inspired by his designs, and those closely modelled on St Martin's are Christ Church, Philadelphia, built in his lifetime, St Michael, Charleston, St Philip's in the same city, and St Paul's Chapel, New York City, where the portico has been moved from the steeple to the eastern end. Others include Christ Church, Massachusetts, the Old Lyme Connecticut Congregational Church, the First Baptist Meeting House at Providence, Rhode Island and Arlington Street Church, Boston. Even the First Parish Church of Framingham, Massachusetts built in 1926 closely resembles St Martin's with its steeple and four-columned portico.

Gibbs was an interesting choice as architect because he came from a Scots Roman Catholic family, being born at Aberdeen in 1682. Patrick, his father, was a merchant whose two mastiffs were called Wesley and Calvin. James left Scotland when he was 18 because a new law had made it impossible for Roman Catholics to inherit property or educate children. He went to relatives in Holland and then in 1703 entered the Pontifical Scots College in Rome to train for the priesthood but he left after a year to paint and also act as a guide showing wealthy young Englishmen the sights on the Grand Tour. This resulted in his making several friends who were to be useful contacts when he returned to London in 1709. By then he had studied architecture under Carlo Fontana, surveyor to Pope Clement XI, and the sculptor and architect Pietro Garroli. John Erskine, the Earl of Mar, who had subsidised his studies, now placed his name on the list of architects who were to build 50 new London churches and in 1714 he became a surveyor of the scheme and designed St Mary-le-Strand, which Mar called 'the most complete little damsel'. In 1719 he was asked to add a steeple to Wren's St Clement Danes and he was responsible for several new houses in Marylebone and elsewhere. Gibbs was never officially a pupil of Wren but they became friends, although Sir Christopher was much older. Both learnt from each other – Wren had never been to Italy and so the younger man's knowledge of Italian architecture was of great interest to him.

The building of the new St Martin's provided Gibbs with several headaches. Soon after work had begun in 1722 he stopped the project as the bricklayer had supplied bad materials and was guilty of bad workmanship. He and the

Clerk of Works were dismissed. The work took four and a half years and cost £33,661, a huge outlay for a church at that time. Originally there were no central pews and the open design allowed everyone to see and hear what was going on. The body of the church is a simple rectangle adorned along its sides with Corinthian pilasters and the east end, a trifle wide for its height, has a triple window. He preferred not to have pews, which he said 'clog up' interiors, but the hundreds of worshippers had to sit somewhere and so he installed galleries.[5] In Rome Gibbs had been educated to naves with empty floors but over the next few years pews were to make an appearance.

After his appointment as architect Gibbs never looked back and he had no further financial worries because commissions, such as the Radcliffe Camera in Oxford, were plentiful. As a producer of memorials an important event for him was the arrival from Antwerp in 1720 of the young John Michael Rysbrack. If Gibbs wanted his memorials erected he needed a good carver and now he had found one and he used him as a sub-contractor, on the Matthew Prior memorial in Poets' Corner, Westminster Abbey for example. Other Abbey commissions followed and the two men, who had become close friends, worked together on monuments throughout England.

Gibbs' influence was extensive, particularly because of his books – *Rules of Drawing* and *Book of Architecture*. They are consulted by builders and designers to this day. He never married and when he died in August 1754 he had no relatives to attend his funeral in Marylebone church, where he is buried. A well built, handsome man, his portrait by Hogarth and his bust by Rysbrack, now in the Victoria and Albert Museum, show a fleshy face with a firm mouth and nose. He was fond of good living and in later life was told by his friend Patrick Guthrie to walk more, 'it would bring down your fat parts purely'. He remains a shadowy figure who kept his religious and political views to himself. His buildings and books reveal his brilliance and profound knowledge of architecture and so they are his memorial. His biographer, Bryan Little, compares him with Wren:

> Gibbs had very great talents, an excellent training, ability to make himself known and to publish his work, a flair at times amounting to genius. Yet he lacked the prodigious, Leonardian range of Wren's knowledge and accomplishments. A Wren is a phenomenon very seldom repeated ... our debt to the Georgians is for a generally tasteful tradition, not for any one supreme creator of dazzling masterpieces. Nor had Gibbs the opportunities of Wren; he was never Court Architect. London in his time had no great fire. It needed no cathedral, though it could have done with a good royal palace. James Gibbs, unlike Sir Christopher Wren to the Stuarts, was politically uncongenial to the Hanoverians ... Where he did brilliantly, and where he performed a good service to the memory of the great architect who had befriended him, was in the transmission of a tradition and the fructifying of some of Wren's ideas.[6]

A final act of kindness was to leave in his will £1,000, three houses in Marylebone and all his plate to Lord Erskine, the son of the Earl of Mar, his great benefactor, who had fallen on difficult times and fled abroad after taking part in a rebellion against the King. He had died in 1732 leaving his son in some financial difficulties. The generous bequest was 'in gratitude for favours received from his father'.

John Hunter, 'The Father of Scientific Surgery' (1728-1793)

Dr Hunter moved into St Martin's parish when he purchased a large town house in Leicester Square in 1783 for his wife and two children. Until then he had lived in Jermyn Street in the parish of St James, Piccadilly where he married Anne Home, daughter of an Army surgeon, in 1771.They also had a country house in Earls Court. Having bought the house at the bottom of his garden in the next street, he installed in his new home a lecture room, picture gallery and museum for his collection of 14,000 anatomical specimens. Many of his students came to his conversaziones and enjoyed viewing the curious objects. He loved talking anatomy with his students, many of whom were to become famous surgeons; among them were John James, William Shippen, John Morgan and Edward Jenner. His angina did not stop him keeping busy with his private practice, hospital duties and with writing articles for learned journals on teeth, sexually transmitted diseases and inflammation. His *Natural History of Human Teeth* (1778) is regarded as the first scientific basis for dentistry.

The youngest of ten children, Hunter was born in Long Calderwood, near East Kilbride, Lanarkshire. After his father, a farmer, died when John was 13 he stayed on the farm for four years and showed little interest in books, preferring country pursuits. This may explain why he later rejected academic speculation, preferring experimentation and observation. 'Don't think, try' was one of his basic tenets. After staying in Glasgow with his sister, whose husband taught him cabinet-making, he rode southwards to London in 1748 to assist his brother William, a teacher of anatomy, in his dissecting room. After watching John carve up arm muscles, William enrolled him in the surgical classes of St George's and St Bartholomew's hospitals, and he became a pupil of the famous William Cheselden at Chelsea Hospital.

Realising that he needed official qualifications he entered St Mary's Hall, Oxford when he was 27, but soon returned to London realising that his 11 years with his brother had been more valuable. During this time he made detailed studies of the structure and use of the lymphatic vessels and of the growth, structure and exfoliation of bone.

He then became an Army surgeon in France and Portugal during the Seven Years War (1756-63) and revolutionised the treatment of gunshot wounds, using his experience to write *Treatise on the Blood, Inflammation and Gun-Shot Wounds* which was published after his death. On his return to England his fame as a surgeon increased and he was made a F.R.S. at the age of 39. He saved lives with a consummate skill founded on a deep understanding of the body's processes, an understanding arising from his profound and ever-widening research. The following year he had another try at a qualification. He studied and was awarded the Diploma of the Company of Surgeons which led to his becoming a surgeon at St George's Hospital. He now began to make observations of live animals – leopards, deer, birds and fish. Queen Charlotte presented him with a bull. He commissioned artists, including George Stubbs, to paint animals for him and his portrait by Reynolds and his statue have pride of place today in the Royal College of Surgeons.

In 1776 he was appointed Surgeon Extraordinary to King George III and in 1790 he became Surgeon-General to the Army, but on 16 October 1793 he suffered a severe heart attack at a governors' meeting in the hospital and died instantly. His funeral took place at St Martin's, his remains being interred in the vaults. Today John Hunter is considered one of the three greatest surgeons of all time, with Ambrose Pare and Joseph Lister, having raised English surgery from a mere technical trade to a position equal to other medical specialities.

His collection of specimens was purchased by the government in 1799 and given to the Royal College of Surgeons in Lincoln's Inn where they can be seen in the museum which was especially designed for them. William Clift, his last assistant, arranged and catalogued it. When a medical society was proposed in 1819 many of the foremost surgeons were former pupils of Hunter, including William Blizard, so it was named the Hunterian Society and is still active today.

In the 1850s, when it was proposed that most of the coffins in the crypt be cleared and reburied in St Martin's cemetery in Camden town, Frank Buckland spent 16 days searching for Dr Hunter's coffin. Eventually it was found among 200 coffins in No. 3 vault. A photograph was taken and many doctors visited the crypt, and on 28 March 1859 the coffin was taken to Westminster Abbey followed by members of the Royal College of Surgeons and other distinguished people. There it was interred on the north side of the nave close to the grave of Ben Jonson. A memorial brass was placed on the floor above it:

> The Royal College of Surgeons of England have placed this tablet over the grave of Hunter, to record their admiration of his genius as a gifted interpreter of the Divine Power and Wisdom at work in the Laws of Organic Life, and their grateful veneration for his services to mankind as the Founder of Scientific Surgery.

A stone bust of John Hunter by Thomas Woolner RA was placed in Leicester Square in 1874, and the Royal College also set up a bust by Nigel Boonham in the south-west corner of Lincoln's Inn Fields to celebrate the Silver Jubilee of Queen Elizabeth II in 1977.

John McMaster, Churchwarden (1906-1919) and Historian

The greatest gift that this formidable man gave to his beloved church was his magisterial *A short history of the royal parish of St Martin-in-the-Fields, London W.C.*, published in 1916. Its 339 pages challenges 'short', but its wealth of detail is still an important resource for anyone needing information about the first 700 years of the parish history. He not only quotes extensively from the Churchwardens' Accounts and Rate Books, but also makes more accessible the Parish Registers containing the records of burials, marriages and baptisms. His personal memories are mostly omitted, but occasionally he allows himself to describe an event like the Beating of the Bounds *c.*1875, when he was a small boy:

> The elder boys went to school at nine and were supplied with long wands, and, with a master and the assistant overseer, went round the eastern portion of the parish, and in the neighbourhood of Drury Lane usually met the boys of St. Giles' parish on the same errand, and in place of beating the boundary stones, whacked each other, and often got a caning from the headmaster the next day for smashing the wands in the morning. On arriving back at the school, prizes were distributed by the Vicar, after which the children attended church. At the close of the service we returned to school where a lunch was provided, consisting of buns, cakes, and lemonade. One old lady told me that when she went perambulating in her childhood she was given good sound ale, none of those sour stuffs that upset one.[7]

In the afternoon the young McMaster and his friends walked behind the beadle and the parish giant carrying the Royal Standard, and any soldier in uniform who saluted as they went by was given a shilling. The verger led the vicar, who walked between his wardens carrying their wands of office, and these were followed by the Vestry and their ladies. Bringing up the rear were the schoolchildren accompanied by the band of the Edmonton Poor Law School. They marched down Charing Cross, through Horse Guards, then across St James's Park to Buckingham Palace. They entered by the garden gate, formed up, and sang the National Anthem to Queen Victoria, who came to a window to greet them. The return journey round Green Park took them through Marlborough House gardens where they saw the future George V and his brother 'receiving their lessons in gymnastic exercises', and so they loyally sang 'God bless the Prince of Wales'.

One cold night in 1887 John McMaster saw a sad, dejected figure in the Strand.[8] He was there the following night so the Churchwarden made room for him in his shoe shop at 14 Panton Street, off Haymarket, and called the doctor, who said there was nothing wrong that good food, warmth and clothing could not put right. The man, who McMaster realised was the poet and writer Francis Thompson, soon recovered and began to work in the shop. A shy, self-centred visionary, suffering from a depressive illness, Thompson had forsaken his medical studies and come to London. He befriended McMaster's orphaned niece and the two of them went out on errands and enjoyed feeding the ducks in St James's Park. He continued to give his address as the Charing Cross Post Office, but stayed several months and wrote several of his earlier pieces in the shop, where the workers treated him kindly.

Unfortunately, he returned to taking drugs and the two men parted company, but in the same year he was befriended by the poet Alice Meynell, who with her husband Wilfred recognised his genius and gave him a home. He published *Poems* in 1893, followed by other poetry and prose of which his best known poem today is 'Hound of Heaven'. He died in 1907 and was buried in St Mary's Roman Catholic Cemetery, Kensal Green. Perhaps it was the kindness of McMaster that inspired these verses in *The Kingdom of God*:

> But (when so sad thou canst not sadder)
> Cry, – and upon thy so sore loss
> Shall shine the traffic of Jacob's ladder
> Pitched betwixt Heaven and Charing Cross.
> Yea, in the night, my Soul, my daughter,
> Cry, – clinging Heaven by the hems –
> And lo, Christ walking on the water
> Not of Gennesareth, but Thames!

McMaster was passionate in his love for St Martin's, and as he had been a loyal Churchwarden for eight years and a friend of Prebendary Shelford, who died in May 1914, he was immensely suspicious of the young, charismatic Dick Sheppard who arrived that autumn. The feeling was mutual, and Dick described him as 'A pompous old devil' that wore a skull cap and made cavalry boots.[9] Dick had never met a man whose attitude to his church, its fabric, its furniture and its ceremonial was one of such blind adoring love, and perceived him as an enemy of change. After several months Dick's charm and McMaster's loyalty overcame all the obstacles, and the 'Irritated and irritating Vicar' and his Warden became friends. Later Dick was to say that no letters which he received at times of joy and sorrow, of illness or loss, were full of more wisdom and loving, courageous sympathy than those from 'Jenks'.[10]

The Chinese Community

Soho has now taken over from Limehouse as the centre of the Chinese community in London although the number of Chinese living in East London was always very small. The arrival in the docks of sailors from India and the Far East gave the area a cosmopolitan flavour, but the local rector after the First World War estimated that the number of Chinese living in his parish was never more than 300.[11] Today the only sign of this community is four excellent restaurants near Pennyfields, crowded every evening with business people from nearby Canary Wharf.

The Chinese community is now very evident in Soho so in May 1964 the Rev. Shui Ying Lee was asked by Bishop Hall of Hong Kong to work with them in London, and St Martin's invited him to hold a service every Sunday afternoon. The first was held in the Dick Sheppard Chapel with 12 people attending. The next Sunday they moved into the crypt, and by the following January the congregation numbered 50 – Anglicans, Baptists, Methodists and members of the Chinese Church of Christ. People, particularly the sick, were visited in their homes, and advice was given on obtaining jobs, and in the autumn of 1964 a social centre was opened at St Anne's in Dean Street. The following year Mr Lee was priested and continued to hold services in Cantonese and to see around fifty people with problems each week. He reported that they worked mainly in restaurants and were depressed by living in a strange environment and climate. Families often remained in Hong Kong and all available cash was sent to them. Many spoke no English, and so he accompanied them to

41 *Dancing in the Bishop R.O. Hall Chinese Centre beneath St Martin's church.*

government offices and lawyers. By 1974 there were 200 members, about a quarter of whom would be in church on Sunday.

On 28 November 1971 Bishop Gilbert Baker, who had been a non-stipendiary curate at St Martin's on Eric Loveday's staff in the 1940s, ordained two women in Hong Kong – Jane Hwang, who was the vicar of one of the largest parishes in the diocese, and Joyce Bennett, Principal of St Catharine's School in the large town of Kwuntong and a member of the Hong Kong Legislative Council. He was following in the footsteps of Bishop Hall who in 1944, to meet a desperate wartime need, had ordained Florence Tim Oi Li and been condemned for it by the Archbishop of Canterbury and the Lambeth Conference. Bishop Baker was also far ahead of other bishops in the Anglican Communion but, gradually, they are following his example. He spent almost all his ministry in China, in Canton, Shanghai and Hong Kong, where he was consecrated their bishop in 1966. On his retirement he returned to England where he preached at St Martin's and assisted with the pastoral work of the Chinese congregation until he died in May 1986.

On 1 July 1984 Joyce Bennett took over from S.Y. Lee, who had retired, and in the 1985 Friends of St Martin's Newsletter reported that Sunday afternoons were exciting since the number of young people was growing and they particularly appreciated their language classes. The Women and Adults' Fellowship was also popular, and a Mission was held to contact men and women living and working in London at which the Rev. Kenneth Wong, minister of the Agape Baptist Church, New York, gave the addresses. The Bishop of London, Graham Leonard, forbade Joyce to celebrate the Eucharist, despite her being a priest, and so a male colleague, usually Charles Hedley, stood beside her at the altar and presumably they said the consecration prayer together. It was to be another eight years before women were ordained to the priesthood in England.

It was estimated in the 1980s that there were 70-80,000 Chinese from Hong Kong living in London so in 1984 the Bishop Ho Ming Wah Association was established to raise money for a community centre. St Martin's offered one and a half vaults in the crypt and Helen Lee, who had married S. Y. Lee's son, Michael, was the centre manager for four years. The centre developed a strong, warm social life. In January 1987 the Association appointed Sandie Ching, who had studied and worked as a social worker in Hong Kong, as a full-time worker and on 11 November the Bishop R.O. Hall Chinese Centre was opened in the crypt and a marble tablet was unveiled by the Bishop's son and daughter. The Bishop who presided over his diocese from 1932 until 1966 was given the Chinese name Ho Ming Wah, meaning 'Hall who understands the Chinese'. Events were now held in the Centre and special care was given to a group for the elderly which met two afternoons a week, when a monthly visit from a doctor was particularly welcome. For nine months Joyce was helped by Rinson Lin, who had grown up in Hong Kong and never had an English name. As he was reading *Robinson Crusoe*, he chose Rinson. His congregation in Vancouver allowed him to come to London but soon afterwards, in August 1988, the Rev. Gilbert Lee arrived as chaplain. Accompanied by his wife, Grace, and six-year-old son Thomas, he was Cantonese-speaking and met a congregation which also included Vietnamese, Japanese and Korean Christians. His first 12 confirmands included four students from Hong Kong and two elderly ladies who had lived for many years in London without learning English.

During 1989 it was realised that the English and Chinese congregations shared very little contact with each other, so three people from each group met and made recommendations. Four joint services were held and members assisted at each other's worship, helping in ventures like the Scrub Club. (This began in 1957 when 73 people, including a curate, a brigadier and two titled ladies, decided the building needed a regular clean!) The vicar also suggested that services on Sunday afternoon be held in the church instead of the crypt, where much scene shifting had to take place before worship could begin. This meant that the Chinese congregation now felt more a part of St Martin's.

In 1995 Sandie Ching told the *Review* that many people come to the Centre with practical problems but in talking they could discuss deeper issues. Two years later a social worker, Miss Emmet Wong, was appointed to help with this and also to develop services aimed at supporting immigrants from Hong Kong, which was now under Chinese rule. Every week 150 people used the Centre and activities included translation, Tai Chi classes and language teaching. Today there are three full-time workers and one part-time chef.

On 19 March 2001 the Rev. Paul Lau joined the staff and after consultation with the Diocese was appointed associate vicar (Chinese). A year later he reported a significant increase in the number of Mandarin speakers in the congregation so there is now another service in Mandarin every Sunday.

The Chinese congregation, which had an electoral roll of 142 adults in 2004, finds that fellowship can be strengthened through Bible classes, prayer meetings and small groups such as those for women, the elderly (Evergreen) and young people – the Timothy, Jonah and Noah groups. Lay leadership is strong and was greatly enhanced when seven members attended the All Souls, Langham Place Training Course. Paul and Edith Lau regularly call on members in their homes and are often accompanied by lay visitors.[12]

42 *The Rev. Paul Lau, Associate Vicar (Chinese), with members of the congregation, 2004.*

The congregation is now made up of retired people who used to work in Soho restaurants, second- and third-generation locally born men and women, immigrants from Hong Kong and about 38 students. Many live in outer London and may travel an hour to come for worship. Paul is an associate chaplain of the Universities in London and visits Chinese students studying in them.

When the new development is completed there will be a new Chinese Day Centre and the congregation will have the use of the church, the parish hall, which will accommodate 150 people, and other meeting rooms and offices.

The Pearlies

On the first Sunday in October members of the other royal family in London come for their Harvest Festival in St Martin's. Tourists reach for their cameras because it is a glittering occasion, full of colour and tradition. To many people these kings in their suits smothered with pearl buttons and their queens in huge, cartwheel hats trimmed with dyed ostrich feathers represent the best of British life, because they have a very definite function – not just to look magnificent, but to raise funds for the poor and vulnerable. Hospitals, children's homes and hundreds of charities including The Connection at St Martin's have benefited by their efforts. Austen Williams invited them to make the church their home in the 1950s and they are still here. (He was given a pearl-buttoned black stole to wear at the Services.) In 2003 they came with their princes and princesses, and the lesson at the service was read by Lyn Nutley, Pearly Queen of the City

43   *The Rev. Canon Geoffrey Brown, Vicar 1985-95, welcomes the Pearly Kings and Queens to one of their special services.*

of London. The Pearly regalia is unique – a garment could be decorated with 30,000 buttons! All outfits are different and may contain designs including stars, suns, moons, diamonds, flowers, fertility symbols, Eyes of God or Trees of Life. Good luck signs such as horse-shoes, crosses and hearts rub shoulders with anchors, bells and crowns. The circle frequently appears symbolising eternity, the wheel of fortune, money or the wheels of a donkey-cart.

The Pearlies will also be in church on the third Sunday in May to commemorate their Founder, Henry Croft, whose great-granddaughter is the present Pearly Queen of Somers Town, near Euston. Most London Boroughs still have a Pearly royal family, and they come together for great events like the Queen's Golden Jubilee and the late Queen Mother's 100th birthday. On Derby Day at Epsom Racecourse they arrive in a decorated donkey cart – with their collecting tins!

Henry Croft, who shared his birthday with Queen Victoria, was born on 24 May 1862 and, never knowing his parents, was brought up in a local orphanage in Somers Town. It was a very depressed area of London and many thousands of people were losing their homes because the three local railway stations, Euston, St Pancras and King's Cross, required more land. The poor were displaced but not removed, so stayed on in overcrowded, stifling buildings. Aged 13, Henry left the orphanage to work for the local council as a road-sweeper and rat-catcher, which led to his spending much time in the markets. There he watched the costermongers selling fruit and vegetables

I   St Martin Dividing His Cloak *by Francesco Solimena (1657-1743).*

II   The Wedding of Stephen Beckingham and Mary Cox, *1729, by William Hogarth.*

III   *Interior of St Martin's looking westwards, John Bowles, c.1750.*

IV   *Lucinda Rogers' impression of the new development, upstairs and downstairs.*

V *The Rt Rev. and Rt Hon. Richard Chartres, Bishop of London, with the Rev. Nicholas Holtam after his Induction and Institution as Vicar, 13 September 1995.*

VI *The present organ of St Martin's installed in 1990 by J.W. Walker & Sons.*

VII *James Gibbs, Architect, 1682-1754, by Andrea Soldi.*

VIII *The Three Kings from the Christmas Crib designed for St Martin's in 1999 by Peter Eugene Ball.*

from their barrows. He was most impressed by their outfits and the way they collected for charity. Their 'flash boy outfits' included a row of bead buttons down the outside seam of their trousers and beads on their caps and waistcoat pocket flaps. He decided to go one step further and cover – smother – all his clothes with pearl buttons, and in 1974 this suit made of heavy brown material in a checked pattern, with a collared waistcoat and flared trousers, was found in an attic in Romford. Fortunately he was good with a needle, and at this time there were about 200 factories in the East End turning out mother-of-pearl buttons and beads, so they were available very cheaply. Henry was less than 5ft tall – shorter than his broom – but the effect of his outfit was stupendous, and people at carnivals and meetings would give him cash for the orphanage where he had been brought up.

Henry, who obviously had an outgoing lively personality, visited the local pubs and collected huge sums – it is reckoned that in his lifetime he collected over £5,000 (which would be around £250,000 today). He was made the first Pearly King of Somers Town and began to recruit his Pearly royal families from among the coster tradesmen in every part of London. He was joined by men like Mike Satwick (Pearly King of Holloway), George Dole (St Pancras), Frank Caulfield (Essex), Bert Matthews (Hampstead), Alf Parker, Fred Tinsley (Southwark) and John Pritchard Marriott (Finsbury). It was hard work responding to all the invitations to attend fairs, carnivals and horse shows as, soon, no Bank Holiday event or Lord Mayor's Show was complete without the Pearlies and their collecting tins. Succession is by inheritance and so the titles pass from parents to children.

War broke out in 1914 and sadness struck Henry because one of his sons and a grand-daughter were killed. In the 1920s John Marriott, the first Pearly King of Finsbury, organised two great Pearly Balls at the Pithead Baths, Finsbury for the two royal families, and the first was attended by the Duke and Duchess of York, later King George VI and Queen Elizabeth. The guest of honour at the other was Princess Marie-Louise, a grand-daughter of Queen Victoria, who took a great interest in their affairs, and gave John Marriott a crimson velvet arm band in recognition of his charity work. Several Pearly daughters were named after the Princess, and Beatrice and John's daughter, Marie-Louise, later Pearly Queen of Finsbury, was the Princess's god daughter.

Henry died on 1 January 1930 and the Pearlies gave him a superb send-off in one of the most magnificent funerals London has ever seen. Four hundred of them in full regalia followed his coffin in decorated donkey-carts, with banners, flowers, feathers and bagpipes. A statue of him was erected in the St Pancras and Islington cemetery, but because of vandalism this is now in the Gallery below the portico for safe keeping. On his grave in the cemetery there is now a marble slab bearing a photograph of the statue.

The Original Pearly Kings and Queens Association, re-formed in 1975, is now based at St Martin's and their motto is 'One Never Knows'. They continue their magnificent fund-raising work and occasionally visit Trade Fairs abroad to help boost exports. No large London event is complete without them.

7

The Parish – Places

The Vicarage

There are three buildings in the magnificent terrace to the north of the church in St Martin's Place. The Transactions of the Commissioner of Woods and Forests made provision in 1826 for this land and all three were built around 1830 as part of the Charing Cross improvement scheme.[1] Nash's early plans proposed a carriageway instead of the present passage between them and the church. Number 6, on the western corner opposite the National Portrait Gallery, was built as a vicarage for the then vicar, the Rev. George Richards, who himself paid £3,000 for his new house. By a Grant of 20 July 1833 a rent of £1 p.a. is paid annually for all three buildings to the Crown Estate which owns the freehold.[2] In 1886 an extra floor was added to the vicarage to accommodate the large family of John Kitto, taking it to its present height. The London Diocesan surveyor, Gordon Macdonald Hills, was responsible for this work. The present vicar and his family live on the two top floors and the ground and first floor are used as meeting rooms and offices. The third-floor flat is used for staff. In one of his radio programmes Professor Laurie Taylor voted No.6 his dream home because, when he lived there briefly in 1971, he enjoyed the views and could not believe people lived so centrally.

The first parsonage of St Martin's stood near Burleigh Street to the east of the parish, but in the reign of King Edward VI (1547-53) it was demolished so that Sir Thomas Palmer could build a mansion on the site. The next vicarage stood at the north-east corner of the churchyard, and was being built by the vicar, Christopher Hayward, when Thomas Davyes was accused of taking away into the neighbouring garden of Mr Styward 'dyuerse peces of Wood and framed tymber'.[3] The vicarage was rebuilt in 1666/7.

In 1960 the Mews to the north of the vicarage were demolished to build a new development including a Post Office. There were many objections but the building designed by Fitzroy Robinson was eventually erected, and an anonymous writer in the *Review* commented, 'It's just a square lump. It's like modern women – they have good shapes but cover them up in shapeless sacks.' The vicarage itself was renovated in 1988 with the proceeds of the sale of Rysbrack's bust of James Gibbs.

The Vestry Hall

In the middle of this white stucco terrace is the Vestry Hall with a pedimented front. Inside, the room's dark panelling and portraits of past incumbents make for a solemn atmosphere. It is the third such building, the first being erected in 1614 in the graveyard as an annexe to the old church on the south side. The Vestry met in the upper floor and the school on the ground floor. When this was demolished to make way for a new church the rebuilding committee held their meetings in various houses, or at Tom's coffee house, or at the St Martin's coffee house nearby. The second vestry room was erected in 1728 on the south-eastern corner of the yard and this was torn down in 1828 to make way for Duncannon Street. The Crown Estate was reluctant to let the Vestry have the present site although it is not clear what they wanted for this 'prominent situation'. Eventually the parish was told that they would have to pay the additional cost of making it of 'uniform height with the two adjoining buildings, so that the height and general character of the buildings may be in unison'. An initial offer of £200 was rejected but eventually terms were agreed and Nash provided a drawing showing the whole façade as it is today. In April 1830 he noted that the wainscoting from the old Vestry Hall would be insufficient for the new Hall. Some new wood was added and today most of the present panelling with its inscriptions provides a link with the earlier room.

The School Building

Across the top of the façade of the 1830s building is inscribed 'St Martin's National Schools. Built by Subscription on Ground the Gift of His Majesty King George IV. MDCCCXXX.' In 1966 the school closed and in the early 1970s the building was altered to become a centre for young people in London. The architect, Paul Koralek, blended the classic exterior with an interesting, functional modern interior. It is now the home of The Connection at St Martin's which works with homeless people of all ages.

The Admiralty

On the west side of Whitehall is the Admiralty which is hidden or, as Horace Walpole thought, 'deservedly veiled', behind a splendid Screen (1759-61) by the youthful Robert Adam. The three-storeyed building was designed by Thomas Ripley and built in the 1720s to provide residential accommodation for the First Sea Lord and his officers. Next door to the south is Admiralty House, by S.P. Cockerell, which was built as a residence for the First Sea Lord in 1786-8. It has no front door and can be reached only from the Admiralty. Winston Churchill lived here twice, in 1911-15 and 1939-40, before he moved into Downing Street. The building was severely damaged in the Second World War but restoration was completed by 1958.

Many residents of the Admiralty have attended services at St Martin's, their parish church, and the 'inscrutable and sphinx like' Admiral Fisher, who was a Presbyterian and friend of Dick Sheppard's father, would worship when he was First Lord. However, when Dick placed a cross on the altar, he sent a pained letter of protest and never came again. The relationship between the Admiralty and its parish church has always been cordial – Dick held a service in St Martin's to commemorate the inauguration of the Women's Royal Naval Service, WRNS, in 1918 and for many years an annual Trafalgar Day Service was held. The last First Lords to sit in the Admiralty box (to the south of the chancel) were James Thomas, later Viscount Cilcennin (1951), and his successor Lord Hailsham – during the Suez Crisis in 1956.

William Bridgeman, Joint Secretary of the Admiralty, presented a font in 1689 and this was transferred to the present church and is still in use today. In May 1726 the Board of Admiralty directed the Navy Board to supply a standard out of His Majesty's Stores, and they have been supplied regularly ever since. The White Ensign was not at that time the exclusive or even the senior ensign of the Navy, but may have been considered, with its St George's Cross on a white background, as a more suitable gift to a church than the Red Ensign. In 1772 the churchwardens informed their Lordships at the Admiralty that, 'the flag used and hoisted from the Parish Church upon King's Birthday and on all other publick occasions being quite worn out and rendered unfit for further service', they needed a new flag.

In 1866 the Admiralty gave a 40ft flagstaff, and further White Ensigns measuring 7½ft by 15ft were given in 1922, 1934 and 1949. In 1954 it donated an Admiralty flag (a yellow anchor set horizontally on a red background) which is still in the possession of the church. The Queen's Colour of the South Atlantic and South America Station of the Royal Navy was placed in St Martin's for safekeeping on 19 November 1967 having been brought back by HMS *Kent* when the station was closed.

The Almshouses

The decision to house elderly vulnerable people was first taken by St Martin's Vestry in 1597. Houses were rented, but on 14 June 1603 it was decided to build on a triangular plot of land owned by Westminster Abbey which was to the south-west of the present Trafalgar Square. It was sandwiched between Cockspur Street to the north and Warwick House Street to the south (opposite today's New Zealand House). This patch of land had already been leased to St Martin's for a pound to keep stray animals and those seized for non-payment of rates in. A small cottage in brick cost approximately £10 to erect at this time but Mr Sidney Greene, a builder, was authorised to spend only £15, although a further £10 was promised in December.[4] The Vestry obviously had problems raising the money, because the plan to have a house especially for children was shelved, and the unfortunate Mr Greene had to wait until the autumn of 1607 to be paid.

The new buildings are mentioned in the Vestry Minutes of 12 January 1611, when Roger and Katherine Merriche, who had lived in the parish 40 years, gave

£10 'to be bestowed towards building one or two rooms … for their succour to dwell in during their lives … building near the almshouse'. They agreed to bequeath this house to the parish for the benefit of the poor.[5] By now there were probably five houses, but the land on which they stood still belonged to the Abbey, so a new lease was signed on 4 December 1611 in which the Vestry agreed to build five large houses on the eastern portion which would be let for £122 p.a., of which £26 would be paid to the Abbey and £96 used for the upkeep of the almshouses. There was still some vacant land to the south, and in 1623 Sir Gregory Fenner was allowed to lease this and build what would later be called Warwick House.

In 1612 Thomas Evans, a parishioner, died and left £50 to the poor and £100 to build a charity house on part of the new burial ground facing the church. This house was put up the following year in Green Street to receive the very poorest of the poor. Despite these gifts financial problems remained, and on 23 September 1613 the Vestry ordered that any poor person living in the Almshouses should convey all their goods to the churchwardens and overseers, and that the men and women had to 'behave themselves quietly, soberlye and honestly'. Weekly pensions, called 'exhibitions' in the Vestry Minutes, were paid to the occupants of all these almshouses so that they could buy food, but they were allowed to look for work. Alice Puttrell, one of the residents, was employed as a Searcher to visit the sick of the parish and report to the wardens.

The same Vestry Minutes record that the Widow Alcocke had bequeathed £10 for another almshouse, but the executor, her son-in-law, was reluctant to pay. Six years of wrangling followed and on 13 June 1619 the Vestry instructed the churchwardens to sue 'Pilcher who maryed the Widdow Alcock's daughter'.

The responsibility of administering the Almshouses must have been considerable, because on 18 November 1624 the Vestry decided that although they would continue to hold both lease and funds they would hand over the day-to-day management to a committee of prominent parishioners. These were asked to 'order the Almeshouses and the Almesfolks according to their discretions, examining their Conversations from tyme to tyme and Reforming their disorders by such means as they shall thinke fitting, and during that time have power to displace and place as they shall find just cause'.

During the Civil War the Dean and Canons of Westminster Abbey fled and a Parliamentary Committee chaired by Sir Robert Harley was set up to administer the Abbey. St Martin's kept quiet about their lease, but at the Restoration it was discovered that it had expired and the buildings had reverted to the Abbey's ownership. When one of the large houses became vacant the Dean and Chapter kept the proceeds of the new lease, which greatly angered the Vestry who had to increase the poor rate. When the Abbey sold leases of the other mansions the following year the Vestry petitioned King Charles II. Lawyers advised them that the Abbey was acting lawfully, but a lease for 15 years was granted at a nominal sum for the Almshouses and the roundhouse, the parish prison which stood next door. With its stocks and whipping post, this must have been a nuisance because the tenants in the large houses persuaded the

Abbey to insert a clause to remove it after only one year, that they 'may not thereby bee annoyed'.[6]

The Vestry now realised that their Almshouses stood on very valuable land and that the Abbey would soon want it, so they looked for a new site. In the 1670s they found it – on the west side of Hog Lane, now Charing Cross Road. The Crown owned the freehold and 'fortunately' the leaseholders, Lord St Albans and Richard Frith, a property developer, both agreed to surrender their interest.

Accordingly, on 31 May 1685, by letters patent, King Charles II granted some land – Kemp's Field or Bunche's Close near Hog Lane, including a church – to Lord Jermyn and other parishioners to be held in trust for the benefit of the poor of the parish of St Martin's for ever. The cost of building the 18 new cottages and two large houses was met by the vicar, Dr Tenison, and Susannah Graham but mostly by Sir Charles Cotterell who lived in Westminster; he also provided an endowment to maintain his gift for the future.[7] Now in his 70s, he was Master of Requests, a powerful position which dealt with applications to the Crown for assistance. He died aged 90 in 1702 and his great generosity – over £4m today according to Dr David Avery[8] – was marked by the Almshouses being named after him.

Work began on the Hog Lane site in 1683 and, because the old Almshouses had to be handed over to the Abbey for demolition, the residents were put in rented accommodation for three years until their new homes were ready. Richard Ryder, the architect, designed three terraces – on the northern, western and southern sides of the site. A year later he was instructed to build two large houses on the eastern side which later, because of the street name change, became 10 and 11 Crown Street. Sixty aged women (increased to 70 after a year) were accommodated, including four known as 'Vicar's ladies' who were of a higher class and lived separately with a female servant to care for them. The building work cost £981, exclusive of architect's fees, and the property endowment probably doubled this figure. The average room size was approx 8ft by 15ft which, although small, was more than most of the residents were used to. On occasions some were happy to share this with a sister or friend.[9]

The Senior Churchwarden was told by the Vestry to 'take care of the Poore People' who moved in, and they were allowed a quantity of coals 'to ayre their Rooms'. The houses looked out on a large garden on part of which the first Greek church in England had been built a few years earlier, in 1677, for Archbishop Joseph Georgines, who with his congregation had been forced to leave the Island of Samos by the Turks. By 1684 this had been taken over by exiled French Huguenots.

By 1818 the buildings were 'in a very old and ruinous condition', so the trustees, who now held the freehold and the endowments, decided to move. An Act of Parliament enabled them to sell the properties and use the money to purchase land on the new St Martin's overspill cemetery in Camden Town, which was still a village. The St Martin's Homes for 'poor elderly spinsters or widows or divorced women of good character' were built in Bayham Street, and the Hog Lane site was sold to Mr E. Allen for £4,102 10s. He promptly re-sold it at a large profit. The new Almshouses were completed in October 1818 for a total of £4,779 4s. 4d. which implies that there were no funds to buy the site itself, and so the vicar and churchwardens gave the land to the charity.

A strip of land at the rear of the houses was sold for £5,000 in 1879 to build a chapel, infirmary, matron's residence, and to give another room to each resident. McMaster archly comments, 'It may, however be considered a debatable question as to whether two rooms are better, as a number of the old people only use one.'[10] Forty-two women were accommodated, all single or widowed – the first resident to marry was Kay Colbourne in 1976 after living there 23 years.

A new name was given to the project on 3 October 1974, The St Martin-in-the-Fields Almshouse Charity, and in December 1980 the charity moved to a new building in St John's Wood Terrace which had 30 one-room flats. The move caused many problems (including squatters) to the Clerk, Lt-Colonel D.L. Searle, who was also Administrator of St Martin's. With the help of the Matron, Mrs Rachel Thornton Lewis, a former Director of Nursing, all residents were re-housed, ten moving into the new building. Upgrading of the flats started in 2002 and by the end of 2004 there will be 15 one-bedroom flats, six bed-sits and a two-bedroom flat for the resident superintendent, Miss Norma Fisher, a former children's nurse who took over on the retirement of Mrs Rachel Thornton Lewis in 1997. Residents care for each other as much as possible, and the Social Services Department are at hand to help. The vicar is an ex-officio trustee and seven trustees are provided by the charity. Westminster City Council nominates six trustees but once appointed they operate with no input from Westminster.

Today the House, with its large communal lounge and conservatory, has a warm, welcoming atmosphere, and thanks to the present Chairman, Sir Peter Jennings, and Clerk, Francis Casserly and their predecessors, the charity has a strong financial future.

OTHER PLACES OF WORSHIP IN THE PARISH

The Quaker Meeting House

A side entrance in Hop Gardens off St Martin's Lane leads to the Quaker Meeting House opened on 8 July 1956, and its pleasant, large rooms are still very much in use. Westminster is one of the oldest Friends Meetings in London and has used various buildings since 1655 when Quakerism came to the Capital. Stephen Hart held a meeting in New Palace Yard which had to be discreet as, until 1688, there were substantial fines for attending. Samuel Pepys noted in his diary for 7 February 1660: 'In the Palace Yard I saw Monk's soldiers abuse Billing and all the Quakers that were at a meeting there; and indeed, the soldiers did use them very roughly and were too blame.'

Hart moved his Meeting to Elizabeth Trott's house in Pall Mall then soon after to Little Almonry in the precincts of the Abbey where it stayed for a hundred years. When the lease ran out a site was purchased in St Martin's Lane near where the Duke of York's theatre now stands. Peter's Court Meeting House, with its commodious, galleried interior, opened in 1779 and cost £2,634, the studio of Roubilliac being demolished to make way for it. Two years later the Savoy Meeting, founded by William Woodcock, merged with the Westminster Meeting. Tsar Alexander I visited Peter's Court on 19 June 1814 and felt 'a communion with the Majesty of all' greater than he had ever known 'in connection with the grandest church ceremonial'. The Society of Friends, as they became known in 1800, taught that the Inner Light was superior to the Scriptures and the Church, and guided by this they became known for their moral probity and for their education and social work.

Another move had to be made when the 100-year lease ran out in 1879. The freehold of 52 St Martin's Lane was purchased by the wealthy congregation – someone unkindly said that in the silence one could hear the stocks and shares rising and falling – and the new building opened in 1883. Attendance was good; 120 children were in the Sunday school, a Band of Hope was started and a Mutual Improvement Union for Young Women was established. In the Second World War an advisory centre for conscientious objectors was opened here, but on 16 April 1941 the Meeting House and caretaker's flat were destroyed by fire bombs. Other rooms were still usable but it was 15 years before everything was repaired.

The Orange Street Chapel

The stables of the Duke of Monmouth, who was beheaded as a traitor after the Battle of Sedgemoor in 1685, were known as the Orange Mews – a reference to the colour of his coat-of-arms. This may explain the name of the street which was partly laid out on the site of those stables, and now extends from Haymarket to Charing Cross Road behind the National Gallery. On its north side is the tiny Congregational chapel built in 1929.

It is an historic piece of land as in 1693 the Huguenot congregation from Glasshouse Street, Piccadilly moved into a small building at the corner of Long's Court and Orange Street known as the Leicester Fields Chapel. In 1776 a Church of England congregation shared it, and for two years until his death the Rev. Augustus Montague Toplady, author of the hymn 'Rock of Ages', preached here twice a week. The building was enlarged in 1790 by taking the house next door on the corner of Orange Street and St Martin's Street; it could now seat 700. The pulpits and organ were placed on the east wall and a new entrance was made in St Martin's Street. The exterior was faced in stucco, the interior having a flat ceiling with a central octagonal lantern light. A gallery which ran round the chapel supported on cast-iron columns contained the organ at the east end with the pulpit in front of it. The Huguenots had neither the numbers nor the funds to continue worshipping here and so sold it to Thomas Hawkes, an Army Accoutrement Contractor of Piccadilly, who converted it into a Congregational chapel. The first minister was the Rev. John Townsend, founder of the London Asylum for the Deaf and Dumb.

The house next door, 35 St Martin's Street, had been lived in by Sir Isaac Newton and Dr Charles Burney, father of Fanny. This and the chapel were condemned as dangerous structures in 1913 so the last service was held on 31 August. Both buildings were demolished and the present chapel sits on the eastern part of the site.

The Queen's Chapel, Saint James's Palace

Inigo Jones set to work to prepare this chapel for the wedding of Charles I to the Infanta of Spain in 1623, but when the marriage negotiations broke down building work stopped. Three years later Princess Henrietta Maria, a Roman Catholic, arrived from France and the chapel was finished for her and the courtiers who came with her, who included a bishop and 29 priests. It became a focus for Roman Catholicism much to the horror of Charles who sent 440 of his wife's retainers back to France. The chapel was refurnished in 1662 for Charles II's wife, Catherine of Braganza, a Roman Catholic.

The chapel stands in Marlborough Road opposite St James's Palace, whose Friary Court housed a friary of Capuchin monks to serve it. Until 1809 there was no road and the Court extended to the chapel. The first church in England to depart from the Perpendicular Gothic style, it 'is unhesitatingly and uncompromisingly classical, and it is furthermore of a simplicity and beauty rarely matched in the more ingenious and complex designs of Wren'.[11] Of Inigo Jones's time is the communion rail and the large chimney-piece on the large west gallery which was the royal pew. The last restoration in 1950 brought the building back to its 17th-century grandeur. 'Proportion, exactitude, control, balance and calm show here as they do in everything Jones built.'[12]

The coffin of Queen Elizabeth, the Queen Mother rested here before it was taken to Westminster Hall for the Lying in State, 5-8 April 2002.

Prayer Book services are held on Sundays between Easter and the end of July and this is almost the only time the chapel may be viewed.

The Chapel Royal, Saint James's Palace

Priests and choirs known as the chapel royal would accompany medieval sovereigns on their travels, but, when court life became more settled, the chapels were established in royal palaces. In St James's Palace the original Tudor Closet was a gallery on stilts and here Elizabeth I said her prayers at the time of the Armada as she had decided to remain in the Palace to receive progress reports from the south coast. Charles I made his communion here before his execution. Happier occasions have been royal weddings: Victoria married Albert in a simple ceremony on 10 February 1840, and the Duke of York married Princess Mary of Teck (later King George V and Queen Mary) on 6 July 1893.[13]

Much of the present building, which stands between Colour Court and Ambassadors' Court, dates from Tudor times, but it was altered in 1836 to provide side galleries and a new ceiling. Pews were installed in 1876.

The Chapel Royal has always been considered one of the cradles of English church music and among its many organists and composers have been Thomas Tallis, William Byrd, Orlando Gibbons and Henry Purcell. George Frederick Handel was appointed 'Composer of Musick of His Majesty's Chappel Royal' by King George I on 25 February 1723, and his 'Zadok the Priest' has been sung at every coronation since. Today the six Gentlemen and the ten Children Choristers, who wear State Coats on great occasions, sing the Sunday services and accompany the Queen to the Royal Maundy Service held each year in one of the cathedrals. Services, which are drawn from the Book of Common Prayer, are held from September to Good Friday and at other times one can visit the chapel only by appointment since the Palace is not open to the public.

The coffin of the much-loved Diana, Princess of Wales rested here in September 1997 before her funeral in Westminster Abbey.

In October 2002 Queen Elizabeth's Jubilee was commemorated by a re-furbishment of the chapel which included installing a stained-glass window, designed by John Napper and made by Goddard and Gibbs, and a new oak reredos, designed by Martin Ashley and incorporating an early Tudor triptych, and cleaning the Holbein ceiling. At the same time the side windows of 1858, which had been blocked up in the 1970s, were reopened.

The Banqueting House, Whitehall

This breathtakingly beautiful building, designed by Inigo Jones and completed in 1622, is all that is left of Whitehall Palace destroyed by fire in 1698. It bore no resemblance to anything ever built in England before and is the result of Jones's study of Palladio's work at Vicenza.[14] The colonnaded hall received the ceiling it deserved when Charles I commissioned Rubens to paint nine massive canvases on it in 1634. Fifteen years later the king was to step out of one of the windows to be beheaded on a cold January morning.

The Hall, adapted by Wren, was used as a chapel royal from 1698 until 1890, and in 1809 a second gallery was added so that the Horse Guards stationed opposite might worship here. There were, however, difficulties. Sir Robert Peel, a regular worshipper, always asked for copies of the sermon because he said that the acoustics were so appalling he had no idea what was being said.

8

Schools

The first mention of a school in the parish is in the Churchwardens' Accounts of 1571 when a quarrel – a diamond-shaped piece of glass – was fitted in a lattice window at a cost today of approx £48:

> payd to geyls quarrel for setinge the scolhowse wyndowe & for vj newe q'rels … iijs ijd.

The building stood near the church and its most famous pupil was the poet and dramatist Ben Jonson, who lived with his mother and stepfather Thomas Fowler, a builder, in Hartshon Lane near Charing Cross. His father, a priest, had died a month after he was born on 11 June 1572. He went on to Westminster School and then, disliking brick-laying, enlisted in the Army to go abroad. On returning to England he became an actor and playwright, writing masterpieces such as *Volpone* and *The Alchemist*. A large, unwieldy man, he was sincere, brave and quarrelsome, a good hater – he had killed the actor Gabriel Spencer in a duel – and 'a good lover, copious in speech; keenly critical in insight, a careful scholar with a fine touch of poetry in his composition'.[1] He died on 6 August 1637 and was buried standing up in Westminster Abbey as he had once asked King Charles I for a favour: 'Give me eighteen inches of square ground.' 'Where?' 'In Westminster Abbey.'[2] The inscription on the marble slab is 'O Rare Ben Jonson', and when Dr John Hunter's bones were transferred from St Martin's to the Abbey in 1859 they were interred next to this spot and Jonson's bones could be clearly seen.[3]

The tiny school was moved in 1614 into the ground floor of the new Vestry Hall which was built on the south side of the church. Two years later there were disagreements so the Vestry, which met upstairs, picked a committee of gentlemen to oversee the affairs of the masters and scholars in consultation with the vicar, Dr Mountforde. The school remained there until plans to rebuild the church were being discussed, so in 1693 the staff and children formed the nucleus of Dr Tenison's new school.

Archbishop Tenison's School and Library

John Evelyn noted in his diary on 15 February 1683/4, 'Dr Tenison communicated to me his intention of erecting a Library in St. Martin's parish, for the public use, and desired my assistance, with Sir Christopher Wren, about the placing and structure thereof.' The following year the vicar told the Vestry that there were a number of ministers, studious persons and noblemen's chaplains in the parish and there was no library for their use. Could he have permission to build one at his own expense? This was unanimously approved and Wren erected a building on the east side of Castle Street (which in 1886 became part of Charing Cross Road). As it was built on land given to the parish by James I in 1606 a Faculty had to be granted by the Bishop of London. At first Tenison suggested that the parish fire engines be kept on the ground floor but the Vestry wanted it adapted for the use of the parish charity school, 'with Seates to be taken downe, and Planks to be taken up, upon any occasion of Burialls.' This would have produced not only an income

44 *Archbishop Tenison's Library and School, Castle Street, Leicester Square, 1850, by T.H. Shepherd.*

45 *Students from Archbishop Tenison's School present a cheque for the Social Care Unit to Roger Shaljean (centre) and Colin Glover (right), 2003.*

but a smell, as it did in the Sir John Cass School, Aldgate which had a similar arrangement in 1710.

The school and the usher's room were on the ground floor, and above was the library – the first free library in London. Tenison gave his collection of books to form the nucleus of the library and £1,000. Nine trustees were appointed, three of whom had to be the vicar and churchwardens, and the master, who had to be in orders and was paid £10 p.a., was also the librarian. He was expected to teach ten boys free of charge, whilst the usher taught 20 boys chosen by the trustees.

The trustees were reprimanded by the Vestry in 1835 for neglecting their duties. The library now contained between 5,000 and 6,000 books with 300 valuable manuscripts, but these and the buildings were in a poor condition, so a public appeal was launched and large sums were collected including a gift of £30 from Queen Victoria. With its 58 scholars, of whom 30 were free, the school flourished under its master, the Rev. W. Eyre, until 1852 when its income collapsed and closure was suggested. A protest meeting of parishioners was held on 11 October 1856 and two years later it was decided to sell the books to keep the school open. This was done with the approval of the Charity Commissioners in 1861, but five years later the building was compulsory purchased for £9,000 to extend the National Gallery. This enabled a site to be bought for £5,700 on the south-east side of Leicester Square where Hogarth had lived. The new buildings were opened by the 5th Duke of Northumberland on 24 July 1871 and cost £5,167 9s. 11d. The first Head not in orders, Mr Arnold, stayed 30 years to be replaced on his death by Mr C.B. Rusbridge, and under both men the school served well its two parishes, St Martin's and St James.

Meanwhile the Public Libraries Act had been passed and a site was purchased for a library in St Martin's Lane. The foundation stone was laid by the Prince of Wales in March 1890, and it was opened by Mr Gladstone on 12 February 1891. After the First World War, when most of the rooms were used for offices, there was a proposal to incorporate the library building into the City Hall which backed on to it, but Dr Sheppard took the Council to court to force them to provide a replacement, which was eventually built in St Martin's Street, close to the Orange Street Chapel.

After years of discussion the children and their teachers moved to Kennington Oval in south London, and on 13 July 1928 the new building, designed by A.H.R. Tenison, a direct descendant of the founder, was opened by the Prince of Wales, later briefly King Edward VIII. During the Second World War the school with its 230 pupils was evacuated to a large, thatched house in Woodley near Reading, which was just as well as the building was severely damaged three times and had to be re-built in 1947/8. The VI form went to Reading School and for the first time girls were admitted, brothers being allowed to take their sisters.

Archbishop Tenison's is today a thriving Voluntary Aided Church of England school with 514 students, aged 11-19, drawn from 50 feeder primary schools in Brixton, Elephant, Kennington and Camberwell. 'All four corners of the world are represented so there is a rich cultural diversity' says Louise Fox, the first woman to be Head. Having been Deputy for four years, she was appointed in 2003 when the school received Specialist Arts College Status, which means that extra government resources will be received to construct a new art complex on the roof. The spacious classrooms and corridors are already filled with colourful banners and paintings; it is a warm, welcoming place. The Tenison Brooke VI form has girl students, and a link is kept with St Martin's, whose vicar is an ex-officio governor.

Saint Martin-in-the-Fields High School for Girls

In May 1699 Dr William Lancaster, Vicar of St Martin's, and some of his parishioners appealed for funds to open a school for the children of the poor. They were so successful that in August the first pupils were admitted to a large room in Hungerford Market, south of the Strand, which had been used as a Huguenot church. Days began at 7 a.m. (8 a.m. in winter) and, with a two-hour break at 11 a.m., finished at 5 p.m. (an hour earlier in winter). The following year it was decided that the girls should have separate premises so a house was leased in Castle Street, near Leicester Fields, and the first mistress appointed. The Minute Book for 9 January 1700 records that:

> Mrs Mary Harbin, lodging at ye sign of the Coffee Mill and Sugar Loafe in St. James' Street came to apply for the school, being recommended by Mr Gaywood. Being examin'd she says she is a single woman aged abt 40, of the Church of England, has in her apprentishipp recd the Sacrament once a month, since that once a week: has read (besides the Bible) Bishop Taylor's, Dr Sherlock's Books;

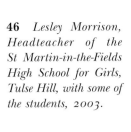

46 *Lesley Morrison, Headteacher of the St Martin-in-the-Fields High School for Girls, Tulse Hill, with some of the students, 2003.*

has for these 20 years past brought up severall children, and has made it her chief business to instruct them in religion, so that all, but one, has (being first brought to ministers) recd the Communion at 15 years of age; writes a very good hand, and understands knitting and plane work.[4]

The school was a success and in March 1704 moved to a larger house nearby in Hunt's Court, Castle Street where 44 girls were admitted. However, the accession of the German King George I did not please Mrs Harbin, who refused to pray for him. The Minute Book records on 25 November 1716 that she 'is of Nonjuring Principles, Disaffected to the present happy Establishment and has refused the Oaths to the Same'. Four days later she was told to leave, but given a glowing reference for her teaching ability.

Funds gradually increased and the school flourished so much that when Hemming's Row was widened the vicar and churchwardens gave part of their burial ground for a new building – where today's National Portrait Gallery stands. This opened in September 1797 for 50 girls and 40 boys, all of whom had to attend St Martin's twice every Sunday. When the girls reached 15 they were sent into service and given £5 for clothing.

The school was forced to move when the National Gallery was extended northwards, but compensation of £7,500 was given so a new building was erected on the west side of Charing Cross Road. Now known as the St Martin's Middle School for Girls it opened in January 1875. By 1910 only 14 of the 150 girls came from the parish so it was decided to move to a four-and-a-half acre site in Tulse Hill, South London in 1928. The new building accommodated 300 girls and during the 30-year headship of Miss Bannister, who supervised the move from central London, the school grew to 500 pupils. She retired in 1942, when half the children had been evacuated to Leatherhead.

Each decade after the war new buildings were erected, and in 2004 a VI form centre will admit boys as well as girls. In 1996 the school received specialist status for technology. Always over-subscribed, there are at present 760 girls from

Brixton, Dulwich and as far away as Croydon, including a sizeable minority of Muslim students. A Church of England comprehensive, it has girls with a Caribbean, West African and Portuguese heritage, which reflects the local area. The Head, Lesley Morrison, says that she tries to respond to ever-changing government initiatives and is particularly proud that a recent OFSTED report gave no key issues for improvement, and that the Chief Inspector's annual report said results were above the national average. A link is kept with St Martin's because the vicar is an ex-officio governor and usually vice chair.

Saint Martin's National Schools, Adelaide Street

Although the land to the north of the church was given by King George IV in 1830 – as the inscription on the façade points out – it was his successor, William IV, whose Deed of Grant dated 20 July 1833 enabled the schools to be established. The vicar and wardens only had to pay £1 p.a. so that poor children could be educated according to the tenets of the Church of England. The school soon needed more space and the Vestry agreed in June 1841 that the rooms above their Hall could be extra classrooms, so a door was made between the two buildings. In 1859 the Vestry asked for the rooms back, but the vicar, the scholarly William Humphry, persuaded it to change its mind.

By the end of the century there was no local secular school in the parish, so the various Church of England ones educated all the children except for the 80 who attended the Roman Catholic school in the former *General Elliot* public house at 1 Bedfordbury. Mr Kitto told Charles Booth in 1898 that he did not care if a Board school were opened as he could always beat them 'by supplying a better article'. He visited regularly, daily catechised in St Martin's and was proud that two-thirds of the pupils attended Sunday school.[5]

In August 1907 the building was reconstructed at a cost of nearly £2,000, raised by donations, and the schools now came under the control of the London County Council, who paid the teachers' salaries. The managers, as in all church schools, were still responsible for the upkeep, maintenance and general well-being and by 1910 there were 475 pupils on the roll. The schools were closed during the Second World War when the children went to Cambridge and the building was used by organisations connected with Civil Defence. They reopened in 1953 and by 1957 had become a Secondary Modern with 229 pupils on the roll – and 159 applications for 60 vacancies. The churchyard was used as a playground and sports had to be played in Regent's Park, Hampstead or Clapham Common. Unfortunately the number of local children declined rapidly, so in July 1966 the school was closed by the Inner London Education Authority and the pupils moved to Pimlico School.

Bedfordbury Mission School

In the 1850s nearly 4,000 people were crammed into the slums surrounding Bedfordbury, the poorest and most densely populated part of the parish, its four acres containing houses where nearly all families lived in one room.

Those who had work were tailors, shoemakers, labourers or porters, but many were unemployed. The curate responsible for this part of the parish, the Rev. Henry Swabry, was appalled by what he saw, and wrote to his vicar, William Humphrey, in November 1859 after one year asking that a church and school be opened:

> You know my feelings about our schools – that the very fact of the presence of a class of children who are better clothed than the very poor, practically excludes those who form my particular charge. Again you know what I feel about church accommodation. I cannot bid the poor of Bedfordbury to Saint Martin's because I know that they cannot get there in any numbers.[6]

Mr Swabry suggests that the new chapel should hold 500 people and that no pew rents should be charged. Prebendary Humphrey, who had been in post four years and would stay another 27, acted quickly and on 29 September 1860 he and the churchwardens bought 17, 18 and 19 Bedfordbury, demolished the houses and built a chapel and school, appealing for funds. The Queen sent £250 towards the £3,000 needed, and the building was completed and opened on 14 November 1861 – only two years after Mr Swabry's letter. In 1864 there was a Roman Catholic school next door at No.20, which moved to No.1 around 1871.

The school, which was free, was a great gift to the poor as it was not until the Education Act of 1870 that free education was provided for children up to the age of thirteen. Miss Maria Cope, the Head for the first 15 years, and her two untrained teachers taught around 130 pupils in one large room. When more wanted to be admitted the managers decided in 1885 that boys over eight should go elsewhere. After this the roll began to drop dramatically as people moved out of the parish. Soon there were only 50 boys and girls, so the school closed on 17 February 1893.

Saint Martin's Northern Schools

On 17 October 1850 Dr Blomfield opened yet more church schools in his diocese of London when, after preaching at St Martin's, he walked, followed by the first pupils, to Long Acre for lunch with those whose subscriptions had paid £2,500 for the new building. The Mercers' Company had granted a 999-year lease for £2 p.a. in 1848. There were already 363 church schools in his diocese – of which 151 survive today – and three-quarters of the children in England were being educated in Church of England schools, so the two new ones were soon full. By 1915 they had become one, with 325 boys and girls, several of whom were killed and injured in an air raid. The year before, the Mercers' Company gave further land at the side and back for a playground, replacing the one on the roof which the authorities thought was no longer suitable. By then the school stood in the parish of St John, Broad Court, Drury Lane which had been inaugurated in 1855 and whose incumbent joined the vicar of St Martin's on the trustees. In 1928 the roll was 256, and this dropped dramatically over the next few years.

The vicar wrote to the Mercers on 11 November 1949 telling them that the building had been badly blitzed during the war and would not be rebuilt as the children had been transferred to the National Schools. The school managers surrendered their lease in January 1951.

Bedfordbury Ragged School

'Some villainous looking fellows who seemed to have come for the purpose of having a row' faced the vicar, Henry Mackenzie, at a meeting in the 'Berry' to establish a school there in 1848. Fortunately he was accompanied by several theological students from King's College who had come with their Principal, Dr Jelf, and the Rev. Professor F.D. Maurice. It was their idea to establish and pay for one of the first free Ragged Schools in London, in which they would teach. Three rooms had been rented in 41 Bedfordbury, of which two were knocked into one as a classroom and the third was a washing-room. Classes were held from 7-9p.m. and on the first evening 120 people arrived, most of whom had been working, but they had to be pared down to sixty. Cast-off clothing was given so that the men could look presentable after their 6.30 scrub, and prayers began and ended the lessons in reading, writing and arithmetic. 'Formidable levity' could ruin the proceedings but the culprits would be expelled so that others could fill their place. The Bishop of London was profoundly impressed and said that he hoped this new movement would be the first fruits of widespread exertions for educating the poor on the only sound basis, that of the established religion.[7] The school was, however, closed after a few years.

St Martin's School of Art

Dr Henry Mackenzie, vicar of St Martin's 1848-55, and his parishioners were concerned that industrial education should be developed and allied to the religious and general education already provided by church schools. They also thought that art education should form part of the industrial instruction for apprentices, so in 1854 the vicar helped found the St Martin's School of Art on the top floor of St Martin's Northern School in Castle Street (now Shelton Street), north of Long Acre. Boys from the age of 13 onwards were admitted and most classes involved the teaching of design skills. The School became independent of the parish in 1859, and by 1884 the number of male and female students had reached 100, with courses including drawing, painting and sculpture.

By 1913 numbers had risen to 300 so new premises were leased on the site of St Mary's church in Charing Cross Road. In 1989 the School, known for its fashion and fine art, merged with the Central School of Art and Design, forming the Central St Martin's College of Art and Design. They were joined in 1999 by the Drama Centre, London, and in 2003 by the Byam Shaw School of Art, so today this world-famous College has five centres, including Charing Cross Road, and students of all ages from 65 different countries.

9

Organs and Organists

The present organ was installed in 1990 by J.W. Walker & Sons, which firm, under the inspired leadership of the late Robert Pennells, had achieved a very high reputation as a builder of fine instruments. The cases in American Red Oak were designed by David Graebe, who followed the outline of the earlier Shrider cases but added 16ft towers at the sides to accommodate the pedal organ. Much of the ornamentation is based on material found in Gibbs' *Rules for Drawing*. The instrument is flanked by two mitres and surmounted by a crown – from the original 1726 case – symbolising Church and State. The consultant was Dame Gillian Weir, a leading recitalist, who was helped by her husband Larry Phelps, a Canadian organ builder. Dame Gillian particularly asked for the wide gaps between the front pipes. On 6 June 1991 a Royal Gala Concert was held in the presence of Diana, Princess of Wales and the programme was carefully chosen to demonstrate the versatility of the new instrument. Simon Preston was the soloist and the evening ended with a rousing 'Jerusalem', after which the Princess asked for the second verse to be played again. '1,100 pairs of eyes were focused on me,' said Mark Stringer, the organist, 'it took me a few minutes to find the place then away we went.'

Organs, known as regals, began to be used in church in the 15th century, although they were known to the Greeks and Romans. The first mention of one in St Martin's is in the Churchwarden's Accounts in 1526:

> Glewe to mend the organs . . . . .jd.
> M' Watts for his Child to pley at Organs byal that yere . . . . xvjs viijd.

The following year the child was only paid seven shillings for half a year and in 1533 Nicholas, the parish clerk, was organist for a year, being paid 12s. 3d. The clerk usually led the singing, although singers were employed on Festivals – 'Georg, ye syngeng man' was paid 12 pence 'for helping ye quyer the holy days'. For the next 14 years regular payments were made to the maker, but only once is he named – John Howe in 1542. Known as Father, he was a member of a famous organ building family and his name appears in the accounts 20 times before 1569.[1]

The old instruments were discarded when the second St Martin's was built around 1544, and a long list of benefactors who included Sir Humfrey

Foster, Mayster Stowe and Mayster Hayle subscribed to the cost of new organs – £6 13s. 4d. Mr Fortescewe headed the list of subscribers with an amount five times as great as the next largest gift and he probably arranged for the instrument to be built by Howe.

In 1553 Queen Mary presented 'a payre of Regalls' to St Martin's but the wardens had to pay eight pence to collect them. Various entries appear for repairs, tuning, etc., and six years later money was paid for 'tow new skyns for the bellows, a pounde of glewe, new springes, tow new stoppes, new wyer and springes'. There is then a long silence in the accounts until Dr Mounteford, the vicar, in 1602 'Did moove the Vestry about the Organs, at Mr Woodlockes'. Money was paid but there is no indication what for.

Members of the Vestry visited St Giles-in-the-Fields in 1637 to see the work of a new maker, William Hathaway, and then asked him to insert a new instrument in their old case, which was moved from the gallery and placed 'upon a fframe of timber' apparently in a loft at the east end of the north side of the nave, between the pulpit and chancel. Sums were paid for this work to Mr Ryder, carpenter; Jeremy Kellat, joiner; Zachary Taylor, carver, and Hathaway himself received £12 12s. George Hudson was appointed organist, followed in 1639 by Ambrose Oakeley, and in 1641/2 John Jackson was paid 20 shillings 'for blowing the bellows'.

Sometime in the 1670s George Dallam installed in St Martin's an organ which had been removed from St George's Chapel, Windsor and his name appears in the accounts from 1677 to 1684 as the maker in charge.[2] At the Restoration there were few organ builders in England so the government offered premiums to foreign builders to encourage them to come here, build instruments and train craftsmen. Father Smith arrived from Germany with his two nephews, and Thomas Harris and his son Renatus from France. (The latter's only work for St Martin's was in 1695 when he was paid £190 for repairs and improvements.) Father Smith's best workman, Christopher Schrider, married his daughter and inherited the business on Smith's death in 1708 and five years later he was appointed at a salary of £4 p.a. to look after the organ at St Martin's. When the church was demolished it was put in the temporary tabernacle, and then sold for £30 to Schrider who, after renovating it, sold it to Dr Christopher Pache, who gave it to St Peter's, St Albans.

The new building needed a new organ so the Vestry advertised for makers to bring proposals forward, and King George I offered £105 towards the cost, apparently wanting to salve his conscience for resigning as a churchwarden. The contract went to Schrider and early in 1726 the instrument was ready. It had three manuals, pedals, 22 stops and was enclosed in a fine case designed by James Gibbs. Handel, who had been employed as Kapellmeister by King George when he was Elector of Hanover, played at the opening and was so pleased with it that he often returned to play the Sunday voluntaries himself. Dr Charles Burney, the father of Fanny who lived nearby, noted, 'It was the fashion for the first musicians in London to frequent that church; I have often seen Mr Handel there.' Tuning and oversight remained in Schrider's hands until his death in 1751, when Gerard Smith took over until 1765 when Mr Byfield was appointed. Thirty-two years later he was told that as he had neglected it he must hand over to Robert Cooke.

47 *The organ of St Martin's, 1726-99, built by Christopher Schrider with a case designed by James Gibbs.*

The Vestry for some reason decided on 29 May 1799 to sell the organ complete with its inscription 'The Gift of His Most Sacred Majesty King George. 1726.' An advertisement appeared in several newspapers:

> Capital Church Organ for Sale.
> St. Martin's, London, having contracted for a new organ to be built on a larger scale than the present one, which is in the cathedral style with a separate choir organ in front. The organ contains twenty-two stops, three rows of keys, and pedals, etc. The organ can be seen on application to the churchwardens –
> Mr Thomas Goodall, Bricklayer, Chandos Street.
> Mr Christopher Brown, Pawnbroker, Long Acre.[3]

It was bought for £200 by the Rev. D.W. Tattershall for St Mary, Wotton-under-edge, Gloucestershire. William Gray made a new one of similar size which was paid for by the church rate levied on all households in the parish. Over the next few years there was much dissatisfaction with this instrument, which was not thought to be equal in tone or appearance to its predecessor, so on 10 August 1853 the Vestry approved plans to build a new organ with money raised by public subscription. The old one was sold to the Roman Catholic Cathedral in Plymouth, and at a cost of over £1,000 it was replaced by a much larger organ by Bevington and Sons, with double cases designed by Thomas Allom.

Messrs W. Hill & Son, later Messrs Hill, Norman & Beard Ltd, took charge of it in 1869 when the organ was reconstructed, retaining the case. This organ was entirely rebuilt by Hill in 1912 because, as the *Messenger* reported, 'it is of an obsolete kind, being devoid of the mechanical and other features which have revolutionised the art of organ building'. The vicar already had £600 so appealed for another £600 for the instrument to be rebuilt with a new tubular pneumatic action – the tubes, he said, would stretch 2½ miles. On 10 June it was rededicated and the *Messenger* proudly announced that

> the console, the whole of the interior work and many of the pipes are new. The console now contains 3 keyboards, usual pedal board, 41 stops controlling 2,292 speaking pipes, 12 couplers, 34 combination pistons and pedals. To provide the wind a fan revolving 800 times a minute and driven by a 4h.p. electric motor is under the belfry immediately behind the organ and separated from the instrument by an asbestos-lined partition.

The cases of 1853 were retained.

In 1927 it was decided to modify the tonal characteristics for congregational singing and music recitals – two recitals were given by Dr Albert Schweitzer. Ten years later, under the direction of Sidney Ambler, a musician, the tubular action was converted to electro-pneumatic operation and a remote console was placed at the east end of the north gallery. A so-called 'Altar' division of 11 stops was added at gallery level on the north side of the sanctuary. The detached console featured patent luminous stop-tablets that, when on, glowed in various colours according to their function. It was likened by one critic to the console of a 1930s railway signalbox. The work was carried out by R. Spurden Rutt of Leytonstone, but by the late 1960s the console had become unreliable and the Altar division unplayable. A third of the instrument had been out of action for over five years but *ad hoc* repairs enabled it to continue until the present organ was installed in 1990.

J.W. Walker's 1990 organ was commissioned as a 48-stop instrument that could be played at concerts, provide appropriate accompaniment for the extensive choral programme and lead hymn singing for dozens of carol and other popular services, often packed to capacity. The goal was to fulfil these requirements, avoiding tricks or gimmicks, and so create an instrument of musical integrity. The church is much admired for its intimate acoustic and well known for its suitability for chamber music, but when filled with 1,200 people singing heartily the organ needs to hold its own, and it does. 'The organ handles an enormous repertory with staggering ease.'[4]

The new case design follows the outline of the Schrider main case, but was somewhat altered from the original design to allow more sound to pass through the fronts. The instrument employs mechanical key-action and electric stop-action with an extensive combination action for recital purposes. The coupling is mechanical, with optional electric assists. So remarkable is the touch that these latter have proved to be unnecessary. Interchangeable parallel and radiating pedal boards have been provided. The French stoplist was chosen to indicate a consistency of nomenclature rather than identification with any particular period or style. A conscious effort was made to ride above the invention of neo-classicism and to base the instrument solidly on classical principles. Simple classical balances were adhered to as the basis on which voicing decisions were made. In the recent past, so-called classical balances often meant that choruses were cold and hard. This instrument shows that these balances can be maintained whilst producing Principals that are warm and rich, yet clear and singing.

Combined with the classically balanced choruses are French-style reeds; a combination which proved so successful in Alsatian organ-building. The instrument also draws ideas from the earlier French Classical period, particularly in the form and style of the mutation stops. All this combines to ensure that a scheme, not necessarily devised originally for liturgical work, will nonetheless serve the fundamental requirements of a church organ. The enclosed *Récit* provides a convincing English Swell effect. This seemingly eclectic combination of styles is actually a well-considered synthesis, united into a style of its own. It has been said that Germanic music suffers less on stops that are broadly scaled and voiced with warmth, than French music played on narrow North German scales. In so far as this is true, the scaling of the organ has bowed to this belief. Voicing techniques employed for polyphonic music serve to best advantage in the French Classical and romantic repertoires.

The organ has 5,000 pipes ranging in length from one inch to 32 feet, with those in front constructed of pure tin and others variously alloyed. There are three 61-note manuals, flanked by 48 stop buttons arrayed at each end with

32 pedal keys below. The manuals are associated with three different types of organ depending on the volume and quality of sound desired. One is the Grand *Orgue* which uses the largest flue pipes. The *Positif* is linked to a smaller array of pipes directly opposite the manuals. The pipes of the *Récit* are enclosed in a box with a louvre which can be adjusted by the organist to create a 'swelling' effect. The specification is:

Grande Orgue		*Pédale*	
Bourdon	16	Montre	16
Montre	8	Soubasse	16
Flûte Harmonique	8	Prestant	8
Bourdon	8	Bourdon	8
Prestant	4	Doublette	4
Flûte Ouverte	4	Fourniture	IV
Doublette	2	Contra Bombarde	32
Cornet (from a)	V	Bombarde	16
Fourniture 19.22.26.29	IV	Douçaine	16
Cymbale 26.29.33.36	IV	Trompette	8
Trompette	8	Chalumeau	4
Clairon	4	*Tremblant*	
Tremblant		*Récit to Pédale*	
Récit to Grand Orgue		*Grande Orgue to Pédale*	
Positif to Grand Orgue		*Positif to Pédale*	

Récit Expressif		*Positif*	
Diapason	8	Bourdon	8
Flûte à Cheminée	8	Prestant	4
Viole de Gambe	8	Flûte à Fuseau	4
Voix Céleste (from g)	8	Nasard	2 2/3
Prestant	4	Doublette	2
Flûte Conique	4	Quartre de Nasard	2
Nasard	2 2/3	Tierce	1 3/5
Octavin	2	Larigot	1 1/3
Tierce	1 3/5	Fourniture 22.26.29.33	IV
Plein Jeu 15.19.22.26.29	V	Cromorne	8
Basson	16	*Tremblant*	
Trompette	8	*Récit to Positif*	
Hautbois	8		
Voix Humaine	8	*Compass*	
Clairon	4	Manuals: C-c⁴ 61notes	
Tremblant		Pedals: C-g¹ 32notes	

Mechanical action with optional electric coupling; electric stop action and Solid State pistons with 8 memories and independent sequencer. There are 8 divisional pistons for each department and 8 general pistons.[5]

David Hardwick, churchwarden 1981-92, has described some of the headaches surrounding the purchase of this grand instrument:

> When the order was placed it increased the pulse of the Music Department from *andante* to *allegro accelerando*. A fund had been established by Austen Williams, but it totalled no more than £110,000 – less than a third of the cost. The entire spectrum of Walker's resources was now concentrated on this project which entailed a pre-assembly mock-up in their factory. Then the flow of City money which had reached £120,000 suddenly ceased ... Geoffrey Brown summoned his astute Churchwarden, Matthew Portal, to be the midwife for a difficult birth. At this point the diocesan authorities felt that this was the ideal moment to send in the experts: those in suits searched our books to see if we had overreached ourselves and those in bow ties demanded that our flue pipes should be gold plated. The former came and retired satisfied and the latter had to agree that tin was better than gold. It was in this darkest hour that a substantial legacy came from Redvers Green, a faithful member of St Martin's for many decades. Even more significantly, the new Enterprise had at last moved into profit under the firm control of Caroline Graham-Brown and was able to make up the shortfall.
>
> One of the consequences of the new organ was that it increased the load on the supports from 2 to 7 tons. It was difficult to obtain reliable advice on how to sustain the heavier load because any two consultants would provide three options. Eventually a steel platform was constructed and partly supported by the two existing cast iron columns that pass down through the wardens' pews to the bookshop below. The cost of this together with the consultants' fees was roughly £35,000.
>
> There was still the problem of the *putti* which cavort at the top of the case: fat, pink and naked. They were sent back and returned marginally less pink. They were sent back again and returned, this time with little white loin cloths.[6]

In 1995 J.W.Walker built a portable chamber organ – funded by the Enterprise, this is primarily for the accompaniment of early church music and for use as a continuo instrument in concerts. The specifications are:

Manual

Stopped Flute 8
Chimney Flute 4
Fifteenth 2
Mechanical action; transposing device (A440-A415)

Organists and Masters of the Music

1525   'Mr Watts his child.'
1533   'Nicholas, our Clarke.'
1636   George Hudson.
1639-40 Ambrose Oakeley.
1674   Christopher Gibbons (1615-76). Second son of Orlando Gibbons. 1638 organist of Winchester Cathedral where in 1642 he witnessed the 'faire organs in the Minster broken down by the souldiers' of the Parliamentary forces. 1660 Private Organist to Charles II and

Organist of Westminster Abbey. 1664 Master of the Choristers. DMus Oxon. One of the most influential English keyboard players of his period and an outstanding figure in Restoration music. Anthony Wood described him as 'a person most excellent in his faculty, but a grand debauchee'.[7] St Martin's paid him £5 per quarter out of which he had to pay 'ye bellowes blower'.

1676?   Bernard 'Father' Smith (c.1630-1708). Having worked in Germany, where he was probably born, and Holland, he first came to England in 1666. One of the most illustrious of English builders – his name is associated with over 70 instruments, notably Great St Mary's and Trinity College, Cambridge; St Paul's and Durham Cathedrals. 1676 Organist at St Margaret's, Westminster. 1681 King's Organ Maker. McMaster says that Smith built an organ for St Martin's and was appointed Organist but there is no mention of this in the Account Books or Vestry Minutes.

1708?   Robert King. 1676-1728. Violinist, composer and concert promoter. 1689 Composer in Ordinary to the King and his four successors.

1714   John Weldon (1676-1736). Pupil of Henry Purcell, Organist of New College, Oxford (1694). He was also Organist and Composer to the Chapel Royal. In February 1727 St Martin's appointed an assistant instead of doubling his salary as he had proposed. 'A composer of considerable talent who never quite fulfilled his early promise. His melodic range was wide, from gay tunes to intense declamation. His word-setting was often sensitive and rhythmically subtle though he over-indulged in lengthy roulades and certain favourite turns of phrase.'[8]

1736   Joseph Kelway (1702-82). Composer, harpsichordist. Pupil of Chilcot and Geminiani. Eminent musicologist Charles Burney, who tried unsuccessfully to succeed him at St Martin's, described his playing style as one of 'masterly wildness ... both rapid and fanciful'. Much admired by Handel who came to the church to hear him play. He was music instructor to Queen Charlotte. 'A composer of considerable originality and boldness.'[9]

1782   Benjamin Cooke (1734-93). Eminent composer. Pupil of Pepush. At the age of 12 he became Deputy Organist of Westminster Abbey then Master of the Choristers (1757) then Organist (1762). Librarian then Conductor (1752) of the Academy of Ancient Music. MusD Cantab. 1775, DMus Oxon. 1782. 'Though not in the very first rank he was an admirable glee composer. His Service in G, written for the Abbey organ when pedals were first added in 1780, keeps his name alive.'[10] There is a memorial to him in the Abbey where he is buried in the cloisters.

1793   Robert Cooke (1768-1814). Son of Benjamin. Composer of sacred and secular vocal works. Organist and Master of the Choristers at Westminster Abbey (1802). Like his father he held these appointments whilst at St Martin's. He drowned himself in the Thames, 13 August

1814, after an unhappy love affair and is buried in the same grave as his father.

1814   Thomas Forbes Walmisley (1783-1866). Composer, teacher. Pupil of Attwood. Secretary of the Concentores Sodales from 1817 to its dissolution in 1847 when the Society's stock of wine was given to him. Despite being at St Martin's for 40 years he had a long running battle with the Vestry about his salary. It began at £40 and rose to £90 in 1828. When he asked for another rise the Vestry suggested £50 as he was 'a favoured and fortunate individual'. He was pensioned off with £35 p.a. 'Remembered chiefly as a glee writer, he produced 59. They are written with masterly skill and elegance.'[11]

1852   William T. Best (1826-97). Resigned to be Organist of Lincoln's Inn. 1840 Organist, Liverpool Philharmonic Society. Known for his solo performances. 'One of the great organ virtuosos of the 19th century, his powerful improvisations and fine pedal technique being especially admired ... his real genius lay in the interpretation of secular music. He holds a distinguished place among the new class of civic musicians brought into prominence by the installation of concert organs in large public buildings.'[12]

1854   William Beale (1784-1854). Composer. 1821 Organist, Trinity College, Cambridge. 1816-20 One of the Gentlemen of the Chapel Royal.

1854   Henry Bevington. One of the Bevington family – Soho organ builders – who built the new instrument for St Martin's in 1854.

1855   Edward Collett May (1806-87). Teacher. Pupil of Cipriani Potter. 1837-69 Organist, Greenwich Hospital. 1879-83 Professor of Vocal Music, Queen's College, London.

1857   W.H. Adams (1820-1914). During his 42 years at St Martin's he helped found the College of Organists and was elected a Fellow in 1865.

1899   W.J. Kipps. FRCO, ARAM Professor at the Royal Academy of Music.

1920   Martin Shaw (1875-1958). Composer. Assisted Vaughan Williams in his research for Percy Dearmer's English Hymnal and had a profound influence on 20th-century church music. His Anglican Folk Mass and hymn tunes are widely used, and with his brother, Geoffrey, and others he produced *Songs of Praise* (1925), and in 1928 *The Oxford Book of Carols*. 1932 Lambeth DMus, 1955 OBE, 1958 Fellow of the Royal College of Music. 'As a composer he mainly cultivated stage music and choral music. Though with few exceptions his prolific output of songs leaves the impression of good taste without strong character they were welcomed by fastidious singers of their day.'[13]

1924   Arnold Goldsbrough (1892-1964). Conductor, teacher. Formerly Sub-organist, Manchester Cathedral and 1920-27 Westminster Abbey. 1924-29 Director of Music, Morley College. Founded the Goldsbrough Orchestra which became the English Chamber Orchestra.

1935   John Hewlitt Alden.

1939   S. Drummond Wolff. Later Organist, Montreal Cathedral.

1948   John Churchill. Helped found the Academy of St Martin in the Fields. 'The performances so far from being damped or dimmed by the absence of applause were at once more inward and more lively than some we have heard just across the river on the south bank.'[14] He left to be Professor of Music, Carleton University, Ottawa. Died 1997.

1967   Eric Harrison. Concert pianist. Taught at Melbourne University and whilst at St Martin's taught at the Royal College of Music. 1968 Returned to Melbourne University.

1968   Robert Vincent (1941-.) Professor of Organ and Theory at the Guildhall School of Music. 1978 Organist and Master of the Choristers, Manchester Cathedral.

1977   Christopher Stokes. Organist and Master of the Choristers, Manchester Cathedral.

1989   Mark Stringer. Head of Music, Speech and Drama Examinations, Trinity College, London. Mark had been assistant organist at St Martin's where he achieved fame before Liberace's Memorial Service by sewing tinsel stars on Christopher Stokes's surplice. These could not be removed before the service began so caused much merriment.

1996   Paul Stubbings. Had been assistant to Mark Stringer. Director of Music, St Lawrence College, Ramsgate. One of the outstanding organists of his generation.

2001   Nicholas Danks. Had been Organ Scholar, Corpus Christi College, Cambridge then assistant at St Martin's. He has broadened the choir and parish music in the tradition of Martin Shaw.

Music Today at St Martin's

Lunchtime concerts which are free take place in church every Monday, Tuesday and Friday at 1p.m. and feature an extraordinarily wide range of performers and repertoire. Evening concerts are often by candlelight. 'Our speciality,' said a member of staff,

> is the repertoire of the baroque and classical eras. You may hear a Mozart or Haydn symphony, perhaps a lively Bach oboe or violin concerto, chamber works for piano quintet or string quartet, or maybe even the thrilling sounds of a Handel anthem, performed by full chorus with organ.

Tickets are available at the box office or may be ordered on-line.

10

The Bells of St Martin's

There were at one time five churches dedicated to St Martin in the square mile of the City of London – Orgar, Outwich, Pomeroy, Vintry and Ludgate (which still stands). There are several contenders for the five farthings of the nursery rhyme, which probably was written in the mid-18th century. However, since St Martin's has possessed bells for at least 500 years it has a chance! The Elizabethan building had a Sanctus bell, which when rung told everyone that the priest had consecrated the bread and wine in the Mass, and three other bells. Repairs to these are noted in the Accounts:

1525 Payde to Mr Wyncote for bell ropes ... iiij s vij d.
1530 paide to John Young, saddeler, for bawd-deryks for the bells ... ij s vij d.
     paide to John Brooke to truse the grete bell ij dayes at viij d the daye
      ... xxi d.
     payed for mending of the claper of the Middel bell ... xvj d.
     payed for a corde for the santes bell ... ij d.

In 1539 a new set of bells was cast and hung, the cost being paid by parishioners, and soon after the ringers were paid four pence for greeting King Henry VIII as he rode by. When his daughter Queen Mary 'came to Whyte Haull' the ringers received ten pence and when she died seven pence. In 1583 eight new bells were cast by Robert Mote, the bell founder, who received £17 7s., and they rang for the Armada victory on 17 November 1588. Ten years later some had cracked and were exchanged with another founder, Lawrence Wright. Oliver Cromwell was not averse to having bells rung in his honour because the 1653 accounts record:

Paid for ringing when the Lord Protector went to dine in the City ... 5s.

When the tower was rebuilt in 1663 the bells were overhauled and some recast, and the Accounts mention the bells frequently before the building was demolished in 1721. They were then sent to Abraham Rudhall of Gloucester to be recast and formed the fine new peal of 12 bells and a Sanctus bell. The Vestry had intended to have only eight, but in 1724 the Prince of Wales, later George II, offered to pay for ten, and when the Duke of Somerset donated 100 guineas it was decided to have twelve. In London only St Bride's had so many.

They were not ready for the consecration of the church but were installed on 28 May 1727. The following March there was a ringing match between the Society of College Youths and the Society of London Scholars. On the 14th the Scholars set a record by ringing the longest 12-bell peal – 6,000 Grandsire Cinques. The next day their rivals rang 6,314 in the same method. There is no record of what the nearby parishioners thought of this marathon.

On 6 October 1788 the College Youths rang the first ever peal of Stedman Cinques, the most difficult technical achievement in campanology of the century. The Union Scholars, who had rung at St Martin's since 1736, disbanded in the 1750s, and there was a split between the older and newer members of the College Youths. By 1756 the senior branch had made the church their home, but in 1788 they ceased and the juniors, from which the present Ancient Society of College Youths is descended, came to St Martin's. They stayed until 1849 when they moved to Southwark. In their place came the Society of Cumberland Youths, founded in 1747, and named after the Duke of Cumberland. The name Royal was added to their title to reflect their ringing at the Royal Parish Church.

In October 1728 one of the gudgeons of the tenor bell broke and the bell crashed to the floor. The treble bells were replaced in 1758 and a third was recast. The bells were marked:

Treble RECAST BY A.R. 1758
2nd M:HART & W:CHAPMAN CHVRCHWARDENS 1770:T R:
3rd RECAST by A R 1758
4th AND IN EARTH PEACE 1725
5th GOOD WILL TOWARDS MEN 1725
6th ABR: RVDHALL OF GLOVCESTER CAST VS ALL 1725
7th PROSPERITY TO THE CHVRCH OF ENGLAND 1725
8th PEACE AND GOOD NEIGHBOVRHOOD 1725
9th PROSPERITY TO THE PARISH OF SNT MARTINS.1725
10th FEAR GOD HONOVR THE KING 1725
11th JOHN WALKER & JOHN SAWCER CHVRCHWARDENS 1725
Tenor ZACHARIAH PEARCE D:D VICAR 1726
WALTER TVRNER & WM: HOVSE CHVRCHWARDENS

In 1912 H.B. Walters in *Church Bells of England* noted that 'the floor of the ringing chamber oscillates considerably during the ringing of the peal', but it is unlikely that this was cured by the overhaul and re-hanging that year paid for by some of the money received from letting the churchyard for stands to view the coronation procession.

It was decided in 1984 to spend money on the bells, which were hung too high and were difficult to ring. On practice nights Churchwarden David Hardwick, who was on the staff of the Faculty of Civil Engineering at Imperial College, London, disappeared into the tower clad in protective clothing and festooned with technical apparatus. He advised that the bells should be lowered to the clock room immediately below the ringing chamber and that the John Leroux clock, only 33 years younger than the bells, should move up a floor. A new frame would have to be designed for the bells as the room was smaller, and a semitone bell added to give the ring greater flexibility. Meanwhile the Parochial Church Council had decided the bells should be re-cast at the Whitechapel Bell Foundry, which had been established in Houndsditch in 1420 and moved to its present address in 1738.

Overnight things changed dramatically when the Australia and New Zealand Association of Bell Ringers asked if they might mark the Australian Bicentenary in 1988 by transporting the bells to the University of Western Australia in Perth. A new tower would be built for them capped by a concrete and glass spire. The offer was accepted, the last peal rung in August 1987, and dismantling began.

Renison Goldfields Consolidated Ltd sent to London 12 tonnes of Australian copper and tin to provide the new bells and fund-raising began. By June 1988 the new bells, cast at the Whitechapel Bell Foundry, were ready. They were hung a stage lower, making ringing easier, and they have these inscriptions:

Treble IN MEMORIAM. RICHARD KENNETH SIBSON, 22 JANUARY
    1967 – 14 JUNE 1971
#2nd GIFT OF AUSTRALIA AND NEW ZEALAND ASSOCIATION OF
    BELLRINGERS
2nd 40 YEARS LOVE AND GUIDANCE, MURIEL SILVER GREEN
3rd GIFT OF THE ASSOCIATION OF THE FRIENDS OF ST MARTIN-IN-
    THE-FIELDS
4th GIFT OF THE LADIES' PEAL BAND, NOVEMBER 1983
5th GIFT OF THE SAINSBURY CHARITABLE TRUSTS
6th GIFT OF THE CITY OF WESTMINSTER
7th AUSTEN WILLIAMS, VICAR 1956-1984
8th GEOFFREY BROWN, VICAR 1988
9th R.W.J. KEAY
J.D. HARDWICK
CHURCHWARDENS 1987.
10th GIFT OF DEREK SIBSON
11th GIFT OF THE ST MARTIN-IN-THE-FIELDS BAND OF RINGERS
Tenor GIFT OF THE SOCIETY OF ROYAL CUMBERLAND YOUTHS

The tower is still the headquarters of the Society of Royal Cumberland Youths who every Sunday provide members to ring for the two morning services, and visitors are often drawn to the church by the cascade of joyful sound which even the traffic cannot muffle.

The 12 old bells together with six new ones now hang in the Swan Bells tower near the Swan River in Perth, and are numerically the largest set of bells for change ringing in the world. The ringers can be seen through the glass panels and above the seven-storey chamber rises a crystal glass spire to a height of 82 metres. The lower parts of the tower are enfolded by curved copper sheets in the form of sails to celebrate both the nautical and the mining heritage of Western Australia.

Peal Boards

Of the 16 boards only five are of interest:

1727   14 March. The Society of London Scholars rang the first complete peal of S. Thowland Cinques.

1785   It records a peal of Oxford Treble Bob Maximus, 5,136 changes by the Society of College Youths.

1788   6 October. Restored 1988. It records the ringing at St Martin's of the first ever peal of Stedman Cinques, 6,204 changes by the Society of College Youths. It took four hours and 47 minutes.

1862   It records a peal of Stedman Caters, 5,050 changes by the Royal Society of Cumberland Youths in honour of the Prince of Wales's majority.

1887   It records a peal of Grandsire Cinques, 5,015 changes by the Royal Society of Cumberland Youths to commemorate Queen Victoria's Golden Jubilee.

11

St Martin's Possessions

Silver

Theft and auction have removed nearly all of the church's historic plate. On 25 September 1649 all the silver was stolen, and only one piece – a large Charles I flagon dated 1634 which had been given on that Good Friday by John Wandrake – was recovered, despite the wardens paying £1 to an informer, Thomas Madgwith, a prisoner in Newgate prison, 'in hope to heare of some more of the plate'. The Account Books of Francis Bramwell and Christopher Parsons, churchwardens, refer to 'Disbursements in persecution of Robt Fielder and others that robb'd the church Sept: ye 25. 1649.'

Fielder had been found guilty of robbery a month earlier but 'asked for the book' – a literate person could escape full punishment. He was branded on the left thumb with a T to show he had escaped the Tyburn gallows. Two other men, Edward Tooth, who kept an alehouse south of the church called *The Bermudas*, and John Levett appeared with Fielder at the Old Bailey on 10 October. The gaol clerk noted against Levett's name 'Put himself on his country, not guilty,' but Fielder is marked 'confessed the indictment, to be hanged.' Tooth's name is crossed out and the document lists seven witnesses. The total cost of prosecuting them was £14 5s. 2d. but there are no details of when Fielder was hanged. He was a thief and a highwayman who frequented Tooth's alehouse, and when Colonel Pride's men raided the tavern he had the flagon with him. The rest of the silver, which was probably melted down, included: four silver-gilt cups with covers, three silver-gilt pots, one silver charger and one silver-gilt flagon.

Because of the robbery St Martin's, unlike the City churches, had no Elizabethan or Jacobean plate. Over the next few years gifts began to be made by wealthy parishioners such as Mrs Elizabeth Pocock, the widow of Brigadier Pocock, and Mrs Elizabeth Enderson, whose chalice given in 1649 was 'new wrought' for the church in 1726. Almost all of this silver was sold at Sotheby's in London 17 May 1973 to raise funds to repair the building. A suggestion had already been made at a Vestry Meeting of 5 April 1833 that the silver be sold by William Humphry, the vicar, who pointed out that as it was kept in the bank no one saw it, and the proceeds of the sale could maintain the fabric and services of the church. The Vestry agreed with him and a Faculty was applied for, but several influential parishioners stopped the sale. This did not happen in 1973 and £72,760 was raised. There was remarkably little opposition to the sale which, somewhat surprisingly, was supported by Churchwarden Sir Trenchard Cox, Director of the Victoria and Albert Museum, 1955-66. Several of his colleagues made it very clear to him that they disapproved. Some still question the wisdom of selling the family silver, particularly as the George I Dish and Ewer were valued at £1½m in 2003, and attempts are now being made to see if those who bought the plate might lend it for an exhibition in the new Hall. In August 1924 burglars forced their way into the strong room and stole two alms dishes, a paten and a processional cross. Today the plate includes:

A silver-gilt Flagon, engraved with armorials within a ropework and foliate cartouche. Inscribed 'The Gift of my Lady Mason for the use of Trinity Chapel.'
13¾ inches high. John Jackson, London, 1700.

A silver-gilt Flagon, cylindrical with plain body, inscribed Long Acre Chapel.
13½ inches high. Thomas Parr, London, 1705.

Six silver staves. Edward Aldridge, London, 1743.

A pair of silver-gilt staves. Unmarked. 1775.

A silver-gilt spoon. Elias Cachert, London, 1757.

A parcel-gilt alms dish, London, 1926.

Silver plate alms dish, given by the Diocese of Hong Kong and Macao to Bishop Baker on his retirement.

A silver-gilt processional cross, c.1920. Inscribed 'To the Glory of God and in memory of the Officers and Men of the 3rd County of London Yeomanry who fell in the War 1914–1918.'

A number of chalices, patens and ciboria, early 20th-century and 1960s.

The silver sold in 1973 was:

A Charles I silver-gilt Flagon. Baluster body with scroll handle and on spreading foot. Domed cover with urn-shaped finial.
18¼in. high. RS between mullets. 94 oz. 1634.
Underside of foot engraved 'Saint Martyn In the Fields. March 1634.'
This was the only piece recovered after the 1649 robbery.
Sold for £4,000.

Three Commonwealth silver-gilt Wine Cups with deep beaker-shaped bowls, and each on simple spreading trumpet foot.
9¼in. high. RS.
Underside inscribed 'Saint Martins in the Fieldes Aprill the 6th Anno 1650.'

Three circular Patens.
6¾in. dia. William Darker. 1726.
Underside inscribed 'St Martin in the Feilds October ye 26 1726.'
Cups and Patens weigh 99 oz 10 dwt.
Sold for £10,500.

A Commonwealth silver-gilt Wine Cup.
  9¼in. high.1653.
  Inscribed 'St Martin in the Feilds Aprill ye 6th 1654.'

A Paten.
  6¾in. dia. William Darker. 1726.
  Cup and Paten weigh 34 oz 12 dwt.
  Sold for £1,780.

A Charles II silver-gilt Wine Cup, a corded band at the base of the bowl.
  5½in. high. I.C. with mullet below. 5 oz 18 dwt.
  Inscribed 'VIC FOR PRIV: ST MARTINS IN THE FIELDS MARCH y17 1679/80'.
  Sold for £2,000.

A Charles II silver-gilt Salver on foot with reeded borders.
  12in. dia. I.C. with mullet below. 1682. 36 oz 17 dwt.
  Inscribed 'St Martin in the Fields March the First Anno 1682/3'.
  Sold for £1,850.

A Pair of Charles II Chalices and Patens.
  Chalices 5¼in. high. M.K. 1683. 13 oz 18 dwt.
  Undersides inscribed 'St Martins PAR: for PRIV. COM. April 10 1684'.
  Sold for £3,200.

A William and Mary silver-gilt Wine Cup, Paten and Salver on foot en suite each engraved
with a rayed nimbus incorporating Gloria Deo Trino Uni.
  Cup 9½in. high with beaker-shaped bowl and on knopped trumpet foot.
  Paten 6¼in. dia on capstan foot.
  Salver 11½in. dia on similar foot with moulded border.
  Mark: D. 55 oz 12 dwt. 1691.
  Sold for £2,100.

A William III silver-gilt Salver with a reeded border on a trumpet foot.
  10in. dia. Charles Overing. 1699. 24 oz 14 dwt.
  Inscribed 'Long Acre Chapple – St Martins in ye Fields 21 Dec 1699'.
  Sold for £950.

A George I silver-gilt sideboard Dish and Ewer.
  Ewer 13¼in. high. 80 oz helmet-shaped engraved with some armorials.
  Dish 27¼in. dia. 237 oz 7 dwt.
  Lewis Mettayer 1720.
  Both inscribed 'The gift of Madam Pocock at the desire of her late Husband the Honble
  Brgr Gent Pocock St Martins in the Fields 1732'.
  The Arms are those of Pocock.
  Sold for £26,000.

A George I silver-gilt Salver on foot.
  8¾in. dia. Petley Ley. 1720. 16 oz 2 dwt.
  Inscribed 'The legacy of Mrs Lydia Edridge to St Martin in the Fields Westminster'.
  Sold for £580.

A Pair of George I silver-gilt Flagons with domed covers.
  14¾in. high. William Darker. 1726. 108 oz 14 dwt.
  Undersides inscribed 'The Gift of Mrs Eliz. Enderson to St Martin in the fields 1649
  – New Wrought October 20 1726. Walter Turner, William House Church Wardens'.
  Sold for £3,000.

A George II Chalice and two companion Patens showing traces of gilding.
> Chalice 8¼in. high, bell-shaped on trumpet foot.
> Circular Patens 6in. dia. each on capstan foot.
> ?Jeremiah King. 1746. 39oz 3dwt.
> Undersides inscribed 'The Gift of Mrs Eliz. Pocock to ye Parish of St Martin, Westminster 1746'.
> Sold for £1,350.

A Pair of massive George III silver-gilt Flagons, leaf-capped double-scroll handles, baluster bodies with gadroon girdles repeated on foot, detachable domed covers.
> 20½in. high. John le Sage. 1746. 523oz 10dwt.
> Undersides inscribed 'The Gift of Mrs Eliz Pocock to ye Parish of St Martin, Westminster 1746'.
> Sold for £14,000.
> Now in the Gilbert Collection.

A Suite of three George III silver-gilt Salvers on foot with gadroon borders.
> Pair are 8in. dia, the other 12¼in. dia. Robert Garrard. 1815. 92oz 16dwt.
> Undersides inscribed with names of Vicar (Pott) and wardens, J.C. Parker and F.W. Barron.
> Sold for £1,450.

The Heriot Lamp.

A notable funeral took place in the church on 20 February 1624 – that of the immensely wealthy George Heriot, jeweller and goldsmith to King James I. Born in Edinburgh, he was already the Queen's Jeweller when aged 40 he moved with the Court to London in 1603. He was known as 'Jinglin' Geordie' because of the coins rattling in his pockets. Both his wives died young so he died childless, and after private legacies he bequeathed his large estate for the establishment in his native city of a hospital for the upbringing and education 'of puire fatherless bairnes, friemenes sones of that toune of Edinburgh'. Today George Heriot's is an Independent School with approximately 1,700 boys and girls. A large silver sanctuary lamp made in 1953 was presented shortly afterwards to St Martin's in his memory by past and present pupils of the school and on the first Monday in June the London Heriot Club holds a service in the church.

Furniture

A PAIR OF GEORGE I LIBRARY CHAIRS
Made c.1726, these may have been commissioned by King George I for the royal box. They are mahogany, of exceptional quality, and may have been made by Benjamin Goodison of Long Acre. The detail of the ear pieces and the flowers and foliage is very fine, and the legs are carved at the knee with lions' masks. They were restored in 2002 by Peter Holmes.

A GEORGE III MINISTER'S CHAIR
Commissioned by the wardens, this was made in 1774 by John Bradburn of Long Acre and cost £20 – the church possesses a copy of the original bill. Bradburn

supplied furniture to the royal households in 1764-7 when he was working for the royal cabinet-makers in St Martin's Lane. The chair is surmounted with the King's coat of arms, and today is used as the Bishop's chair in the sanctuary.

Paintings

King George I by the Studio of Kneller, *c.*1716. This was probably acquired by the Vestry to mark the King's generosity to St Martin's. Good carved frame of 1735 possibly by Gosset or Dufort.

James Gibbs by Andrea Soldi. The Vestry Minutes of 17 January 1800 record that this was given by John Gregory of Chelsea. The architect of St Martin's is portrayed with his *Book of Architecture* and the plans for a circular building, probably the Radcliffe Camera in Oxford, which is seen in the background. Restored in 2002, the painting framed is 108cm. wide by 141cm. high. The 1868 Vestry Minutes wrongly attribute it to Hogarth. The portrait is on loan to Duff House in Scotland and will be returned in 2007.

St Martin and the Beggar by Solimena (1657-1747). There is no record of provenance. Pevsner thought it 'dark and agitated' and probably 18th-century. It is on loan to the National Gallery and a copy hangs in the church. It is a version of a wall painting in the monastery of St Martin, to the north of Naples, in which the saint's cloak is so large that he would scarcely have missed half. Perhaps it is Solimena's joke at the opulent monastery's expense. On the opposite wall is a second painting showing the beggar returning to Martin as Christ in a dream.

Dick Sheppard by Sir Gerald Kelly, PRA.

Paintings of Clergy

The church possesses a large number of portraits of former incumbents. Many of these are copies and few are of any distinction or value. Among them are:

Thomas Lamplugh (1670-6). Given to the Vestry by Dr Pearce, 1730, and paid for by the income received from the Oxendon Chapel. It cost 28 guineas.

William Lloyd (1676-80). Given by Dr Pearce.

Thomas Tenison (1680-92). Given by Dr Pearce. A Copy.

William Lancaster (1694-1716). Given by Dr Pearce. A Copy.

Thomas Green (1716-1723). First mentioned when cleaned in 1750 but probably earlier.

Zachariah Pearce (1723-56) 1750. Probably a copy of the painting by T. Hudson at Lambeth Palace.

Erasmus Saunders (1756-76). Finest of all the portraits. First mentioned 1799.

Anthony Hamilton (1776-1812) by T.Kettle, 1776.

Joseph Pott (1812-24) by William Owen, *c.*1826.

George Richards (1824-34) by C. Ross, 1832.

Sir Henry Dukinfield (1834-48) by Sir M.A.Shee.

Henry Mackenzie (1848-55). Cleaned 1866.

William Humphrey (1855-86). First mentioned at cleaning 1891.

John Kitto (1886-1903).

Leonard Shelford (1903-14).

Sculpture

RYSBRACK'S BUST OF RICHARD MILLER

John Michael Rysbrack, aged 26, the son of a landscape painter, arrived in England from Antwerp in 1720 and six years later he was asked to sculpt this bust of one of St Martin's benefactors. He was the foremost monumental, architectural and portrait sculptor in England, until two younger men, Roubiliac and Scheemakers, came to prominence. He retained the loyalty of his own patrons, and continued to produce high quality work. He has 16 monuments in Westminster Abbey and tombs in parish churches throughout England. He often obtained commissions through Gibbs, who was at this time building the new church. Gibbs was to design many of Rysbrack's busts and monuments including his Ben Jonson, John 'Portland' Smith and Dr John Friend in Westminster Abbey and the Edward Colston memorial in All Saints, Bristol. In Gibbs' Radcliffe Library the bust of Dr Radcliffe is by Rysbrack.

The Vestry on 2 December 1725 asked Miller to sit for his portrait, 'in consideration of his many great benefactions', but he told them he preferred a bust, which the Vestry ordered and paid for (Vestry Minutes, 4 February 1726). The bust may have been worked from a terracotta one owned by Queen's College, Oxford, of which Miller was also a benefactor. Beneath the bust is inscribed:

> The effigies of Richard Miller who had given to ye Charity Schools of this Parish £500 to the Library and Free School £300 and for the building of the Vestry House £300. In memory of whose uncommon Benefactions ye Vestry in his Lifetime has caus'd to be made and set up his Effigies. A.D. 1726/27.

The Vestry to which Miller contributed stood at the south-eastern corner of the churchyard, and was pulled down in 1828 to be replaced by the present Vestry Hall. Miller was given part of a vault under the old hall as a burial place for himself and his friends.

The bust was cleaned in 1864, and again at an unknown date when a stainless steel bolt was inserted.

MARBLE BUST OF THE REV. DR GEORGE RICHARDS

William Behnes, who sculpted this, is best known for his statue of General Havelock in Trafalgar Square. Dr Richards was vicar 1824-34, and this bust of him, signed and dated 1830, was exhibited at the Royal Academy that year.

RYSBRACK'S BUST OF JAMES GIBBS

Carved when Gibbs was completing the present building, it shows him bewigged with a firm, well made face. It did not come into the church's possession until 60 years later, and was sold to the Victoria and Albert Museum for £465,000 in 1988. The P.C.C. had decided to sell it two years earlier to renovate parts of the buildings which had not been covered by the 1982/3 Appeal, but the Council for the Care of Churches was reluctant to give permission, suggesting that as the bust was too valuable and vulnerable to be put on display it should be loaned to the National Portrait Gallery. Eventually the matter came before the Consistory Court of the London Diocese presided over by the elderly Chancellor George Newsome. Known for his conservative views and his impatience – he once asked if a controversial case could end by 4.30 p.m. as his train to Sevenoaks left at 5 p.m. – it did not seem that he would agree to the sale. The vicar, Geoffrey Brown, his churchwarden Dr Ronald Keay, and their barrister appeared before him on 15-17 December 1987 and must have created a good impression because Newsome eventually agreed that although the bust could not be sold on the open market it could be purchased by a national collection. Everything had to be taken down in longhand, hence the length of the hearing.[1]

The bust, which was the gift of William Boore, an antique dealer and silver merchant in the Strand, stood for many years at the west end of the nave, but following some minor damage in 1969 had been moved to the Vestry Hall and was no longer on view. Now it is publicly displayed and properly cared for.

Rysbrack worked closely with his friend, James Gibbs, his near neighbour in Marylebone, and the bust of Gibbs is particularly fine. Dr Margaret Whinney, who wrote *Sculpture in Britain 1530-1830*, commented in 1964:

> The James Gibbs is of special interest since it is an early work. It is a shorter, wider bust, far less antique in inspiration and, though the dress is informal, the full curling wig is a splendid setting for the arrogant face. This must have been a highly satisfactory portrait to the sitter, for it shows him as handsome and assured, with a far greater firmness in the mouth than is to be seen in the painting by J.M.Williams in the National Portrait Gallery.

IN THE BEGINNING

Associate vicar David Monteith and Rachel Leigh-Wood led a small group which in 1999 commissioned Mike Chapman to create this sculpture in place of the traditional Christmas crib as part of the preparation to celebrate the Millennium. Standing in the Portico, this Portland stone block with a roughened top about 130 million years old reveals a new born baby with its umbilical cord running back into the stone. (Rachel's infant son Tobias was the model.) Its purpose is to persuade men and women to think again about the way in which God is present at the beginning of the third millennium. 'Look unto the Rock from which you are hewn.'

MEMORIAL TO THE VICTIMS OF APARTHEID
Chaim Stephenson's bronze figure of a young man in full stride carrying the dead body of a child was inspired by a photograph taken after the shooting of 13-year-old Hector Peterson in Soweto, 1976. It was dedicated in St Martin's on 25 October 1994 by Archbishop Desmond Tutu, who spoke of the pain and struggle of his people to sustain their faith in a brighter future during the 46 years of apartheid.

THREE WOODCARVINGS WITH THE ROYAL COAT OF ARMS OF AMSTERDAM
These were possibly donated by exiled Huguenots living in the parish in the 17th and 18th centuries.

The Font

The handsome, oval, marble font was given to St Martin's by William Bridgem, a parishioner, in 1689 and was transferred to the new church in the 1720s. Tradition says that after 20 years of married life a son had been born to his wife and this gift was a thanks offering. It has a carved oak cover which, for security reasons, is stored elsewhere. The elaborate wrought-iron railing around it was brought from the demolished St Matthew, Spring Gardens in 1885.

Altar Rails

These are in wrought-iron, divided into bays with inter-spacings of balusters, and finished with a mahogany moulded rail. They are almost certainly the original rails but their shape has changed over the years. They received their present shape in 1876 when T.H. Lewis made them run straight across the sanctuary instead of being bowed.

48 *The Font given by William Bridgem in 1689 and later transferred to the new church. Its carved oak cover is stored elsewhere.*

The Pulpit

Originally a three-decker with an elaborate sounding-board above, it lost its reading desk, clerk's pew and board during the renovations of Prebendary Humphry (1855-86), and soon after moved from the north side of the church to its present position. Made of oak, hexagonal, and supported on a hexagonal-shaped stem with a high based moulding, it is entered by an exquisite staircase with carved spandrel brackets, spiral balusters, three to a tread, and a moulded handrail. The five panels are inlaid, one with the sacred monogram IHS and the others with sunbursts – 18th-century glory. The preacher, who stands six foot above contradiction, might feel alarmed at its slight movement but can be reassured that this is one of the finest pulpits in London. Pevsner dates it as early Georgian and Dr Friedman suggests it was designed by Gibbs, and that Charles Griffith the joiner's bill for making a 'pullpet in Right Wainscott' for £80 still exists. Thomas Bridgewater carved the decorative work on it.

49   *The Pulpit, early Georgian and possibly designed by James Gibbs. Originally it was a three-decker with an elaborate sounding-board.*

Memorials

CHURCH

Gibbs' new building was considered such a fine example of the Grecian style of architecture that an unwritten rule was instituted that no monuments or ornaments should be fixed to the walls and this still applies. A royal command from Buckingham Palace in 1838 brought the first exception. Queen Victoria wished to commemorate in her parish church a much loved servant, so under the organ gallery is a plaque:

> Sacred to the Memory of
> Louisa Louis
> For many years the faithful and devoted servant of
> Her late Royal Highness the Princess Charlotte
> of Wales, and from earliest infancy honoured by the
> affectionate attachment of Her Majesty Queen
> Victoria, by whose gracious command this tablet
> has been placed in St. Martin's Church.
> Died at Buckingham Palace, 1838.

Mrs Louis, 'a very respectable woman', was throughout her life dresser and personal maid to Princess Charlotte, daughter and heir of George IV, and she loved her mistress dearly, probably because, as she told a friend, Queen Caroline never showed the least affection for her daughter. When Charlotte became pregnant Louisa thought that the confinement would be normal as the Princess was 'uncommonly well'. Like everyone in England, she was devastated by her death in November 1817.[2]

In 1872 Victoria reminisced about the 'brightest' interludes of her 'otherwise rather melancholy childhood' when she visited her beloved uncle Leopold, widower of Princess Charlotte, at his home, Claremont, near Esher. Too young to attend dinner parties, she would listen to a chamber orchestra play in the hall, and she could be 'doted on' as 'too much an idol in the House' by old Mrs Louis and the other servants. 'Up to my fifth year I had been much indulged by everyone and set pretty well all at defiance. Old Baroness de Spath, the Devoted Lady of my Mother, my Nurse Mrs Brock, dear old Mrs Louis – all worshipped the poor little fatherless child whose future then was still very uncertain.'[3]

Permission was given for another plaque to be placed in church during a time when there was no incumbent – Prebendary Kitto had died and Prebendary Shelford had not been appointed.[4] On 22 November 1903 a plaque on the west wall was dedicated:

In Memory of
Officers, N.C. Officers, and Men of the
18th, 21st, and 23rd Bns, 'Sharpshooters',
Imperial Yeomanry.
Killed in action or died of disease in the South African
War, 1899-1902.

Major-General (later Lord) Robert Baden-Powell, the hero of Mafeking who was to found the World Scout Movement, unveiled the tablet and paid tribute to the courage of the 'Sharpshooters' who had been founded by Royal Warrant on 24 December 1899. After the disastrous setbacks at the outbreak of war it was realised that mounted infantry were needed in large numbers to counter the fast-moving, hard-hitting Boers. The Yeomanry, a voluntary organisation that had been in existence throughout England for 100 years, was asked to create companies of 115 men to form the new 'Imperial' force. Over the next five months the original contingent of 550 officers and 10,371 men sailed for South Africa, where they met their regular army comrades. The two groups differed greatly. The volunteers, half of whom were upper- or middle-class, provided their own horses, saddlery and clothing, whilst the government supplied ammunition, arms, camp equipment, transport, and paid them at cavalry rates with a capitation grant for horses, clothing, etc. Not many of these men, who had to be 20-35 years of age, were good marksmen or riders so the delay at the Cape gave them an opportunity to learn and to acclimatise. Fortunately the war was over in two years – the Peace Treaty was signed on 31 May 1902 – but many lost their lives.

In 1908 the title 'Imperial' was dropped, and, as the 3rd County of London Yeomanry (Sharpshooters), they fought with distinction in both world wars. In 1961 they amalgamated with the Kent Yeomanry and six years later were reduced to squadron strength as part of the Royal Yeomanry. Their Headquarters is now in Mitcham Barracks.

A plaque and standard have been placed in the north-east corner of the church, where there is also a glass case containing two blocks of teak which were part of sleepers taken from the Burma-Siam railway built by prisoner-of-war labour. In 1942 Japanese forces advancing towards India needed supplies and the Irrawaddy River which runs the full length of Burma was too slow. A railway was proposed but engineers estimated it would take five years to build. By then the Japanese had taken over 100,000 prisoners, which meant that they had a workforce, so construction began in October 1942, and was completed ten months later. It claimed 6,540 British lives, together with over 80,000 Asian labourers, 2,830 Dutch P.O.W.s and 2,710 Australian P.O.W.s.

CRYPT

A number of gravestones dating from 1770-1820 are set into the floor of the crypt near the south-west entrance, and under the portico – in the gallery – there are 30 memorials which have recently been remounted on the walls, 11 of which were in the old church demolished in 1721. The saddest is that of John and Utrecia Tompson's family – they lost their daughter Utrecia aged one month on 9 December 1684, then on 10 July 1686 their other daughter, Frances, aged three years and four months. The oldest commemorates Thomas Evans, who was messenger to two Lord Chancellors of Queen Elizabeth I, and a monument of significance is the bust of Sir Theodore Turquet de Mayerne (1573-1654/5).

Born in Geneva, the son of a protestant French historian, he studied medicine at Heidelberg University and then moved to Paris where he became one of the royal physicians. In 1606 he came to England where he became physician to Queen Anne and a few years later to her husband James I. Elected a Fellow of the Royal College of Physicians in 1616, aged 43, his practice thrived, he wrote books and was knighted in 1624. The following year he was appointed first physician to King Charles I and Queen Henrietta Maria. He became famous for his copious case notes and in one which survives he records in 1628 seeing a 29-year-old MP, Oliver Cromwell, who had a variety of symptoms – coughing, excess of phlegm, digestive problems and 'Valde Melancholicus'.

Mayerne remained in London at his house in St Martin's Lane during the Civil War, attending patients. On the execution of Charles I he was made nominal first physician to Charles II, but did not live to see the Restoration, dying at his retirement home in Chelsea on 22 March 1654/5. His body was interred in St Martin's near the bodies of his mother, first wife, and five of his children. The inscription on his monument was written in Latin by his godson, Sir Theodore des Vaux.

A tablet with a frontal bust held by two putti commemorates Elizabeth Macdowall, 1670, and a very fine marble profile of Maria Augusta Murray, 1 May 1810-26 March 1840, has inscribed under it:

> If e'er pure spirit rose unto the skies
> Wafted to heav'n on friendship's deep drawn sighs
> Her pious soul to God hath wing'd its flight,
> And left behind but sorrow, gloom and night.

The LCC Survey of London lists 144 monuments and wall tablets in the crypt with their inscriptions, and a key plan shows their original positions.[5]

Alison Hardwick has described the heraldry of some of the other memorials:

> Most of our heraldry is to be found only on small and, unfortunately, largely nameless fragments. However, the design on one shield is almost as distinct as the day it was carved, with two-headed eagles, a lion rampant and sharp arrow heads, a crest of helmet and winged horse all enveloped in abundant and stylish mantling. Nearby is another shield ringed by a garland of fruit and flowers and, although broken, a closer look will show that the left-hand half of the design is identical to that on the first shield. A subsequent generation had had the good fortune to marry well, when the husband would have 'impaled' his wife's family arms with his own. In general the greater the number of 'quarterings', the greater the number of heiresses preceding generations had managed to collect in marriage – indeed, an inherited talent for such alliances can lead to those almost impossibly complicated arms which display 32 different devices – a sort of heraldic manifestation of name-dropping.
>
> A lone example of a painted shield livens things up considerably and on the memorial to Johanna, widow or relict of Lord Henry Powlet, although the armorial details are no longer visible, a variation is illustrated by the 'lozenge' or diamond outline. Women are not allowed to display their arms on a shield, having no business to tangle with military associations (the single exception being the Queen). Around another example of a lozenge are ribbon braids tied into a neat bow at the top – a decoration sometimes used to denote a single woman using her father's arms.

CHURCHYARD

Near the south-east corner stands a stone fountain with two lion's heads in memory of John Law Baker, 1789-1886, formerly of the Madras Army.

Glass

The new church was clear glazed except for the east window, which was designed by James and William Price at a cost of £130 and inserted in a wooden frame designed for it by Gibbs in 1726. It was geometrical in design and brightly coloured. This remained until 1867 when stained glass depicting the Ascension of Christ was installed in the three panels by Messrs Clayton & Bell, who with Messrs Lavers & Westlake of Endell Street filled the north and south windows with glass over the next forty years.

UPPER NORTH WINDOWS:
St Martin. 1898. Erected by William Stone, formerly of this parish.

St Andrew. 1899. In Memory of James Christie, given by his friend Matilda Evans, Guardian, Overseer, and Vestrywoman.

St George. 1898. In Memory of George James, former Churchwarden.

St David. 1899. In Memory of Thomas Woodley Marshall, former Churchwarden, given by his widow and son.

St Patrick. 1906. In Memory of Prebendary Kitto, 'A man greatly beloved'.

LOWER NORTH WINDOWS:
Jesus on the lake. 1899. Erected by William Stone.

John the Baptist. 1899. In Memory of James Christie, given by Matilda Evans.

The Crucifixion. 1900. In Memory of Edward Stanford and Mary Nesbitt, his wife, former residents of the parish. Given by their son.

Visit of the Magi. 1901. In Memory of Thomas Prescott, MRCS, a guardian and member of the Vestry and formerly Churchwarden.

The Nativity. 1906. In Memory of Prebendary Kitto.

UPPER SOUTH WINDOWS:
St John. 1889 by Ion Pace. To commemorate Queen Victoria's Golden Jubilee.

St Luke. 1892. In Memory of William Henry Smith (MP of the Borough).
Our Saviour. 1888. In Memory of William Gilson Humphrey, Vicar.

St Mark. 1898. To commemorate Queen Victoria's Diamond Jubilee, given by Lt. Col. Clifford Probyn, JP.

St Matthew. 1901. In Memory of Robert Cross, MD, and Eliza Hannah, his wife, erected by their surviving children.

LOWER SOUTH WINDOWS:
Our Lord's commission to Peter. 1893. Erected by George James, former Warden.

Our Lord at Emmaus. 1892. In Memory of William Henry Smith, MP.

The Angel appears to the two Marys. 1888. In Memory of William Humphrey, Vicar.

Jesus appears to Mary Magdalene. 1894. To commemorate Queen Victoria's Diamond Jubilee. Given by Lt. Col. Clifford Probyn, JP.

Jesus at the Sepulchre. 1898. To commemorate the reign of Queen Victoria, given by Thomas Robert Hill, churchwarden.

In 1913 the upper windows at the east end of the galleries were filled with stained glass as a gift from the Earl of Coventry, one of whose ancestor's memorials had been moved to the crypt when the church was built. The inscription read:

> To the Glory of God, and in Memory of the Right
> Honourable Sir Henry Coventry. Buried in the Chancel
> Of this Parish Church, Dec, 1686. Aged 70.
> He was Secretary of State to Charles II, Ambassador
> To the Court of Sweden, 1664 also to the Dutch
> Court, 1667.
> This window is dedicated by the Earl of Coventry
> In place of a monument removed to the Church of
> Croome, Worcestershire, 1913[6]

All this glass was lost by bomb blast in the Second World War, and despite a Faculty being granted in 1944 it was not replaced.

The Church Clock

When the church was completed in 1726 there would probably have been a clock with a single hour hand, but the present clock dates from 1759 and its main structural features remain to this day. The brass plate on its frame is inscribed:

> John Leroux and Son
> Charing Cross
> London
> MDCCLIX

Jonathan Betts, from the Royal Observatory, Greenwich, suggests that while Leroux was a fine maker of watches, the clock's movement was probably built by William Smith of Upper Moorfields. David Hardwick researched the history of the clock with Viscount Middleton of the British Horological Institute and Mr Betts, and reported:

> The new mechanism was housed in a wrought-iron frame rising to a central peak from which the pendulum was suspended. Frames of this form with their protruding levers on either side of the peak are sometimes called pagoda-style movements. Three separate processes, each driven by a falling weight, were housed in the frame: the going train powers the hands of the clock, the striking train drives the hammers which strikes the hours and the quarter striking train which originally merely subdivided the hours. Each week or so, the weights would have been cranked up wooden shutes constructed through the floors of the tower; in a later development, constant torque during winding was communicated to the movement by a secondary mass beneath the going train mounted on an endless chain devised by the 17th-century polymath, Christian Huyghens. The cranks were located on the east side of the frame while the leadoff work which drives the clock hands were taken from the west side, passing through an annular hole in the rod of the original pendulum! The vertical rod which takes the drive up to the level of the clockfaces is equipped with a universal joint to allow for any misalignment of the long shaft.

Ten metres above the mechanism – where only the most intrepid spiders can survive in the wind that funnels through the louvres – the vertical rod, slowly revolving on its axis minute by minute, terminates in a nest of bevel gears which turns the rotation through ninety degrees along a horizontal drive shaft. One end of this shaft controls both the minute hand of the east dial and a 12:1 gear train which powers the hour hand through an annular, concentric link. Counterweights balance the dead load of the clock hands. At the other end of the shaft a second nest of bevels permits drives in three directions to the north, west and south dials.

In the 1890s greater accuracy was achieved through the introduction of the ingenious 'Grimthorpe double three-legged gravity escapement'. This elaborate device consisting of wheels and arms maintains a constant impulsing force on the pendulum and eliminates the effects of unsteady wind-loads on the clock hands which would otherwise alter the pendulum's amplitude. A further increase of accuracy was achieved by installing a new pendulum with a shaft formed of an inner steel rod with an outer concentric zinc tube. Rod and tube are so arranged that temperature variations cause equal changes of length in the two metals such that the overall length of the pendulum remains constant. It seems likely that at this time a chiming train – working on the principle of a music box – replaced the quarter striking to mimic Big Ben's popular Westminster Chimes.

In the 1950s electric motors were introduced for each of the three trains, and in 1989 when the bells were relocated five metres lower to reduce tower sway, the clock movement was taken to pieces, serviced and re-sited above rather than below the bells; this necessitated new linkages to the hammers which strike the hours and quarters, and resulted in a now rather lethargic Westminster Chime. At the same time an electrical switching device was installed to silence the clock when the Vicar is asleep.

What we now have is a clock movement which has been greatly adapted – sometimes perhaps a little crudely – but which nevertheless is both accurate and reliable. It is moreover a valuable feature of St Martin's heritage and an important example of horological development.[7]

Other Treasures

ROYAL COAT OF ARMS
This is wooden with a crest and the supporters are a unicorn and a lion with a suitably fierce mien and his tongue hanging out. There is a motto, DIEV: ET: MON: DROIT., mantling, and the design may be of the Stuart period. At present it hangs in the Vestry Hall.

CHEST
In the Churchwardens' Accounts for the Michaelmas Quarter, 1597 there is an item 'ffor making of a newe stronge Cheaste to stand in'. It is made of elm and is 22in. by 5ft 7½in. by 24in. with a lid 2½in. thick.

MODEL OF THE CHURCH
Having approved the final design for the building on 23 May 1721, the Vestry asked Gibbs to make this model which cost £71 10s. A work of superlative craftsmanship, it has a removable steeple, six portions of the roof can be lifted,

and it shows the crypt by means of a sectional view on the south elevation and a removable portion of the main floor. The Vestry Minutes of 3 May 1749 record that the vicar, Dr Pearce, was asked to keep it in a convenient place in the vicarage, but on 15 November 1756 it was ordered that a proper recess be made for the model at the west end of the Vestry Room. In 1930 it was restored and a new glass case was made which could be lit inside by putting a coin in the slot. In 2004 the model was on loan to the Royal Institute of British Architects but on display at the Victoria and Albert Museum. It will return in 2007.

THE CHRISTMAS CRIB
Peter Eugene Ball, whose work can be seen in many cathedrals including Winchester, Birmingham and Southwell Minster, created a set of crib figures for St Martin's in 1999. Peter takes his inspiration from artists such as Richard Wentworth and Jean Dubuffet and uses ordinary and discarded objects in his work such as driftwood and even railway sleepers. David Monteith, curate then associate vicar, who has a great interest in the Church and Art, writes in the 1999 Newsletter of the Friends:

> Society lacks any single cohesive identity and so Peter's work manages to reflect something of the disparate nature of contemporary culture while pointing us to more mystical and universal paradigms. In this sense his art is both ancient and modern. One senses the delight he has had in creating these rather quirky figures from the little copper nails in their shoes to the startling pantomime-esque buttons; the hats and staffs and caskets crucial to any crib are formed from his found objects. The human figures together with the appealing animals beautifully express some of the St Martin's concerns. The curvaceous, coloured figures are bright and somewhat gaudy in keeping with our baroque surroundings. The shepherds' hats and poses allude to the many characters who make up our community. The kings deliberately reflect the multicultural and international atmosphere which we enjoy, and the roof of the stable with its bare rafters, reminds us that the Christ child, like so many of God's children, found no place to lay his head.

A WHIPPING POST
This dates from 1751 when it was set up by the churchwardens to punish offenders.

12

Churchwardens and Lay Officials

Today the word Vestry implies a small room where clergy vest for a service and the vestments and silver are kept, but until the late 19th century it described either the actual meeting of parishioners who governed the local area or the body of parishioners themselves. (In the Episcopal Church of the United States this is still the case.) The meeting was usually held in the church vestry, but if a village was far removed from the building the members would meet at an inn. The first recorded meeting of the St Martin's Vestry was in 1530, when the Churchwardens' Accounts were presented and passed, and three members present signed and three put their marks. A dinner followed. A minute book was started in 1546 to keep a record of proceedings and from 1561 the wardens had to render account to the 'Masters' of the parish, which might be a description of the Vestry.

Today's churchwardens have responsibility only for ecclesiastical functions – caring for ecclesiastical property and finances – but in earlier times they were also responsible for local government. They had great responsibilities and were elected annually at Easter, the meeting being attended by all the parishioners whether they belonged to the Church of England or not. If there was a dispute the incumbent would appoint one and the parishioners the other. Once elected they could not resign without the Vestry's permission, except for ill health. On resignation a fine had to be paid, and in 1589 Mr Poultney had to pay the large sum of 20 shillings to St Martin's for not fulfilling his obligation; when he resigned after a few months King George I gave an organ to the church. In 1775 Messrs Robert Drummond, James Payne, Richard Roycroft Wrathor and Henry Allon were fined £20 each for refusing to serve, and in 1800 £100 was received for five refusals.

Until 1868 the Vestry was able to levy a rate to repair the building and maintain the churchyard. Parishioners often paid their rates partly in kind, and each farm in the parish had also to supply hay for Queen Elizabeth's stables in the mews. It was agreed that every year three loads, each containing 35 trusses, must be delivered. The number of trusses sent by a farmer, who had to pay carriage, depended on his acreage and so:

Mr Poultney, the ffarmer of Saint James ffarm xij Trusses.
Mr ffletcher of Drurey house xij Trusses.

> John Dawnst of strond xij Trusses.
> Richard Coxshott of St. Gilles xij Trusses.
> Richard Darlowe of St. Martines ix Trusses.

After 1868 a voluntary rate was sometimes levied (it still is in some City of London parishes) but in most places collections and subscriptions had to suffice to keep the church in repair. The Vestry kept its civil powers until 1894 when local, elected councils were set up to make decisions on matters such as sanitation, the lighting and maintenance of roads, education and policing the parish. The Vestry's responsibilities had already been gradually eroded in the 19th century by various Acts of Parliament and so now the real government and administration of the parish of St Martin's passed to the London County Council and, eventually, to the Westminster City Council. The Vestry, however, continued to meet as an advisory body to the incumbent and wardens until 1921 when a Parochial Church Council was set up with legal powers.

St Martin's churchwardens were thus very important people, and their names are recorded on the boards near the stairs leading to the south gallery. They were required to wear gowns, and on 3 April 1740 the Vestry suggested that their shabby gowns should be replaced; in 1824 £21 was paid for new ones. Sidesmen, who were paid, also wore gowns, and someone suggested their duties might be:

> To hear and see and say nowt,
> To eat and drink and pay nowt;
> And when the wardens drunken roam,
> Your duty is to see them home.[1]

The Churchwardens' Accounts of St Martin's date back to 1525 and for nearly 250 years they were written on and bound in vellum, the earlier ones recorded by professional scriveners, and are beautifully illustrated. The entries give an idea of their duties, which were laid down in Canon 89, 1604. In the 14th century they had been told to take charge of the church revenues, goods and ornaments, and to tell the Bishop of any heresy. Accordingly, in 1584 they took Carrie Hilton to him for this offence, and three years later 'presented' the vicar, Christopher Hayward, as being unfit for office.

Plagues brought problems. In 1563 it was estimated that 20,000 Londoners died and the St Martin's books record 300 burials that year. Corpses were buried in sheets but a coffin was provided for the journey to the church and graveside. The churchwardens appointed three men and three 'discreet women' as examiners and searchers who would visit a house to ascertain the cause of death. If it was the plague they were notified, and those living in the house given a three-foot red wand to carry should they go outside. Notices were fixed to the doorposts. Two married couples were employed for this task – 'Goodwif Bellows and Goodwif Baylie' – who were paid 17 pence each, sixpence more than their husbands, John and William. For fear of their spreading the plague another man was employed for two shillings and fourpence to kill all stray dogs.

There were further outbreaks of the plague in 1625, 1630, 1636 and 1647 and then the Great Plague of 1665. Entries in the Burial Book marked 'P' or 'peste' showed this cause of death, and the churchwardens themselves suffered because in one year four new men were elected to fill the place of those who had died. With great thankfulness they noted on 30 January 1666 that 'not one of the sickness in this parish, praised be the Lord'.

The nearby Royal Mews meant that the roads were often dirty and almost impassable so the wardens, as part of their civil duties, had to collect fines from those who fouled the highways. The 1573 Book records a sum of two shillings and three pence. 'Receyued the viij daie of Februarye of Mr Jenningns of the Bore Hede in part of payment because our church was indyted for layinge the dounge in the Queene's highe waye.'

A fine of a shilling was levied on any parishioner not attending worship on Sundays or Holy Days, and the constables had to collect these after the wardens had given them the information. In 1572 fivepence was 'Payde to the Sexton for ffetchinge of Robert Morton and Neale to the church.'

The churchwardens were also responsible for seating worshippers according to their rank and station, and this occasionally caused problems. When the Vestry, in a Minute of 21 January 1629, noted that neither Warden 'shall henceforth place any person or persons of the rank of esquire or upwards', the Bishop agreed with them, but on his visitation of 29 March 1631, he wrote in the margin of the Account Book that he cancelled his order and supported the churchwardens.

Punishing offenders was part of the Vestry's responsibilities, and on 18 July 1602 they handed £20 to their wardens to make at Charing Cross 'a cage house of correction, or lock-up with the bedel's chambers over'. Stocks had to be purchased but the first reference to these is not until the Vestry minutes of 4 February 1618: 'two pairs of stocks to be made strong and sufficient to be placed – one pair at the Ragged Row and the other at Drury Lane'. The St Martin's pillory stood at Charing Cross but was abolished in the 1830s. Executions had taken place on the same spot, and nine of those who had signed the death warrant of Charles I were executed there in 1660.

'Beating the Bounds' began with medieval processions round the parish to bless the crops at Rogationtide. In 1526 the wardens paid nine men one penny each 'for bearying of the cross and banner in the crosweke'. Priest and people perambulated round the parish for the three days before the Feast of the Ascension, but Queen Elizabeth restricted it to one day with one priest officiating. In 1584 the church accounts record a payment of 12 pence 'to childes men for carrying planks'. These were used to cross ditches, and when the boundary stones of the parish were reached the boys were whipped with canes and paid twopence each for their pains! This tradition – without the whipping – carried on till the late 19th century, and Churchwarden McMaster, then in his teens, describes in his book what he had to do in the St Martin's procession which took place every three years.[2]

Another duty of the wardens was to provide the means of extinguishing fires in the parish, and in 1600 the Accounts show that 17 pence was paid 'unto vj poore men for helping home with the buckets and ladders from Durham house where the stables was afire'. By 1700 St Martin's had an engine, usually painted every year in the wardens' colours, which may not have been very reliable as the engineer was paid a reward not exceeding thirty shillings and his assistant ten shillings if it arrived in good condition!

An unpleasant duty of the wardens was to issue certificates to people suffering from scrofula or 'king's evil'. This enabled them to attend a ceremony when the Sovereign would touch them and they would be given tokens or touch pieces. The practice was eventually discontinued after 700 years by George I in 1714.

The churchwardens were responsible for a good water supply and in 1551 they rewarded Mr Martyn, a bricklayer, for 'his good furtherance towards our water', but things went awry in 1573 when a fine was levied for pollution. Three streams flowed from north to south across the parish and one of these caused problems to Gibbs when he built the new church. It was still flowing underground in the 1880s and caused problems to the foundations of both the new Town Hall and the Garrick theatre in Charing Cross Road.

A dispute raged at St Martin's for 160 years concerning who should be members of the Vestry. In 1660 some parishioners were opposed to the restoration of the monarchy and so, to exclude them, the other members asked Gilbert Sheldon, Bishop of London to issue a Faculty to establish a Select Vestry, which he did on 28 June 1662. Some of the old members did not know of this petition but Nathaniel Hardy, the vicar, supported it and he and the wardens joined the 49 members of the new body. By 1715 these Vestries, which were self selected not elected, had a bad reputation in London, so the House of Commons instituted an enquiry and St Martin's was chosen to be looked at first. The committee found that the account books were so muddled and complicated that 'It was impossible to say what was fictitious and what was real, because of the large number of names in the books ... the money is used for the wrong purposes ... the methods used are such as are liable to great frauds, being without check or control, and the money is often diverted from its primitive use.' Armed with this information and other criticisms in the report, several parishioners petitioned the House of Commons to come to their aid and abolish the Select Vestry. Nothing was done and in 1742 a case was brought in the Court of King's Bench, airing all the grievances, but the powers of the Select Vestry were upheld. The parishioners renewed their attack in 1790, and even elected a rival pair of churchwardens who tried unsuccessfully to enter the official pew. The courts again ruled against them.

Things quietened until Easter Monday 1833, when the police were called because parishioners had broken down the Vestry door and were interrupting a meeting. The next year a large mob occupied the Vestry room and two separate meetings had to be held with proceedings of both bodies being entered in the minutes. Mr Henry Simpson now brought an action against Mr Churchwarden Holroyd to test the legality of the Select Vestry's control of parish affairs. The case was heard before the Lord Chief Justice who ended its reign. He pointed out that both the Vestry minutes of 1575, which had just been discovered in the roof of the building, and the Churchwardens' Accounts of 1525 clearly showed that they had always been elected 'with the consent, wish, and agreement of the whole bodie of the Parish'. The Judge said it was unfortunate that the documents had not been produced before.

The custom of all parishioners electing the churchwardens had been re-instated, and the bells were rung! The new Vestry immediately appointed a committee to enquire into parish affairs and the report was critical. It queried everything including the number of beadles employed, the amount spent on lighting the church, and how often the bells were rung: 'Ringing of Bells, £38 17s. This amount differs more or less every year; but your committee consider it generally a great charge for an useless service; and your committee recommend churchwardens to be more careful of this item, and make less noise in this way in future.'

The Vestry became a corporate body when Parliament passed the Metropolitan Management Act, 1855, and the three wards of the parish, Park, Long Acre and Strand, elected 12 members each, who joined the ex-officio vicar and wardens. Its powers and functions were now more clearly defined on matters such as street lighting, paving and refuse removal. In 1894 all elected vestries were abolished, and the civil and ecclesiastical functions separated so that the incumbent no longer took the chair. The responsibilities were now considerable and the substantial expenditure was funded by rates levied on parishioners – £85,000 for general and sewer rates, and £40,000 for the poor rate. The chairman of the new council was Colonel Clifford Probyn who had been a member of the old Vestry.[3]

The Council lasted only five years as the 1899 London Government Act enabled Westminster City Council to take over the administration of all parishes in its area. A Mayor, Aldermen and Councillors were elected, and the new Town Clerk asked the Clerk of the Vestry to prepare a statement of the assets and liabilities of the parish. The final meeting was held on 31 October 1900, when the Medical Officer of Health gave his report, road repairs were authorised, votes of thanks were passed and proceedings ended with the singing of the National Anthem. Some lobbied for the new City Hall to be in Mayfair, which drew a swift response from former Churchwarden Edward Watherston who pointed out that 'St George's is quite a modern parish', and the Hall should be near St Martin's. Did not Dr Johnson say that 'The full tide of human existence is to be found at Charing Cross'? Westminster City Hall was built in Charing Cross Road.

St Martin's vicarage was the venue of a meeting which was to have a profound effect on the structure of the Church of England. During the First World War several clergy became angry that the institution was not facing up to the challenges of the war and seemed incapable of adapting itself to modern living. Amongst them were Dick Sheppard and his great friend William Temple, vicar of St James, Piccadilly. They convened a meeting in the vicarage in March 1917 to form a ginger group which became the Life and Liberty Movement. Both men agreed that the Church must have more freedom to order its affairs and, fortunately, Temple's careful wisdom balanced Dick's practical enthusiasm. Hensley Henson, the acerbic Bishop of Durham, dismissed the group as shell-shocked chaplains, young men in a hurry, and some later nick-named them the Lovely Libertines, but many others, including Maude Royden, the feminist Congregational minister, cheered them on. Encouraged by Archbishop Garbett of York, Temple resigned his living to become the Movement's first full-time secretary and results came quickly: three years later Parliament passed the Enabling Act which set up the Church Assembly, now the General Synod. The Assembly, often absorbed in trivial internal concerns, was to disappoint, disgust and infuriate Dick but it brought a whiff of democracy to ecclesiastical life, and in 1921 the Parochial Church Councils (Powers) Measure set up an elected council of laity in each parish.[4] An electoral roll was set up by the first St Martin's Council, which had 40 members. Women soon took their place on the committees and in 1940 Joyce Hollins and Clara Elizmar were elected the first woman churchwardens, each serving for ten years. In 2004 the wardens are Jeff Claxton and Andrew Caspari (Tricia Sibbons having withdrawn after eight years' devoted service) and the St Martin's P.C.C. has 20 members whose primary duty is 'to cooperate with the incumbent in the initiation, conduct, and development of church work both within the parish and outside'.

Guardians of the Peace

In the 16th century the parish constables were responsible for keeping order in the fields and roads around St Martin's. In charge of them was an official called the headborough, a rank similar to an alderman, who was an important local figure – in 1578 Robert Pennythorne, carpenter and headborough, was given an imposing funeral in the church. St Martin's had three such men, who had power to hear, examine and punish, and they were assisted by one or two paid constables who collected fines in their ward. A bellman was also appointed who went round the parish at night calling out, 'Take care of your fire and candle, and be charitable to the poor, and pray for the dead'. Not all of these were conscientious as the 1599 Accounts reveal: 'Paid to Fisher's wife for her husband's watch about the parish in the night, being appointed when the bellman was in trouble … 2s. 6d.'

In 1736 conditions on the crowded streets around St Martin's had deteriorated so badly that a special Act of Parliament was passed authorising the Vestry to appoint a Watch Committee who would employ able-bodied men as watchmen and beadles to patrol the parish. A rate was levied, and 41 men were paid £12 each year to stand in their sentry box armed with an ash staff. The watchmen were given a definite area to patrol, and had to be on duty in the summer from 10 p.m. to 5 a.m., and in winter from 9 p.m. to 6 a.m. They had to arrest offenders, and every 90 minutes walk round the streets making sure all premises were secure, and in a clear, distinct voice declare the time. Eight beadles supervised these men, and they had to record any incidents which occurred during the night and report to the wardens in church on Sunday. A uniform was supplied, and in 1743 the men wore a blue greatcoat trimmed with red plush and laced with gold, a gold-lace hat and scarlet stockings. By 1828 St Martin's parish had 68 watchmen and eight patrolmen but they were eventually replaced by Sir Robert Peel's new police force.

13

The Least, the Last and the Lost

The care of the poor has been one of the most important functions of St
Martin's congregation since earliest times. When in the 1530s the monasteries
and convents which had provided most of the relief were destroyed by King
Henry VIII, parishes throughout England found that they had to increase their
practical care. In 1547 the churchwardens, who had already taken collections
for the poor, paid Robert Pennythorne seven pence for installing a box in
the choir to collect alms for those in need. wardens were now empowered to
issue licences to beg, but were told to beware of 'sturdy beggars' who ought to
be working. If these were caught begging they were to be whipped; a second
offence meant the right ear was cut off and a third meant death. In 1572
£29 0s. 8d. was distributed to the poor and two years later a rate was levied
on the 164 householders in the parish, and this, added to collections, realised
£36. There were 15 special collections for 'maimed or lame soldiers' at the
end of the century and the Churchwardens' Accounts for 1593 record many
such practical gifts, including apprenticing boys to a trade:

> Paid for the new hose and doublet for Edward Thrasher at his binding unto Dawson
> the joiner ... x pence.
> Paid for new hose and shoes for him ... 1 shilling v pence.
> Paid with him unto his master ... xx pence.
> Paid unto Bellows for ye board of ye said E. Thrasher ... iii shillings.

The Parliament of 1597, which devoted much of its time to social legislation,
passed five statutes dealing with old and infirm beggars, vagabonds, wounded
soldiers and poor relief in general, and their provisions were enshrined in
the great Poor Law Act, 1601, which enabled wardens to levy a rate for the
relief of the necessitous poor in their parish and remove itinerant strangers.[1]
Overseers were appointed to see that this was done and to make sure that those
in receipt of money were wearing a badge with 'P' on it. Owing to the great
number of poor people who flocked to London an Act was passed in 1662 to
help the Cities of London and Westminster cope financially.

The Minutes of St Martin's Vestry for 20 July 1664 record that the Earl
of Newport and others asked that a workhouse be built and this was done,
but oddly it was under-used so it was let in 1683 on condition that another

be provided if the need arose. Another was needed, and in 1724 the Vestry passed an estimate for £607 10s. to build a new one. Another huge three-storey workhouse was built in 1772 on the south side of Hemming's Row and trustees were appointed. It stood on the part of the National Portrait Gallery which looks up Charing Cross Road but was demolished in 1871 when the National Gallery was extended northwards.[2] The inmates helped with the tasks of the house; the women cared for their children and for the elderly, and some of the men went out to work.

The 1601 Act, which lasted until 1834, introduced Laws of Settlement so that to receive benefits a person had to have resided in a parish for at least a month. After the 1662 Settlement Act people could obtain this right by marriage, apprenticeship, being in domestic service for a year, or paying rent of £10 p.a. or more. Anyone not fulfilling these criteria could be removed to their original parish. Applicants would be examined and the St Martin's Settlement Examinations, which give us much information about people coming for help, are contained in 74 volumes held at Westminster City Archives. Men and women travelled from all parts of the British Isles and some came from the West Indies and America. They included children abandoned by their parents, widows, old people, deserted wives and people out of work. There were many difficulties – children could be separated from their mother if she had married for a second time and then sought help, and a widow could be sent to her husband's place of settlement which she may never have visited.[3] There are some 30,000 case studies available in the St Martin's examinations, and each tells a heart-rending tale. One concerns children caught up in the turmoil of the Seven Years War:

> 26th May, 1761. Jane Styles, wife of Thomas, a soldier. Examined in the Workhouse, on oath she described how she, her husband and six children, John Bell, aged 8 years, Elizabeth Charles, 7, John Clements, 5, William Watley, 5, John Brigaduff, 4, and Diana Myers, 6, embarked on a small two-masted sailing ship, John and Sarah hired to bring sick and wounded soldiers from Bremen to London. On arrival they landed at Chelsea where a Constable told her that there were no billets for women or children. The Parish Officers for relief took them to the Workhouse for four days then told them to leave but gave her a shilling, told her not to say what he had done and advised her to leave the children elsewhere, promising that he would give her something more. She went with the children to the Office for the affairs of Chelsea Hospital in Scotland Yard. On being told the Board could do nothing she went her way leaving the children there. They were taken to St Martin's Workhouse, and their subsequent fate is unknown.[4]

'The immoral conduct of the Rev. Mr Tillston, chaplain of the workhouse,' caused alarm to the authorities in 1819 so, after receiving proof, the gentleman was dismissed but no details are given. The same year the overseers, much concerned at the plight of the infant poor, asked the churchwardens, Mr Cleaver and Mr Kep, to lease a large house they had found in Highwood Hill near Hendon for £210 at a rent of £35 p.a. This was done on 6 September 1819, but the first matron only stayed three months so a replacement was sought who had to be unmarried and under thirty-five. There were 40 applicants for the post and Mrs Elizabeth Talbot was appointed and told that she could have her mother live with her. The house, now known as Highwood Ash, still stands but as the lease expired on 11 December 1834 St Martin's had to vacate the premises, leaving only coal and potatoes behind.[5]

In 1832 the industrious, ubiquitous Blomfield, Bishop of London, was asked by the Chancellor of the Exchequer to chair the Poor Law Commission to sort out the fearsome tangle of ineffective devices and regulations. He attended every meeting, and two years later the recommendations were published. These became law in April 1834, when poor relief was taken out of the hands of Vestries. Local ratepayers would now elect a Board of Guardians who would appoint a Poor Law Officer. The St Martin's Board, who inherited most of the overseers' functions, remained until 1868 when several parishes formed the Strand Union. Then in 1913 the City of Westminster took over. In 1886 many fragmented and diverse schemes for relief were rationalised and are now part of the St Martin-in–the-Fields Almshouse Charity.

The award for the church's best beggar must surely go to Mr Walsh, a Welsh miner blind for 28 years, who in the 1890s sat with his back to the church wall accompanied by his pepper and salt mongrel Nell who sat at attention beside him. When someone threw a penny on the pavement she would retrieve it and take it to her master. Each morning she met him off an omnibus near St James's Park. In May 1893 she was abducted but as she was so well known the culprit was soon discovered and given six months' hard labour. When Walsh died two years later his daughter received many offers for the now disorientated Nell, but she refused to sell.[6]

The amount given to the poor in 1896 amounted to £220. 'I am afraid,' said the vicar, Mr Kitto, 'that we dispense relief as Mrs Gamp dispensed medicine, judgmatically, that is without any very fixed principles.' When he arrived in 1886 he discovered that each day clergy doled out shilling tickets indiscriminately, so he instituted a more thorough examination in order that, if necessary, sums up to £20 could be given.[7]

The Open Door policy adopted by Dick Sheppard and his congregation in the First World War set the pattern for St Martin's care for the poor and the vulnerable from then on. Tired and weary soldiers arriving from the Front in 1915 found a warm, friendly crypt containing a canteen staffed by volunteers where they could stay. They were followed in the 1920s and 1930s by out-of-work civilians, many of whom had been in the services and were now unwanted and forgotten. They came with their sick children and hungry wives. Volunteers under the guidance of Miss Whitmore, a trained social worker appointed in 1931 by Pat McCormick, interviewed and helped hundreds of people in distress in the south-west porch. Meal tickets, food, clothes and hostel vouchers were given out, and a house in Grosvenor Road where 30 men could be given emergency accommodation was leased for three years from 1925. Its residents included the son of an archbishop; a man who had owned his own racing stables; doctors, soldiers, porters and painters.[8]

50 *Mr Walsh, a blind beggar, with his mongrel Nell at their pitch outside St Martin's,* The Daily Graphic, *14 December 1895.*

The 1930s brought no improvement and in the year ending March 1933 workers interviewed 854 homeless men and 606 others; 5,281 meal tickets and 433 bed and food tickets were distributed; 144 passed through the hostels and 717 received clothing; 48,555 men, 6,395 women and 41 children slept in the crypt.[9] No one could stay more than three nights as it was not a registered hostel.

The Second World War brought crowds to the crypt seeking shelter from the air raids and in need of a friendly place to sleep and eat. In 1948 the establishment of the Welfare State meant that government formed a partnership with churches and voluntary bodies to care for the poor, but it soon became evident that there was still much to be done by charitable agencies, who had to be careful not to let the state avoid its responsibilities.

In 1948 Mervyn Charles-Edwards employed two full-time welfare workers, Eileen Sprules, who had first come to St Martin's in 1918 when she was working with MI5, and Frank Lambert. They were responsible for relief work in the 1950s and soon established links with the London County Council, the Church Army, Salvation Army and the Family Welfare Association. By 1951 eighty callers arrived each week wanting food and money, and the workers felt that their short interviews were not sufficient to cope with the mental and physical problems facing each caller. Much constructive work was done and the following year 3,100 people were interviewed and employment was found for 240 men. 'We need to know our limitations,' said Eileen. Letters also came in from families needing help. The vicar's Christmas Appeal on the radio, which attracted £29,000 in 1962, enabled them to receive grants, and also helped pay for the Unit – as it still does. In 1962 Eileen retired and the Rev. John Pudney, a Baptist minister who had served with the RAF, took charge of the Social Care Unit. Men and women continued to pour into the crypt for help, and after three years he reported that there were now 25,000 record cards in the Unit.

The House of St Martin at Norton Fitzwarren in Somerset was opened by John in September 1963, and 18 people from the Unit were able go there for rest and rehabilitation. Standing in four acres of land, it had a resident warden and two assistants. There was no fixed time for residents to stay, and some were able to get a job locally and then move into their own flat. One resident described the House as a place where 'new desires are born, old habits lost, and life is gradually taking on a new meaning'. In the 1970s the House was handed over to another charity to administer.

The 1966 Friends' Newsletter, having reported that between 500 and 700 people came to the soup kitchen in the crypt every Sunday between 11 a.m. and 6 p.m., asked, 'What have they come to find? What should we give them?' The service, originally started for 'down and out' men, was now also a meeting place for young people who had opted out of society and who enjoyed coming to this warm, welcoming place where no questions were asked, and where they received free soup and bread. The writer, who was probably Austen Williams, felt that a contact – a bridge – had been made, but more constructive help was needed. Norman Ingram-Smith, who had been on the management committee for two years, took up the challenge.

51   *The Social Care Unit, 1982.*

Norman joined the staff in 1965 as a co-director and then, when John left to be a prison governor three years later, he became Director. Over the next 20 years this gentle, avuncular man and his staff had a profound influence on both the church and the Care Unit, making St Martin's work with the homeless known and respected in London and beyond. Having worked in hostels for ex-borstal boys and then been in charge of St Luke's alcoholic rehabilitation centre in south London for five years, he had all the necessary gifts and skills needed by the director. He lived simply in an Aladdin's cave filled with books and papers which is now the George Richards Room in 6 St Martin's Place. He was one of the founders of NACRO and advised on the setting up of the Prince's Trust. Challenged with being a professional do-gooder he replied, 'It seems to me that you can only do good or do bad. Personally I'd rather try to do good.'[10] Austen asked him to preach regularly and his gospel-based sermons and articles in the *Review* were always

52 *Norman Ingram-Smith, the much loved and respected Director of the Social Service Unit, 1965-85.*

illustrated by his experiences. The two men liked and respected each other, and worked extremely well together. Norman's deep faith informed everything he did, and time and time again he focused on the need for friendship – 'Here at Saint Martin's we make friends, and we sustain each other by friendship.'

In 1965 a hostel for eight men was opened in Clapham. It had two staff flats and became a valuable resource to the Unit. wardens included Stephen Mitchell, who was later ordained, and David Curry, who became a psychotherapist and tragically died in 1995. This house was rebuilt in 2002 and the London and Quadrant Housing Association have leased the 16 bed-sits there to the Unit. Another house was purchased by Austen in the early 1980s, but it proved too difficult to administer them both and it was sold after a few years – at a good profit! The vicar's tender conscience was troubled but, of course, the money helped boost funds.

For five years from 1967 St Martin's with the Salvation Army Rink Club in Soho attempted to help homeless young people who were coming in droves to the Capital in search of money and glamour. Bitterly disappointed, they were sleeping on the streets or in derelict buildings. Tom Gaston, a local man born in the Charing Cross Hospital, brought up in Bedfordbury and now one of the vergers, found them waiting in the cold when he opened the church in the morning. He told Carolyn Scott how he felt: 'Sometimes I feel sorry for them. With others I feel they're so foolish and it makes me mad. Why don't they look for a job?' When I ask them what they will do when they are my age, they say they will be dead by twenty-five. One did say, 'This isn't living, it isn't even existing,' and went back to Scotland. Norman Croucher was in charge of the project which in one year saw 7,000 young people passing through. Of those 400 were found jobs, 200 accommodation, 200 went home and 250 were given emergency treatment for drug overdoses.[11] They entered the primitive, tiny rooms of the Undercroft (now the Gallery) with a multitude of problems, and the workers, having formed good relations with the police, probation service, doctors and a host of caring agencies, were able to refer them to the appropriate place. Norman Croucher, himself seriously disabled, left after four years and is now one of the best known workers in his field.

Posters appeared advertising a 24-hour Openline telephone service in the crypt, and volunteers had to answer questions as varied as 'My Dad has died, do you believe in an after life?' (at 3 a.m.!) and 'Where can I find somewhere to sleep tonight?' A large donation from Cecil King, the press baron and chairman of the International Publishing Corporation, gave this service financial security for its first seven years. He had met someone in Australia who had started a similar venture and witnessed three children abandoned by the roadside being helped by the project, so telephoned Austen when he returned to England and said, 'Why don't you start this at St Martin's?'[12] In 1968 Norman told the *Review* that telephone counselling had been given to 5,840 people. In that same year the Social Care Unit, which now had 17 full-time paid workers and 100 volunteers, interviewed some 16,000 people – 40-60 callers each day. The Sunday soup kitchen continued to serve hungry men and women each week – approx 104,000 cups to around 72,000 people in one year![13]

A typical day in the Unit was described by a member of staff, Heather Flowerdew, in 1974. When the volunteers leave, having taken calls during the night, the day shift arrive and read case-notes and make preparations for the first callers at 10 a.m. Men and women are interviewed all day in small private rooms. Some, mostly regulars, only need company and a hot drink, but a number of vagrant people ask for money and clothing. To refuse brings a variety of responses: 'All right, I'll have to go thieving, won't I?' 'Thought the Church was supposed to help people.' 'Never mind, love. You do your best.' There will be the 'ordinary' person with alcohol or family problems needing time to talk. Mid-afternoon sees a roaring drunk at the door, who is followed by a bruised woman with her arm in plaster. Her husband, having attacked her, has left home. Who will feed the three children and pay the rent money? The Social Security office is phoned. The evening shift arrives at 5.30 and by 10 p.m. over sixty people will have been interviewed.[14]

53 *The Kitchen.*

After nine years in the Unit Norman Ingram-Smith wrote:

> The staff are viewed as saints or fools which usually depends on whether the person making the judgement actually knows someone who visits the Unit. It depends on whether they are aware of the series of cruel blows life can deal to force from a man every vestige of hope and motivation. We make ourselves available daily to offer friendship, help and advice to such a varied collection of problems that there would never be any successful outcome to the work without the constant support and prayers of everyone attached to St Martin's.[15]

No homeless centre can exist without volunteers and these have always been people of all faiths and none, who generously offer their time, talents and friendship. In 1979 one of the most loved of these remarkable women and men died – Nancy Palmer. Having trained at Bart's Hospital she later became Assistant Matron there, and then went to be Matron of the Elizabeth Garrett Anderson Hospital for 15 years. One of the founders of CRISIS, when she retired she spent two weeks sleeping rough on the Embankment, and with others started the Sunday Soup Kitchen at St Martin's in the mid-1960s.

During Norman's time at the Unit there was a shift in the kind of care that was needed because many people who would formerly have been restrained in mental hospitals were now roaming the streets – failures of the care in the community policies. 'Not being sufficiently ill to be kept in hospital yet they are not always competent to live in the open community even with the financial help of the welfare state,' wrote Norman. 'If you have to live in a hostel which does not provide food and so have to buy meals in London cafés, then the slightest increase in appetite can completely destroy a minimal budget supplied by the government. Your clothes get stolen; you can't wash a pair of socks without pretty certain risk of losing them while they are drying. For people living in

54 *The Art Class.*

this haphazard way, there's a constant need for help.'[16] Unemployment, inflation, redundancies and other tensions including the weakening of family life were causing immense problems, and in 1979 a counselling service was established with a separate entrance in Number 5. A continual stream of callers came to the Unit each day and Carolyn Scott describes in detail the sort of people coming for help – ex-prisoners, drug addicts, compulsive gamblers, mentally ill and alcoholics, people for whom life has got out of hand, twisted and impossible.[17]

Will Carey, a teacher at Westminster School, did some research into the needs of the homeless with the result that the Place Day Centre was established in May 1980. Around forty homeless people were invited into the sitting room of the Unit on three afternoons a week for tea, toast, scrabble and television. The following year Bob Lloyd, a former Franciscan friar, and Ann Jennings were employed to pioneer the project and work with the volunteers helping those who called in. The number of visits increased dramatically from 403 in June 1981 to 2,000 in June 1983. There were very few women callers and the men were all ages, mostly single and unemployed, with a high proportion that had drink-related problems.

Well-known regulars, known to everyone as 'the troops', were still shadowy figures in the side pews despite the fact that sitting rooms were available for them in the Unit. Some visitors found this difficult to understand but Austen and Norman felt strongly that hospitality should be offered in the church itself, particularly in winter time, providing that the person did not eat, smoke, drink or sleep. Shoes had to remain on! One man, an ageing Pole who always wore gloves, had been visiting since 1948. He had fought the Germans when they invaded his country in 1934, been interned, escaped, and joined the Polish and British armies in Italy. His left hand had been badly burned at the battle of Monte Cassino. Next to him might be a 17-year-old girl who had run away from home after an argument with her father. The troops would snooze in the pews during the week but occasionally Austen, worn down by complaints that 'that man is smoking and eating', would suddenly arrive, throw open the doors and say, 'Out, out, you all need some fresh air.' So did the church! Gradually the troops would creep back.

Norman retired to Suffolk in 1985 so Roger Shaljean, who had arrived as a social worker in 1965, shared the post of director with Les Mohrman for a year and then took over himself. He had a deputy, six other full-time social workers, a secretary, accountant and a canteen assistant to help him. The Unit's premises were enlarged but it remained a rabbit warren of offices, interview and counselling rooms, kitchen, lavatories and small halls. In the severe winter of 1987 up to fifty men were invited to sleep in the Unit, and a soup kitchen was kept open all night. Two years later Bob Isles formed the Friends of the Unit and many donors joined so that today there are over 1,000 members who receive three newsletters each year. Since 1994 they have contributed nearly £2m – including many generous legacies – to social care at St Martin's.

A slight change of emphasis now took place in the work. Individual counselling continued but activities and group work were introduced such as art classes and discussion groups. All the staff had been expected to do all the tasks, but now they began to specialise. Other agencies were asked to help and the Day Centre now had a visiting doctor, nurse, chiropodist and housing advice worker. Outings began and in 1991 the first Pilgrimage to Canterbury to lay flowers on Dick Sheppard's grave took place. About sixty volunteers, staff, clients and friends, all sponsored, walked together in the best Chaucerian fashion. Sleeping in village halls, the pilgrims got to know each other, and the venture mirrored Roger's gentle, collaborative style of leadership. Today around 100 people set off and 140 arrive, and in 2003 £17,000 was raised for the work. Roger, who in 2005 will complete 40 years of devoted and skilled service to St Martin's homeless, resigned as director in 1998 but remained on the staff.

'Challenge Anneka', the television programme, visited the Centre in 1993 and Anneka Rice, wearing her bright blue track suit, dashed round London persuading firms to supply and fit kitchen equipment, furniture, etc. free of charge. She had only three days to complete the challenge so she stayed at the vicarage. Everything had to be done with the utmost secrecy so that the programme would have the maximum effect, and the volunteers had a huge shock when they saw the improvements.

The organisation was now becoming more professional. Statutory bodies and other funders demand strict rules for the operation of the Unit, the employment of staff and the assessment of results. In April 2003 came the momentous merger between the Social Care Unit and the London Connection to form The Connection at St Martin's. In No.5 (the former SCU) there are now fewer old people and those who travel long distances are being encouraged to look for day centres locally. The emphasis is more on rough sleepers and those who move in and out of bed and breakfast accommodation. It is expected that the number of refugees, traumatised by war and persecution, will rise and, if their benefits are cut, their needs will grow even more. Those young people who arrive at No.12 (the former London Connection) are quickly linked with a youth worker so that a friendly and helpful relationship can begin and they can feel at home in a safe space.

Chief Executive Colin Glover, who merged three organisations in 1988 to form the London Connection, now has the responsibility to lead the all-age work, and after the redevelopment of the site to settle everyone into the new premises in the old school and cellars of No.6. He has 105 full-time workers, around 200 volunteers and a budget of over £3.5m to administer. Each day 100 young and 150 older people visit the centre, and the staff is divided into groups to help them. There are two day centres, a night centre and an outreach team who work with rough sleepers within a half-mile radius of the church. The multiple needs and the employment/training teams work closely with them. Mick Baker, Director of Client Services, is keeping a close watch on what is provided, and hopes to avoid duplication and streamline what already exists. Accommodation is vital and this is provided at St Martin's House, Clapham, where there are 16 studio flats, but the huge demand for somewhere to live is also addressed by Sarah McLees and the 10 members of the tenancy sustainment team who visit the 500 people who have been found a flat in various parts of London.

Colin is excited by the opportunities of the new organisation and the new building but also hopes that the local community will play a part in assisting those who arrive at St Martin's looking for help:

> Inner cities should feel safe and secure, where residents and visitors do not feel at risk. The challenge to us is to deliver services to the most vulnerable, while managing the impact of our work on our neighbours. We must not be too prescriptive about whom we will work with, but respond to those in a crisis; our role might change, for example we might become more of a sign-posting service.

14

The Academy of
St Martin in the Fields

Alfred Brendel, in the Introduction to Meirion and Susie Harries' splendid book on the Academy, published in 1981, says it took him some years to remember the Academy's full name correctly. 'A group with such an impossible name had either to be dreary, or become a legend. It became the latter.' Over the years there have been several suggestions to change the name but all have been resisted, and today it is a moot point whether people know of the church because of the Academy or vice versa. Because of its concerts and recordings – no day on the radio station Classic FM is complete without its contribution – this ensemble of part-time and pastime players and singers has become world famous. 'Rumour has it,' remarked *The Times* in 1975, 'that the Academy of St Martin in the Fields is nowadays one of the three most famous things about England – the others, in no particular order, are Laura Ashley and Earl Grey.'

John Churchill was appointed Organist and Master of the Music in 1949 and immediately began twice-weekly lunchtime concerts by young professional musicians, but made no secret of the fact that he wanted a permanent orchestra based at the church. The St Martin's Chamber Orchestra was formed but the professional players were unable to give the time commitment needed and the orchestra folded. In 1956 Austen Williams became vicar, and Churchill, with Michael Bowie, one of his ex-pupils, asked him if money could be raised to pay a small group of musicians to play in the church. Two of his colleagues in the London Symphony Orchestra, Simon Streatfeild and Norman Nelson, supported the idea and in the September 1958 issue of the *Review* Austen launched 'An Appeal to All Music-Lovers':

> We have never been able to help the music financially as much as we would like because of our heavy commitments in other fields (social service, overseas work and so on) and since it is clear that the concerts and recitals are going to need a sound backing if we are to go forwards as we would wish, we are launching a special appeal to those who are interested in music and would like it to grow here at St Martin's. John Churchill has the plans – a small professional orchestra is one of them – and we must try to help him.

The Music Committee set to work and raised sufficient funds to begin the venture, approaching Neville Marriner, another member of the LSO, who agreed to lead it. He had experience in chamber music and a detailed knowledge of the baroque repertoire. In the autumn of 1958, at a meeting in a pub near Trafalgar Square, the basic principles which would govern the orchestra were discussed over many pints of bitter, and it was decided to discover and perform some of the many masterpieces which have been forgotten, particularly from the 17th and 18th centuries. There would be 11 string players with harpsichord continuo played by John Churchill. Wind instruments could be added if necessary and there would be no conductor – in true baroque style the group would be led from the first desk of the violins. There would be no full-time players since everyone would be free to work with other ensembles. The group realised it would be difficult to persuade people to take them seriously since there would be no box office nor tickets, just a retiring collection, and the church venue might have suggested an amateur undertaking.

Churchill had no qualms about using St Martin's. 'It is a perfect venue – its position, architecture (contemporary with the music to be played), its vitality, its willingness to accept new ideas and cast its cloak over new groups of people. There could be no other church where the Academy could find so suitable a home.'

What should the new orchestra call itself? A link with the host building was agreed, and eventually it was decided to use the word Academy as throughout Europe in the baroque era Academies were meetings of professional musicians and connoisseurs; their emphasis had been on practice rather than theory, and so musicians would play rather than talk at meetings. There had also been an Academy of Ancient Music established in London in 1710 when a group of professional musicians met on a Friday evening at the *Crown and Anchor* in the Strand. In 1744 they had performed *Messiah* there.

Neville Marriner now began to search for seven players to join John Churchill, Norman Nelson, Simon Streatfeild, Michael Bowie and himself. There would be no star instrumentalists; players had to be of the first-rank and prepared to play for pleasure rather than money. They also had to have the style and sound best suited to baroque music and not be temperamental as a relaxed atmosphere was essential. Eventually rehearsals began with Raymond Keenlyside (violin), Wilfred Simenauer (cello), Kenneth Heath (cello), Malcolm Latchem (violin), Tessa Robbins (violin), Stuart Knussen (double bass) and Anthony Howard (violin).

The first two concerts were held on Sunday evenings in November 1958 with thick fog enveloping London which meant that audiences were small and the double bass player became stuck in a traffic jam. With no rehearsal John Gray stepped in and stayed for 15 years until he emigrated to Australia. The harpsichord was lent by Thomas Goff, the eminent instrument-maker, and the musicians were paid 30 shillings each. Three more concerts followed in church over that winter, the programmes of which were concertos by Vivaldi, Bach, Handel and lesser-known composers such as Manfredini and Albicastro. Soloists were always members – Alexander Murray, the flute soloist in the fourth concert, and Roger Lord, the oboe soloist in the fifth – although a young man, James Galway, once filled in for Murray.

The BBC now offered their first engagement – a half-hour of Handel, Albicastro and Corelli, and a further series of concerts was put on in church the following November. It was not easy to rehearse with the tourists and homeless continually coming in and out and members taking a break would be tapped on the shoulder and asked 'Are you the vicar?' (It is still difficult today because most performers at the music recitals in church are asked 'Say, are you Neville Marinner?') Rehearsals had to be held in the Marriners' drawing room where the cats quickly commandeered the empty violin cases. Proceedings often ended after midnight, but Neville's direction was informal and unobtrusive, consisting of indicating tempo and nuance by his playing.

During 1959 Neville's wife Molly took over the administration of the group, using her kitchen table as a desk – she once remarked that 'A shoe-string would be an exaggeration for what the Academy runs on'. The November concerts were more organised – 'A Survey of the Baroque Concerto'. On 8 December the Academy joined the St Martin's Cantata Choir to give the first performance of the Watkins Shaw edition of *Messiah*. Someone thought there was a bus strike as people were thronging the pavements outside the church, but it was the queue for the concert, which drew a full house. Despite this and despite the fact that the St Martin's Music Committee had begged £1,000 from the Pilgrim Trust, there were now financial problems, so members continued with their other work. They did, however, travel to Dublin to give two concerts in a bitterly cold hall. A paraffin heater was placed behind the second cello's chair, which led him, green and sweating, to retire in the second half overcome by the fumes.

Very soon it was realised that there was not enough work to keep the Academy financially stable, and when the first stereo records were making their appearance in Britain it seemed that the best way forward would be to enter the recording industry. Jimmy Burdett, a BBC producer they had come to know, was asked for help in making an audition tape. For their first (and last) recording made in the church they chose a Handel concerto grosso but had to wait until 2 a.m. for the traffic noise from Trafalgar Square to quieten down. By a stroke of good fortune Neville sent the tape, which had been edited by Burdett, to one of Jimmy's friends, and after a few weeks a single record was offered. L'Oiseau-Lyre, the company making the offer, had been founded in 1932 by Mrs Louise Hanson Dyer, an Australian millionairess, who had trained as a singer but come to France and settled in Paris. A glamorous woman with huge charm and an iron will, she set about promoting music which she loved but felt neglected. Having started by publishing, she then started to illustrate the editions with 78 rpm discs and asked the Decca Record Company to work with her. The Academy's first record was made in 1961 in Conway Hall, Red Lion Square, and the musicians received £5 each for it. The 40-minute programme consisted of rarely heard works by Corelli, Torelli and Locatelli (called the 'ice-cream makers' by the group) together with Handel and Albicastro. The record was a success and *Gramophone* said that it was 'played with precision, care, consummate musicianship, and with more sense of style than all the other chamber orchestras in Europe put together'.

55 *Sir Neville Marriner, who in 1958 with John Churchill and others founded the world-famous Academy of St Martin in the Fields. He was their first Director.*

Mrs Dyer was so pleased that she asked the Academy to make seven more recordings of 18th-century music including Bach, Handel, Vivaldi and Telemann. She did not regard her recordings as profit-making ventures, gave the performers only two sessions to record, and no royalties were paid. It soon became a joke amongst members that she was obviously having to sell a sheep back home to pay for each recording – perhaps appropriate as a cartoon of the Academy shows them playing in a field. Mrs Dyer died in 1962 and Dr Hanson took over the company. When he died a few years later the Academy moved to Argo Records whose Managing Director, Harley Usill, was a friend of Neville. Early in 1965 a recording of Handel's oboe concertos with Roger Lord as soloist was produced by Michael Bremner, who was to stay with the Academy for the next ten years.

The *Gramophone* wrote, 'If Handel had always been played like this, he would never have got the reputation, still held in some circles, of being a sanctimonious old stooge.' By 1968 there were 25 records on the market, and in 1981 this had risen to 250. Today it is double that number, ranging from baroque and classical to the romantic and 20th-century. A complete discography is available to buy from the orchestra's office.

Molly Marriner's informal and unpaid management made for a family atmosphere where friends could make music together at rehearsals before being given a meal, which often had to be prepared between balancing the books and booking halls. If regular players were unavailable she had a list of people willing to play. Her official title of Secretary arrived when headed notepaper was needed and it was at this time that the hyphens of the Academy's name were dropped. Later Neville wrote in the *Review*, 'The players of the group regard the Academy as their escape from conductors and a chance to play music for enjoyment. They play with many different organisations from symphony orchestras to string quartets. We do hope that all those who wanted more music in the Church in 1958 and who raised not only the money but the interest, feel proud of the contribution they originated to the musical life of this country.'

The college choirs of Cambridge had close links with Argo, so in 1964 the Academy recorded a recital of Purcell's 'Music for the Chapel Royal' with the choir of St John's College under the direction of Dr George Guest, followed by a set of Haydn's last six Masses, written *c.*1800, which were taken as a gift for the Pope when the Prime Minister, Edward Heath, visited him in Rome in 1972. Orchestra and choir got on very well and the Academy were invited to record with the choir of King's College under the direction of Sir David Willcocks. This was a particular pleasure to Neville since his son was one of the choirboys. (He had achieved fame at his interview when Sir David asked, 'And how old are you, Andrew?' 'Eight, sir. How old are you?')[1] To the Academy, used to being led from the front desk, being conducted by the Choir's Director was a new experience, but the collaboration worked well and 12 records were made between 1965 and 1974. The echo and the sub-zero temperature of the Chapel were a challenge, and Dame Janet Baker told Meirion and Susie Harries that she remembered Dietrich Fischer-Dieskau muffled in his sturdiest overcoat, his breath coming in blue clouds, but there was a fantastic feeling of joyousness as a group. 'The Academy had an enthusiasm one didn't often find among professional orchestras, the choir was full of young singers eager to enter the profession; you'd hear this marvellous obbligato playing starting up behind you in this superb building – and it would all take off like a jet aeroplane.'[2] Continuo players rarely travelled to King's as the part was usually taken by organ scholars like Andrew Davis and Simon Preston.

Kenwood House was the setting for the Academy's first appearance on television when in 1965 they performed Vivaldi's *The Four Seasons* with Alan Loveday as soloist, and soon afterwards they donned wigs, beards and frock coats to appear in a film about Wagner. They did their first two Promenade Concerts in the same year, often hurrying away at the end to the Dartington Summer School of Music. This Hall in Devon with its beautiful grounds became another spiritual home for the orchestra, complementing the urban St Martin's. It was here that Neville made some of his first appearances as a conductor, taking the Summer School choir and the orchestra through Purcell, Pergolesi, Vivaldi, Mozart, Schubert and Britten. The Harries' book sums up the atmosphere:

> Rossini's String Sonata in C, written by the youthful composer with a comically showy part for the double bass, regularly brought the house down; Richard Strauss's 'Metamorphosen' reduced the audience to tears; and the Academy's playing of Tippett's 'Fantasia Concertante on a Theme of Corelli' moved John Amis to walk, overcome with emotion, out of the rehearsal room and into a plate-glass window.[3]

John Churchill, having completed 19 years as Master of the Music at St Martin's and given the church excellent services, concerts and broadcasts, was appointed Professor of Music at Carleton University in Ottawa. In 1967 he left for Canada. Shortly afterwards Simon Streatfeild and Norman Nelson also emigrated to that country leaving a large gap in the Academy. Alan Loveday, an expert on the baroque style in violin playing, Carmel Kaine and Anthony Jenkins were among those who joined over the next few months. An increasing number of players became involved, and among them was Nicholas Kraemer, who had been doing a summer job in the Dartington kitchens and was to become one of the regular continuo players in the next decade.

Thanks to broadcasts and recordings, the Academy had so far been heard rather than seen, but this was changed by five highly successful concerts in 12 months on the South Bank. Also in 1969 their work began to broaden as they moved into the standard chamber orchestral repertoire of the 19th and 20th centuries. Clarity and precision remained, and Neville remarked that their playing 'is designed to sound like a wrist-watch as compared to an alarm clock – clean, clear and focused'.

The mountain of paperwork and the overflowing box files of music in the Marriners' flat now suggested that paid secretarial help was needed to help Molly, who wrote in the *Review*, 'The Academy's luck worked again. They found in Sylvia Holford a manager who is not only highly efficient, extremely hard-working and devoted, but an excellent musician as well.' As a pianist she had played at one of Churchill's lunchtime concerts in St Martin's. Molly still looked after the music, but the Academy's office now moved to Sylvia's flat in Aberdare Gardens where behind her desk was written 'Lord, Give Me Patience … But Hurry.'

Since then the majority of the orchestra's appearances have been abroad, and players have had to spend months touring all over the world. Over the years the Academy has attracted Canadian, New Zealand, Australian, Czech, Russian and Japanese musicians, and their often hilarious adventures are described in the Harries' book.[4] Loading the members on to a plane was comparatively easy, but taking the instruments on board was a nightmare. They could not be hand luggage, but nor could they face baggage handlers and the sub-zero temperatures of the hold, so they had to have a seat each, although one air line decreed that two cellos needed three seats. One ticket clerk entered them as Mr and Mrs Cello, but the stewardess refused to serve them lunch, much to the consternation of greedy Academy members.

For ten years the Academy had enjoyed having no conductor but now things had to change, even though it might jeopardise the democratic, family atmosphere of the group. The repertoire had to be extended beyond the chamber range, and Alan Loveday pointed out that it was impossible to direct some of the rhythmically more complex chamber works from the front desk by 'the nodding and smiling technique'. Neville had now to take up the baton, which reassured everyone because it meant a stranger would not be called in. But Neville noticed that his friends never hesitated to criticise his performance: 'They tell you if they don't like something, and somewhat pungently too.' It led to the orchestra tackling small classical symphonies with the help of woodwind, trumpets and timpani, all the more reason for a conductor, but Neville still seemed reluctant: 'You could probably do these pieces without a conductor, if you had enough rehearsal time, by discussion and with practice – but no one would ever give you the time to make this kind of experiment.'

A new recording company, Phonogram, now signed a contract with the Academy, although Argo continued their association, and so the number of records doubled. Erik Smith, a close friend of Neville, who had been with him at Pierre Monteux's summer school for conductors in Maine, was the architect of the Academy's career on the Philips label, and his first large-scale project with them was 'The Rise of the Symphony', a set of four records issued in 1971. It became clear from these that there was a place for them in the symphonic field, and over the next ten years the orchestra was to complete the full cycle of Mozart symphonies, make inroads into those of Haydn, and add to the First and Second symphonies of Beethoven a recording of his Fourth which was described in *Records & Recordings* as 'coming uncomfortably close to exuding an aura of perfection'.

Another project initiated by Erik Smith was asking Alfred Brendel to record with the Academy the Mozart piano concertos, which made Roger Covell in the *Sydney Morning Herald* comment, 'There may be a better combination of creative genius and performing talent than Mozart, Brendel and Marriner, but at the moment I can't think of it.' Concerts followed and in 1974 they appeared in two films for the TV programme *Aquarius* produced by Humphrey Burton, who wanted to show how musicians and technicians work together to make a record.

56 *The Academy playing the Mozart Requiem in church, December 1958.*

Although the core of the Academy remained with the 15 string players plus harpsichord, by the early 1980s there were over sixty freelance musicians for Sylvia Holford to call upon. A Chamber Ensemble was formed to play string trios, quintets, sextets and octets. Wind and brass could be added if required. With ensembles now ranging from three to sixty, consistency of style was ensured by careful editing and always having a significant proportion of key players.

The Academy signed a second five-year contract with Philips in 1975 but this time Neville signed a separate contract to conduct and record with symphony orchestras associated with Philips. Over the next three years he came to limit his work with the Academy to recordings of the larger repertoire involving 35 or more players. Iona Brown, a member of the Academy since the mid-1960s and their leader on several European tours, was appointed Director. She was also the Artistic Director of the Norwegian Chamber Orchestra. One critic pointed out that if the United Kingdom could have a lady Prime Minister the Academy could be directed by a lady, especially such a good violinist. In 1986 she was appointed OBE but, sadly, cancer struck her down in her early 60s and she died on 5 June 2004. *The Times* obituary said that her musicianship and zeal were second to none, and 'Under her charismatic leadership the Academy … was able to maintain its position as the leading alternative to the increasingly popular period performance movement.'[5]

It had been difficult to persuade English choirs to accompany the Academy on their various tours. In 1975 Sylvia suggested that they should have their own choir, and the Academy Chorus was born. Laszlo Heltay, who had come to England after the 1956 Hungarian Uprising, agreed to be chorus master, and the search began for 72 singers for the following January's tour. Like the orchestra, the Chorus was not full-time but had a nucleus of regulars. Today it is still made up of lawyers, business people, doctors, students and men and women from all walks of life. They have to be experienced singers with good sight-reading ability, and there are no fees paid although a contribution to travelling expenses is given. Johan Duijck is now the Chorus Director.

The 1975 tour of Germany with the Bach B Minor Mass was a huge success and Hans Ulrich Schmid, who had invited them, described it as 'a sensation, unforgettable, one of my most treasured memories'.[6] It was recorded two years later for Philips with Dame Janet Baker as one of the soloists. An earlier recording – of Handel's *Messiah* – sold 250,000 in three years. Further tours followed, and the Rev. Christopher Walker, for four years a curate at St Martin's, was one of the regular baritones. On the visit to Brussels he had the hotel's largest room, known as 'The Vestry,' and all the social gatherings took place in it.

Recent engagements for the Chorus have included the John Tavener tribute season in the Royal Festival Hall under Richard Hickox, Bach's B Minor Mass in the Rheingau Festival with Ian Watson, and a performance of Haydn's *The Creation* with Neville Marriner in Santiago de Compostela's Cathedral. Their many acclaimed recordings include Mozart's C Minor Mass with Dame Kiri Te Kanawa, Haydn's oratorios and Mendelssohn's *Elijah* with Thomas Allen. The Chorus's regular appearances with Paco Pena in his Missa Flamenca all over Europe, including the Expo Festival in Seville in 1992, were instrumental in winning the Academy its Queen's Award for Export Achievement, the first orchestra to be so honoured.

It took the Academy 21 years to make its first appearance in America although by then every major classical music channel had been playing their records, sometimes for hours at a time. In December 1977 the New York Classical Music radio station took a listeners poll to hear their preference for world orchestras, and the Academy came second after the Chicago Symphony Orchestra, and ahead of the Boston Symphony, the Berlin Philharmonic and the great London orchestras! Once again the name foxed listeners and a San Francisco fan who enjoyed listening while driving wrote to the local newspaper:

> Why does Marriner conduct in the fields? What kind of sadist is he? Dragging those kids and their heavy instruments outside in that God-awful English weather and expecting them to play their hearts out. I must confess that the boys and girls of Saint Martin's do a bang-up job, but the sound of that chill wind roaring off the heath in the background sends shivers up and down my steering-column.'[7]

57 *The Academy playing in the Fields. Cartoon by Kenneth Heath, 1978.*

'Thought we'd like to make you feel at home.'

Conductorless chamber orchestras were unfamiliar in the United States, and reviewers had to explain Iona's role. Neville was already known as a conductor because of his association with the Los Angeles Chamber Orchestra and his appearances at prestigious festivals like Tanglewood. In 1979 he became Music Director of the Minnesota Orchestra based in Minneapolis. A three-week tour took place in 1980, and since then there have been one or two visits to America every year. Members now feel at home in New York, Palm Beach, Sarasota, Boston and Salt Lake City. The American Friends of the Academy was re-launched in April 1999 and its Foundation supports the concerts in the USA, and provides educational opportunities for promising young musicians.

Susie Marriner, daughter of Neville and Molly, was married to Meirion Harries in St Martin's by Austen Williams on 24 November 1979. They were living in Hong Kong at the time, and two years later they published *The Academy of St Martin in the Fields*.

The Academy now offers a wide range of educational workshops and music projects to schools and community groups in Great Britain which vary from one day to several months. *The Green Man*, a large-scale venture for schools in Essex, culminated in an open-air concert featuring Zoe Ball and Elvis Costello. *Rivers* was based on Sally Beamish's Cello Concerto, and *The Soldier's Tale* was a music drama created by students inspired by the themes and images of Stravinsky's *Soldier's Tale*. The homeless work at St Martin's has benefited from a series of music workshops.

In September 1973 the links between church and Academy were strengthened when the first ever Academy Festival was held in St Martin's, and three years later Christopher Walker, curate and Chorus member, arranged a series of concerts to mark the 250th anniversary of the present building and to launch the Organ Fund Appeal. In 1978 the church and orchestra joined in a commemorative concert at which a Fund in memory of Kenneth Heath, one of the Academy's earliest members and their principal cellist for almost 19 years, was launched. The following year Neville Marriner and Austen Williams went together to Buckingham Palace to receive a CBE and CVO respectively. In 1980 the Academy celebrated its 21st birthday with a festival in the church at the end of July which was a happy and memorable week that began with Neville conducting the expanded Academy in Handel's *Firework Music* and ended with the Chorus, under Laszlo Heltay, and orchestra performing the B Minor Mass. For the other concerts the stage was held by the band of sixteen.

The orchestra now divides its time between international tours, education and outreach work, the recording studio and concerts. Today the Academy has three principal partners: Sir Neville Marriner, the Life President who was knighted in 1984, Kenneth Sillito, the Artistic Director and Director of the Chamber Ensemble, and Murray Perahia, the Principal Guest Conductor. The Academy regularly tours the USA, Europe, the Far East and South America, and in June 1997 was invited to Hong Kong to play for the official handover celebrations, which included two performances of Beethoven's Ninth Symphony with Sir Neville conducting. The repertoire continues to broaden, and there have been world premieres of works by Sally Beamish, including her Cello Concerto performed with Robert Cohen, and by Alec Roth – *The Departure of the Queen of Sheba.*

Some of the most recent of the Academy's 500 recordings include Murray Perahia's highly acclaimed *Plays Bach,* Joshua Bell's *Romance for the Violin,* Bernard Stevens' *Chamber Works,* Opera Rara's *Carlo di Borgogna* and the Chamber Ensemble's *Schubert Trout Quintet.* Releases in 2005 include Murray Perahia's Beethoven Quartet no.12 in E-flat Major for Strings, op.127 and Sir Neville Marriner and Andrew Marriner (clarinet) playing Mozart's Clarinet Concerto in A, K622.

Honours have been heaped on the Academy over the years: it has received eight Edisons, the Canadian Grand Prix and many gold discs, 13 for the soundtrack of Milos Forman's film *Amadeus.* Their soundtrack for *The English Patient* won an Oscar for Best Sound. Unlike many major British orchestras it receives no direct government subsidy and relies on its artistic integrity and commercial initiative to survive financially. Fortunately it does receive grants from the Lottery and other foundations which enables it to continue its developmental and educational work, including music workshops for the homeless in the centre and concerts in the church.

There is a deep, symbiotic relationship between church and Academy with both appreciating one another. The congregation are immensely proud of the Academy, even if they might not go as far as an American who called it 'St Marriner's in the Fields'.

15

Vicars of St Martin-in-the-Fields
1275-2005

A document of Henry III's reign, dating from around 1250, mentions 'Williams', Vicar of the Church of St Martin of Charing, but we know nothing about him. John de Hocelive was presented to Richard, the Bishop of London by Sir William Bouquer or Bouchiere, a scholar of the monastery of Westminster, to be the vicar in 1275. The Abbey's records say that Pope Alexander IV agreed to the appointment, and placed patronage in the Abbey's hands.

Listed below are all the incumbents since then, together with some of their other appointments. Nearly all of them held other posts in the Church whilst at St Martin's until the 1830s, when pluralities were forbidden by law. A curate would be paid a paltry sum to take services in the absence of the vicar. At that time it was estimated that a third of the clergy held two incumbencies and some had a third or fourth, but all this was changed by Acts of Parliament brought forward by the Ecclesiastical Commission. Also, until then prebendaries and canons of cathedrals received a stipend, and nearly all of them held incumbencies as well. Today only residentiary canons are paid.

The Civil War, and the Commonwealth period which followed it, were testing times for parishes of the Established Church. Dr William Bray had been inducted as vicar in 1632 and did not die until 1642 when the King had lost control of London. The journal of the House of Commons, 1 December 1642, ordered that the monies of the living of St Martin's be placed in the hands of Sir John Hippisley, S.H.Vane and Messrs Trenchard and Oldworth, who with it should appoint Dr J. Wilcop as Lecturer 'to preach there every Lord's Day in the forenoon'. This seems to have been a temporary measure. Shortly afterwards the Bishop of London was asked to present a Mr Strickland to the benefice, but instead Daniel Cawdry was inducted.

A board with these names can be found on the wall of the south gallery stairs. Some of the earlier dates are tentative – obscured by the mists of time.

1275   John de Hocelive.
1352   John de Kerseye.
1363   Thomas Skyn.
1383   John Atwater.
1383   William Foucher.

1384   John Jakes.
1384   Simon Lambel, died 1390.
1390   John Wymbledon.
1393   Nicholas Sprotte.
1393   John Larke.
1394   John Martyn.
1400   John Loudham.
1406   John Stokes.
1420   John Staynton, died 1420.
1425   Ralph Webbe.
1430   Thomas Laurence.
1433   Dionysius Kyrban.
1434   Richard Jankyn.
1456   Richard Valens.
1487   Robert Everard.
1515   William Sore.
1517   Peter Whalley.
1521   Simon Michel.
1522   William Skinner, MA, buried in the church 8 September 1538.
1538   Edmond Weston, Canon of Westminster,1542.
1539   Robert Beste. Committed to Newgate Prison for singing the Litany in English.
1554   Thomas Wells, buried in the church 25 January 1565.
1565   Robert Beste, reinstated by Queen Elizabeth. Buried in the church, 14 January 1572.
1572   William Wells, domestic Chaplain to Queen Elizabeth.
1574   Thomas Langhorne.
1575   Will Ireland.
1577   Christopher Hayward.
1588   William Fisher, MA, DD
1591   Thomas Knight.
1602   Thomas Mountforde, BD, DD, Canon of Westminster,1578, Prebendary of St Paul's, 1597.
1632   William Bray, BD, Prebendary of Canterbury, 1638. Died 1642.
1643   J. Wincop, DD
1644   Daniel Cawdry.
1650   Gabriell Sangar.
1661   Nathaniel Hardy, MA, DD, born 1618. As a City incumbent (St Dionyse, Back Church) went in 1660 with City deputation to the Hague to pay homage to Charles II and preached before him. Also Dean of Rochester(1660) and Archdeacon of Lewes (1667). Buried in St Martin's, 9 June 1670.
1670   Thomas Lamplugh, MA, DD, Principal of St Alban's Hall, Oxford, 1664, also Dean of Rochester (1672) and Archdeacon of Middlesex and Prebendary of Worcester. 1676 Bishop of Exeter. 1688 Archbishop of York. Died 1691.

1676   William Lloyd, MA, BD, DD, born 1626.1680 Bishop of St Asaph.1688 imprisoned in the Tower by James II for protesting against the King's Declaration. Tried in Westminster Hall and acquitted. King William made him Lord Almoner. 1692 Bishop of Lichfield and Coventry. 1699 Bishop of Worcester. Died 1717.

1680   Thomas Tenison, MA, DD, born 1636. Chaplain to Charles II, also Archdeacon of London. 1691 Bishop of Lincoln. 1694 Archbishop of Canterbury. Died 1715.

1692   William Lancaster, DD, appointed by Bishop of London, but King William claimed patronage and courts upheld his claim to appoint:

1693   Nicholas Gouge, MA, DD, Fellow of Catherine Hall, Cambridge. Died 1694.

1694   William Lancaster, MA, BD, DD. Also Archdeacon of Middlesex(1705) and Provost of Queen's College, Oxford. Chancellor of Oxford University. Died 1717 and buried in St Martin's.

1716   Thomas Green, MA, DD. Born1658. 1698 Master of Corpus Christi College, Cambridge. 1699 Vice Chancellor of Cambridge University. 1708 Archdeacon of Canterbury. 1721 Bishop of Norwich. 1723 Bishop of Ely. Died 1738.

1723   Zachariah Pearce, MA, DD. Born 1690. Also Dean of Winchester (1739), Bishop of Bangor (1748). In 1756 left St Martin's to be Bishop of Rochester. Died 1774.

1756   Erasmus Saunders, MA, BD, DD. 1751 Canon of Windsor, also Prebendary of Rochester (1756) and Vicar of Mapiscombe (1757). Died 1775.

1776   Anthony Hamilton, MA, DD. Born 1738. Also Archdeacon of Colchester (1775-1812) and Rector of Hadham, Herts (1775-1812) where he died in 1812.

1812   Joseph Holden Pott, MA. Born 1759. Also Archdeacon of London until 1842. Left St Martin's to be Vicar of Kensington and Archdeacon of Middlesex (1824) then Chancellor and Prebendary of Exeter (1826). Died 1847.

1824   George Richards, MA, DD. Retired 1834. Died 1837.

1834   Sir Henry Robert Dukinfield, Bart. MA. Also Prebendary of Salisbury. Retired 1848. Died 1858.

1848   Henry Mackenzie, MA, DD. Born 1806. Left to be Rector of Tydd St Mary, then in 1866-70 Rector of South Collingham, then 1870 Archdeacon and Suffragan Bishop of Nottingham. Died 1878.

1855   William Gilson Humphry, MA, BD. Fellow of Trinity College, Cambridge. Prebendary of St Paul's. Died in the vicarage, 1886.

1886   John Frederick Kitto, MA. 1875 Rector of St Mary, Whitechapel. 1881 Rector of Stepney. Hon. Chaplain to Queen Victoria and King Edward VII. Prebendary of St Paul's. Died 1903.

1903   Leonard Edmund Shelford, MA. 1866 Vicar of St Matthew, Upper Clapton. 1886 Rector of St Mary, Stoke Newington. Prebendary of St Paul's. Died 1914.

1914   Hugh Richard Lawrie Sheppard, CH, DD, MA. Born 1880.1909-10 Head of Oxford House, Bethnal Green. 1929-31 Dean of Canterbury. 1934 Residentiary Canon of St Paul's. Hon. Chaplain to King George V. Died 1937.

1927   William Patrick Glyn McCormick, DSO, MA. 1914-18 Chaplain to the Forces. 1919 Vicar of Croydon. Hon. Chaplain to George V, Edward VIII and George VI. Died 1940.

1941   Eric Stephen Loveday, MA. Born 1905. Rector, St Peter, Bristol. Died 1947.

1948   Lewis Mervyn Charles-Edwards.1956-70 Bishop of Worcester.

1956   Sidney Austen Williams, CVO, MA. Born 1912. 1946 Sec. Toc H and Hon. Curate St Martin's. Prebendary of St Paul's. 1961 Chaplain to Queen Elizabeth II. Died 2001.

1985   Geoffrey Harold Brown, MA. Born 1930.1973-85 Team Rector, St Mary and St James, Grimsby. Canon and Preb. of Lincoln.

1995   Nicholas Roderick Holtam, MA, BD, AKC. Born 1954. 1988-95 Vicar of Christ Church and St John with St Luke, Isle of Dogs.

Notes

CHAPTER 1 – WHO WAS SAINT MARTIN?

1   Christopher Donaldson, *Martin of Tours*, 1980.

CHAPTER 2 – THE FIRST TWO CHURCHES

1   John McMaster, *A Short History of St Martin-in-the-Fields*, 1916, p.6.
2   LCC, *Survey of London*, Vol. XX, 1979, p.115.
3   McMaster, *op. cit.*, p.26.
4   F.L. Cross, *Oxford Dictionary of the Christian Church*,1957, p.1016.
5   At this time the New Year began on 25 March.
6   McMaster, *op. cit.*, p 47.
7   LCC, *Survey of London*, Vol. XX, p.112.
8   *Ibid.*, Vol. XX, p.116.
9   McMaster, *op. cit.*, p.179.
10 Christopher Hibbert, *Cavaliers and Roundheads*, 1993, pp.86-7.
11 McMaster, *op. cit.*, p.50.
12 Reginald Colby, *Mayfair. A Town within London*, 1966, pp.66-9.
13 Cross, *op. cit.*, p.557.
14 McMaster, *op. cit.*, p.52.
15 *Ibid.*, p.57.

CHAPTER 3 – PRESENT BUILDING

1   John McMaster, *A Short History of St Martin-in-the-Fields*, 1916, p.72.
2   *Ibid.*, pp.119-33.
3   *Ibid.*, p.76.
4   Bryan Little, *The Life and Work of James Gibbs*, 1954, p.75.
5   Nikolaus Pevsner, *The Buildings of England*, Vol.1, 1957, p.264.
6   McMaster, *op. cit.*, p.82.
7   Drummond chose this area because it was the home of many Scottish families who had travelled south with King James I (and VI of Scotland). The bank moved to its present site south of Trafalgar Square in 1760, and today's building dates from 1877.
8   I am grateful to Sandra Sudak, Archivist of the Episcopal Diocese of Eastern Massachusetts for this information from Mary Kent Davey Babcock's *Historical Sketches of the Colonial Period*, 1723-1775, Christ Church, (Old North) Boston.
9   McMaster, *op. cit.*, p.85.
10 *Ibid.*, p.84.
11 Jenny Uglow, *Hogarth, A Life and a World*, 1997, pp.161-2.
12 McMaster, *op. cit.*, 1916, p.88.
13 LCC, *Survey of London*, Vol. XX, p.10.
14 Uglow, *op. cit.*, 1997, p.358.
15 LCC, *Survey of London*, Vol. XX, p.108.

16   George Vertue, *The Note-books*, Walpole Society, xxx,1934.
17   Ian McIntyre, *Joshua Reynolds*, 2003, pp.30-1.
18   *The Gentleman's Magazine*, 16 September 1801.
19   *The Times*, 17 September 1801, p.2.
20   The overspill cemetery at Camden, opened in the late 18th century, is now a garden opposite All Saints church. One interesting memorial in it, erected in 1880, is that of Charles Dibdin, who wrote 900 songs including 'Tom Bowling' and many sea shanties.
21   Westminster City Archives, St Martin's Parish Records, F 6102.
22   John McMaster, *op. cit.*, 1916, pp.101-2.
23   Horace Mann, *Report on Religious Worship*, 1851.
24   Weinreb and Hibbert (eds), *The London Encyclopaedia*, 1983 p.453.
25   M. and J. Garrod, *North from Charing Cross*, Westminster City Archives, p.3.
26   *The Illustrated London News*, 24 June 1871, pp.619-20.
27   Carolyn Scott, *Betwixt Heaven and Charing Cross*, 1971, p.27-30.
28   McMaster, *op. cit.*, p.105.
29   *Ibid.*, p.107.
30   Booth's Diary No. B244, 27 May 1898.
31   Vicar Kitto's Visiting Book, No. 1831/9, Westminster City Archives.
32   McMaster, *op. cit.*, 1916, p.110.
33   George Lansbury, *My Life*, 1928, pp.37-8.
34   The *Daily News and Leader*, 7 April 1914.
35   McMaster, *op. cit.*, p.112.

CHAPTER 4 – DICK AND PAT
1   R.J. Northcott, *Pat McCormick, A Man's Life*, 1941, p.23.
2   Carolyn Scott, *Dick Sheppard*, 1977, p 41.
3   *Ibid.*, p.63.
4   *Ibid.*, p.68.
5   *Messenger*, June 1911.
6   *Ibid.*, December 1914.
7   *St Martin's Review*, November 1933, p.555.
8   William Purcell, *Woodbine Willie*, 1962, p.104.
9   *Ibid.*, p.222.
10   St Martin's Records, 1831/255, Westminster City Archives.
11   Scott, *op. cit.*, p.166.
12   *Ibid.*, p.235.
13   *St Martin's Review*, November 1927.
14   Northcott, *op. cit.*, p.23.
15   Letter in the possession of Patricia Frank, daughter of Pat McCormick, and quoted by gracious permission of HM Queen Elizabeth II.
16   Letter in the possession of Patricia Frank, daughter of Pat McCormick, and quoted by gracious permission of HM Queen Elizabeth II.
17   Canon McCormick to the Duke of Windsor, Royal Archives DW/3251, and quoted by gracious permission of HM Queen Elizabeth II.
18   Letter in possession of Patricia Frank, quoted by gracious permission of HM Queen Elizabeth II.
19   Philip Ziegler, *King Edward VIII*, 1990, p.363.

CHAPTER 5 – SIXTY CHANGEFUL YEARS
1   Vera Brittain, *The Story of St Martin's*, 1951, p.33.
2   R.S. Lee in *St Martin's Review*, August 1947.
3   George Fearon, *You owe me 5 Farthins*, 1961, p.77.
4   *Review*, April 1951.
5   Fearon, *op. cit.*, p.33.
6   Fearon, *op. cit.*, p 70.

7   Letter to the author, 12 November 2003.
8   Letter to the author, 26 October 2003.
9   *Review*, Oct/Nov 2002.
10 *Review*, Winter 2003/4.
11 The other parishes were St Botolph, Aldgate, St James, Piccadilly, St Mary-le-Bow, and St Marylebone. The author has detailed documentation of the meetings.
12 *Friends Newsletter*, November 1996, p.3.

CHAPTER 6 – THE PARISH: PEOPLE

1   Edward Carpenter, *Cantuar. The Archbishops in their Office*, 1971, p.229.
2   *Ibid.*, p.239.
3   *Ibid.*, p.240.
4   Gibbs, *Book of Architecture*, Plates 29/30.
5   *Ibid.*, p.viii.
6   Bryan Little, *James Gibbs*, 1955, p.175.
7   John McMaster, *A Short History of St Martin-in-the-Fields*, 1916, p.208.
8   *Ibid.*, p.116.
9   Carolyn Scott, *Dick Sheppard*, 1977, p.68.
10 R. Ellis Roberts, *H.R.L. Sheppard, Life and Letters*, 1942, p.132.
11 J.R. Birch, *Limehouse through Five Centuries*, 1930, p.119.
12 Rev. Paul Lau's Report to the Chinese Congregation, 2003.

CHAPTER 7 – THE PARISH: PLACES

1   The statute 7 George IV Chapter 77 authorises a row of buildings to be constructed for school, Vestry Hall and residence.
2   The Grant contains a reverter provision in favour of the Crown Estate which will be effective if there is a breach of obligation by the Church. The owner is responsible for repairs and painting.
3   LCC, *Survey of London*, Vol XX. p.55.
4   David Avery, *The Early History of St Martin-in-the-Fields Almshouses, 1597-1818*, 1989, p.3.
5   John McMaster, *A Short History of St Martin-in-the-Fields*, 1916, p.277.
6   Avery, *op. cit.*, p.11.
7   *Ibid.*, p.278.
8   *Ibid.*, p.20.
9   *Ibid.*, p.20.
10 McMaster, *op. cit.*, p.282.
11 Nikolaus Pevsner, *The Buildings of London*, Vol. 1, 1957, p.435.
12 Elizabeth and Wayland Young, *London's Churches*, 1986, pp.115-16.
13 Weinreb and Hibbert (eds), *The London Encyclopaedia*, 1983, p.137.
14 Pevsner, *op. cit.*, p.473.

CHAPTER 8 – SCHOOLS

1   Arthur Compton-Rickett, *A History of English Literature*, 1953, p.147.
2   Edward Carpenter, *A House of Kings*, 1966, p.162.
3   John McMaster, *A Short History of St Martin-in-the-Fields*, 1916, p.263.
4   *Ibid.*, p.269.
5   Charles Booth's Diary, B244. 27 May 1898.
6   St Martin's Records, 1831/246, Westminster City Archives.
7   *Ragged School Times*, 1849, p.114.

CHAPTER 9 – ORGANS AND ORGANISTS

1   Andrew Freeman, 'The Organs and Organists of St. Martin-in-the-Fields, London' in *The Organ*, July 1921, p.2.
2   *Ibid.*, pp.6-9. Freeman discusses at length the various theories of the post-Restoration organ. There is not space here to rehearse them.

3   John McMaster, *A Short History of St Martin-in-the-Fields*, 1916, p.155.
4   Paul Stubbings, 'The Organs of St Martin-in-the-Fields', unpub. paper.
5   Taken from Walker's specification, 1990.
6   Friends' Newsletter, November 2000, pp.16-21.
7   *The New Grove Dictionary of Music and Musicians*, Vol. 7, 1980, p.352.
8   *Ibid.*, Vol. 20, p.331.
9   *Ibid.*, Vol. 9, p.858.
10 *Ibid.*, Vol. 4, p.709.
11 *Ibid.*, Vol. 20, p.184.
12 *Ibid.*, Vol. 2, pp.662-3.
13 *Ibid.*, Vol. 17, p.234.
14 *The Times*, 21 April 1959.

CHAPTER 11 – ST MARTIN'S POSSESSIONS
1   Ronald Keay in Friends' Newsletter, November 1997, p.10.
2   Alison Plowden, *Caroline and Charlotte*, 1989, pp.87-203.
3   Stanley Weintraub, *Victoria, Biography of a Queen*, 1986, pp.55-6.
4   John McMaster, *A Short History of St Martin-in-the-Fields*, 1916, p.70.
5   LCC, *Survey of London*, Vol. XX, 1940, pp.30-54.
6   McMaster, *op.cit.*, p.139.
7   David Hardwick in Friends' Newsletter, November 1999.

CHAPTER 12 – CHURCHWARDENS AND LAY OFFICIALS
1   John McMaster, *A Short History of St Martin-in-the-Fields*, 1916, p.187.
2   *Ibid.*, pp.207-8.
3   *Ibid.*, p.246.
4   R. Ellis Roberts, *H.R.L.Sheppard, Life and Letters*, 1942, p.119.

CHAPTER 13 – THE LEAST, THE LAST AND THE LOST
1   A.L. Rowse, *The England of Elizabeth*, 1950, pp.399-400.
2   LCC, *Survey of London*, Vol. XX, 1940.
3   Margaret Garrod, 'A Missing Ancestor?', Westminster City Archives.
4   St Martin's Settlement Examinations F5051, p.389, Westminster City Archives.
5   Overseers' Minutes, 1819-1834, F2077, Westminster City Archives.
6   The *Daily Graphic*, 14 December 1895.
7   Charles Booth's Diary B244. 27 May 1898.
8   R.J. Northcott, *Dick Sheppard and St. Martin's*, 1937, p.40.
9   *St Martin's Review*, June 1933, p.277.
10 Carolyn Scott, *Betwixt Heaven and Charing Cross*, 1971, p.74.
11 *Ibid.*, pp.98-101.
12 *Ibid.*, p.72.
13 Friends' Newsletter, November 1974, p.4.
14 *Ibid.*, p.5.
15 *Ibid.*, p.6.
16 *Ibid.*, November 1979, p.6.
17 Scott, *op. cit.*, pp.75-82.

CHAPTER 14 – THE ACADEMY OF ST MARTIN IN THE FIELDS
1   Meirion and Susie Harries, *The Academy of St Martin in the Fields*, 1981, pp.47-8.
2   *Ibid.*, p.51.
3   *Ibid.*, p.62.
4   *Ibid*, pp.117-18.
5   *The Times*, 14 June 2004.
6   Harries, *op. cit.*, p.182.
7   *Ibid.*, p.210.

Bibliography

Anon., *H.R.L. Sheppard* (1937)

Avery, David, *The Early History of St Martin-in-the-Fields Almshouses* (1989)

Binder, Pearl, *The Pearlies* (1975)

Bradley, Simon and Pevsner, Nikolaus, *The Buildings of England, London 6: Westminster* (2003)

Brittain, Vera, *The Story of St Martin's* (1951)

Carpenter, Edward, *Thomas Tenison, His Life and Times* (1948)

Carpenter, Edward, *A House of Kings* (1966)

Carpenter, Edward, *Cantuar. The Archbishops in their Office* (1971)

Colby, Reginald, *Mayfair. A Town within London* (1966)

Donaldson, Christopher, *Martin of Tours* (1980)

Ellis Roberts, R., *H.R.L. Sheppard, Life and Letters* (1942)

Esdaile, Katharine A., *St Martin in the Fields, New and Old* (1944)

Fearon, George, *You Owe me 5 Farthins* (1961)

Garrod, Margaret, *A Missing Ancestor?*, Westminster City Archives

Gater, George and Godfrey, W., *Survey of London*, Vol XX, London County Council (1940)

Hackman, Harvey, *Wate's Book of London Churchyards*, Collins, (1981)

Harries, Meirion and Susie, *The Academy of St Martin in the Fields* (1981)

Johnson, Malcolm, *Bustling Intermeddler? The Life and Work of Charles James Blomfield* (2001)

Joseph, Adam, *King of the Pearly Kings*, Cockney Museum

Kitto, John V. (ed.), *St Martin-in-the-Fields, Accounts of the Churchwardens, 1525-1603* (1901)

Little, Bryan, *The Life and Work of James Gibbs, 1682-1754* (1955)

McMaster, John, *St Martin-in-the-Fields* (1916)

Northcott, R.J., *Dick Sheppard and St. Martin's* (1937)

Northcott, R.J., *Pat McCormick. A Man's Life* (1941)

Purcell, William, *Woodbine Willie* (1962)

Rowse, A.L., *The England of Elizabeth* (1950)

Sadie, Stanley (ed.), *The New Grove Dictionary of Music and Musicians* (1980)

Scott, Carolyn, *Dick Sheppard* (1977)
Uglow, Jenny, *Hogarth. A Life and a World* (1997)
Weinreb, Ben and Hibbert, Christopher, *The London Encyclopaedia* (1983)
Young, Elizabeth and Wayland, *London's Churches* (1986)

St Martin's church strongroom contains the registers of recent baptisms, confirmations, banns, marriages and church services. Nearly all the other important documents, prints, photographs, etc. are held at the City of Westminster Archives Centre, 10 St Ann's Street, London SW1P 2DE, including:

Churchwardens' Accounts, 1525-1821.
Register of Baptisms, 1550/1-1657 and 1660-1965.
Register of Marriages, 1550/1-1968.
Register of Burials, 1550/1-1853.
St Martin's Rate Books, 1599-1900.
Vestry Minutes, 1652-1900.
Day Books including names of people visited, 1679-1696.
Banns Books, 1699-1725 and 1728/9-1966.
Confirmation Registers, 1887-1955.

Index

Compiled by Susan Vaughan

Page numbers in **bold** refer to illustrations

Vicar's General Fund, 89
Vicar's Relief Fund, 94
Victoria, Queen, 40, 105, 119, 123, 127, 142, 151-2, 155, 189
Vile, William, 31
Vincent, Robert, 84, 138
Violante, 27
Visitors' Centre, 90

Wake, William, Archbishop of Canterbury, 18
Walker, Rev. Christopher, **89**, 184, 185-6
Walker, John, 140
Walker, J.W. & Sons, 129, 133, 135
Walmisley, Thomas Forbes, 137
Walpole, Horace, 28, 113
Walpole, Robert, 18
Walsh, Mr, 168, **169**
Walters, H.B., 140
Wand, William, Bishop of London, 71, 76
Wandrake, John, 143
Wantage, Lady, 49
Warwick House, 115
watch house, 28
water supply, 162
Watherston, Edward, 163
Watley, William, 167
Watson, Dr, 19
Watson, Ian, 184
Watts, Mr, 129, 135
weather-vane, 26, 27
Webbe, Ralph, 188
Weir, Dame Gillian, 129
Weldon, John, 136
Wells, Mr, 10
Wells, Thomas, 188
Wells, William, 188
West, Benjamin, 31
Westminster Abbey: burials/ memorials, 3, 102, 104, 121, 136, 148; canon of, 188; Commonwealth Day

Act of Witness, 82; dispute 1222, 3; funeral of Diana, Princess of Wales, 120; land purchased from, 20, 25, 114, 115-16; organists, 136, 137; patronage, 5, 187
Westminster City Council, 36, 42, 43, 76-7, 117, 160, 163
Westminster Hall, xvi, 119, 189
Westminster Palace, 4, 6
Weston, Dr Edmond, 8, 188
Whalley, Peter, 188
Whinney, Dr Margaret, 149
whipping post, 158, 161
White, Dr, 14
Whitehall Palace, 6, 9, 11, 13, 120, 139
Whitfield, George, 30
Whitley, Jane, 84
Whitmore, Miss, 168
Wigram, Clive, 60
Wilcop, Dr J., 187
Wilkens, Chrysostom, 24
Wilkin, Susan, 90
Wilkins, William, 22, 34
Willcocks, Sir David, 181
William I, 18, 100, 189
William IV, xv, 126
Williams, 187
Williams, Mr (farrier), 27
Williams, Daphne, 74, 76, 80, 84, 86, 87, **89**
Williams, Katherin, 14
Williams, Rev. Sidney Austen, **76**, 77-84, **85**, 86-7, 190; and Academy of St Martin in the Fields, 177, 185, 186; bell inscription, 141; ordination anniversary, **89**; organ fund, 135; and Pearlies, 109; St Martin's Fair opening, 95; Social Care Unit, 171, 174; as spare wheel and deputy vicar, 69-70, 71, 72
Wilson, Michael, 32, 86
Wincop, J., 188

window glass, 8, 24, 37, 40, 44, 154-6
Windsor (Berks), St George's Chapel, 130
Wisdom, Norman, 79
With, Messrs, 26
Wolff, S. Drummond, 138
Wolsey, Cardinal, 6
Women's Royal Naval Service, 114
Wong, Emmet, 108
Wong, Kenneth, 108
Wood, Anthony, 136
Woodcock, William, 118
Woodlockes, Mr, 130
Woods, Chris, 84
Woolner, Thomas, 104
Worcester, Bishop of, 10
workhouse, 18, 38, 166-7
World Refugee Year, 77, 79-80
World War One, 46-7, 48, 49-50, 51-2, 53, 57
World War Two, 62-9; see also Blitz
Wortley, William, 9
Wrathor, Richard Roycroft, 159
Wren, Sir Christopher: Banqueting House, 120; children baptised, 14; churches, 14, 20, 22, 23; Gibbs and, 101, 102; library, 99, 133; mason, 22
Wright, Lawrence, 139
Wyatt, Sir Thomas, 9
Wymbledon, John, 188
Wyncote, Mr, 139

Yates, J.A., 35
YMCA, 50
York, church of St Martin, 2
York House, 9
York Place, 6
Youdell, Fr Basil, 89
Young, John, 139
Young & Corner, Messrs, 26

Zoller, Miss, 44